Industrial Purchasing Strategies

Industrial Purchasing Strategies

Recommendations for Purchasing and Marketing Managers

Arch G. Woodside
Tulane University

Niren Vyas
Square D Company

Lexington Books
D.C. Heath and Company/Lexington, Massachusetts/Toronto

Library of Congress Cataloging-in-Publication Data

Woodside, Arch G.
  Industrial purchasing strategies.

  Bibliography: p.
  Includes index.
  1. Industrial procurement. 2. Materials management.
3. Industrial marketing—Management. 4. Purchasing.
I. Vyas, Niren. II. Title.
HD39.5.W66 1987   658.7'2   83-48132
ISBN 0-669-06953-1 (alk. paper)

Copyright © 1987 by D.C. Heath and Company

All rights reserved. No part of this publication may be reproduced or transmitted in any form or by any means, electronic or mechanical, including photocopy, recording, or any information storage or retrieval system, without permission in writing from the publisher.

Published simultaneously in Canada
Printed in the United States of America
International Standard Book Number: 0-669-06953-1
Library of Congress Catalog Card Number: 83-48132

The paper used in this publication meets the minimum requirements of American National Standard for Information Sciences—Permanence of Paper for Printed Library Materials, ANSI Z39.48-1984.∞™

87 88 89 90 8 7 6 5 4 3 2 1

Contents

Figures ix

Preface xi

1. **The Nitty-Gritty of Industrial Purchasing Behavior** 1

   Industrial Purchasing Strategies 1
   Applying Decision Systems Analysis 6
   Major Phases in Industrial Purchasing Strategies 8
   Recommendations for Purchasing Managers 9
   The Good News about Industrial Purchasing Strategies 11

   Appendix 1A: Definitions and Descriptions of Terms 13

2. **Buying Tanks, Ties, and Boxes at Apex Products** 17

   Purchase of Batch Mix Tanks 19
   Purchase of Bale Ties 22
   Purchase of Corrugated Boxes 27

3. **Buying Axles, Motors, and Valves at Chapman Machines** 37

   Purchase of Front Axle Assemblies 39
   Purchase of Hydraulic Motors 41
   Purchase of Directional Valve Castings 45

4. **Buying Castings, Bars, and Blades at Regal Technologies** 55

   Management Structure 56
   Industrial Tool and Railroad Division 56
   Purchasing Organization 57
   Purchase of Investment Castings 58
   Purchase of Steel Rods (Bar Stock) 65
   Purchase of Woodhog Blades 68

5. **Buying Caps, Parts, and Oil at Evans Products   77**

    Purchase of Corrugated Bale Caps   80
    Purchase of Parts for Lift Trucks   83
    Purchase of #6 Fuel Oil   88

6. **Buying Acids, Pallets, and Gaskets at Diamond International Company   99**

    Background   99
    Procurement Function   100
    Purchase of Finishing Ingredients   103
    Purchase of Wooden Pallets   110
    Purchase of Sealing Gaskets   113

7. **Buying Coal, Gases, and Cable at Southeast Electric Company   121**

    History   121
    Service Area   121
    Electric Generating Facilities   122
    Operating Revenues and Management   122
    Regulatory Bodies   122
    Purchasing Department   123
    Purchase of Coal   124
    Purchase of Cooling and Purging Gases   135
    Purchase of 600-Volt Cables   138

8. **Purchase Decision Processes Involving Annual and Long-Term Contracts   149**

    Purpose of Long-Term Contracts in Industrial Buying   149
    Stages in the Purchase Decision Process   151
    Search for Potential Suppliers   152
    Policy on Seeing New Suppliers' Sales Representatives   155
    Inviting Bids   156
    Analyzing Bids   157
    Bid Comparison and Evaluation   157
    Splitting the Volume among Suppliers   159
    Average Time Period for the Decision Process   160
    Personal Factors Influencing the Purchase Decision   162
    Price Negotiations after Awarding Contracts   163
    Centralized versus Decentralized Purchasing Functions   164

9. **Summary and Conclusions 167**

   Research Objectives   167
   Methodology   168
   Discussions of Results and Conclusions   169
   Analysis of Supplier Selection Model for Requesting Quotations   169
   Analysis of Final Supplier Choice Model for Awarding Contracts   175
   Weaknesses Observed in Purchase Decisions   179
   Theoretical Implications   182
   Comparison of Research Findings with Those of Other Studies   183
   Research Findings Unique to This Study   185
   Importance of Decision System Analysis   185
   Managerial Implications   186
   Limitations of the Study   188
   Areas for Further Research   189
   Summary   190

Appendix: Research Methodology   193

References   213

Index   217

About the Authors   225

Figures

1–1. Research Method: Triangulation 3
1–2. Major Steps Observed in the Purchase Decision Process 10
2–1. Apex Products' Purchasing Department: Organizational Chart 19
2–2. Purchase Decision Process: Batch Mix Tanks 24
2–3. Purchase Decision Process: Bale Ties 28
2–4. Purchase Decision Process: Corrugated Boxes 34
3–1. Chapman Machines' Purchasing Department: Organizational Chart 38
3–2. Purchase Decision Process: Front Axle Assembly 42
3–3. Purchase Decision Process: Hydraulic Motors 46
3–4. Purchase Decision Process: Casting for Directional Valve 52
4–1. Regal Technologies' Purchasing Department: Organizational Chart 58
4–2. Purchase Decision Process: Casting for Pneumatic Tool 62
4–3. Purchase Decision Process: Bar Stock 70
4–4. Purchase Decision Process: Woodhog Blades 74
5–1. Evans Products' Purchasing Department: Organizational Chart 79
5–2. Purchase Decision Process: Corrugated Bale Caps 84
5–3. Purchase Decision Process: Parts for Lift Trucks 90
5–4. Purchase Decision Process: #6 Fuel Oil 96
6–1. Diamond International's Regional Procurement Departments 101
6–2. Carolina Regional Purchasing 103

6–3. Purchase Decision Process: Finishing Ingredients (Oleic Acids)   108

6–4. Purchase Decision Process: Wooden Pallets   114

6–5. Purchase Decision Process: Sealing Gaskets   118

7–1. Southeast Electric's Purchasing Department: Organizational Chart   124

7–2. Purchase Decision Process: Coal   132

7–3. Purchase Decision Process: Gases   140

7–4. Purchase Decision Process: 600-Volt Cables   146

9–1. Supplier Selection Model for Requesting Quotations   170

9–2. Supplier Selection Model for Awarding Contracts   172

Preface

The Purchasing Revolution

In the late 1980s, a revolution in industrial purchasing strategy is occurring similar to the marketing revolution of the 1960s. With the recognition and acceptance of the marketing concept (that is, all marketing activities need to be integrated in the firm to achieve maximum profits through customer satisfaction), most large industrial and consumer goods manufacturing firms have created the senior management position of senior vice president of marketing. Strategic marketing planning occurred for the first time in most of these firms in the late 1960s, causing major organizational and strategic planning changes. This marketing revolution was extended to the communications industries in the 1970s (for example, AT&T and GTE) and to the health care industries (for example, hospitals) in the 1980s.

In the 1970s, senior managers in several large organizations upgraded purchasing strategy in response to research evidence on the direct and large impact of purchasing on profitability (see Buzzell, Gale, and Sultan 1975) and the potential cost savings realized by integrating purchasing activities. For example, the director of materials management or director of purchasing would report directly to the chief executive officer. Senior purchasing officers now sit on the highest senior management committees in many large firms in the United States, United Kingdom, West Germany, and other advanced industrial countries.

Thus, changes in corporate culture—philosophy, values, and organization—lead to changes in how purchasing management is organized and purchasing strategies are performed. Hard evidence on the impact of purchasing on profits has led to changes in corporate cultures. As in the case of marketing, purchasing had to prove its importance with evidence in order to gain the attention of senior management. Because of the strong evidence of the impact of purchasing on corporate profit, and because of the purchasing revolution occurring in large industrial firms, fundamental research on planned and realized purchasing strategies is increasing at universities and colleges in North America and Europe (see Mintzberg and Waters 1985). Several books are available now that describe in minute detail how real-life decisions are made in industrial purchasing (for example, Hakansson 1982; Turnbull and Paliwoda 1986; Woodside 1987).

Because of the purchasing revolution, senior executives and purchasing/marketing scholars are giving the same level of attention and recognition to purchasing as marketing receives. We are now eager for more information and expertise on purchasing strategies.

Realized Industrial Purchasing Strategies

This book is about realized strategies—the patterns in streams of industrial purchasing decisions. Inductive and normative approaches are used to answer two questions: (1) How are industrial purchasing strategies made in real life? and (2) What insights for improving strategies can be suggested from learning about real-world industrial purchasing strategies?

Induction

The first question is inductive. Descriptive models of the streams of activities, the communications among persons involved in buying industrial products and services, and the decisions they make are used in this book as building blocks for a general inductive theory-in-use of industrial purchasing strategies.

This inductive approach is a response to Peter's (1981) dictum: "We clearly need to know *what* behaviors people perform before we explain *why* they perform them. Not only has little study been devoted to overt behavior but little attention has been given to delineating the basic sequence of behaviors people must perform to purchase a product or other sequences of behavior of interest in marketing" (p. 144) and in purchasing.

Thus, we advocate the view that valid description of reality must precede proposed prescriptions of improved strategies if the latter are actually to be used and increase purchasing effectiveness.

Normative Theory

The current textbooks on purchasing strategy detail how purchasing should be done. Such recommendations serve a useful function; they are norms for comparing real-life industrial purchasing strategies with recommended, normative, strategies.

Not understanding how purchasing strategies actually occur is the shortcoming in starting with the normative approach. What is really going on in industrial buying processes? For the purchasing manager, how can these industrial buying processes be improved upon? For the marketing manager (and suppliers), how can the firm have more impact in influencing these industrial buying processes?

We believe that gaining a deep knowledge of what is going on in real-life purchasing is useful before advocating improvements or attempting to influence industrial purchasing strategies. This book provides deep level of knowledge for industrial purchasing and marketing strategists.

Though insights are included on improving industrial purchasing strategies and marketing influences on purchasing strategies, the book is not intended to be a textbook on how industrial purchasing *should be done*. It is a book for the strategist on how industrial purchasing *is done*. The book will also provide an excellent reference for practicing marketing managers as to how industrial purchasing decisions are made in the real world. Unfortunately, most salespersons assume they know how these decisions are made. It seems appropriate to quote two British researchers (Hamilton and Wilson 1972):

> Waste in marketing, were it only quantifiable, would, it is suspected, be of astronomic proportions. There are the problems of inadequate advertising, misdirected promotional efforts, expensive, over-elaborate and wasteful catalogues, abortive journeys and sales visits, junk direct mail; also the days and weeks of detailed planning, the operating and monitoring of complex marketing strategies, which are doomed from the outset to failure or at best to limited success because of the lack of understanding in buying.

Successful suppliers are observed to have differential access to the purchasing company's power structure. It is equally evident they have differential knowledge of its operation. Most salespersons making routine sales calls do not even bother to find out if their company's name is on the bidders' lists. These are critical factors for a successful supplier's success. Most salespersons' training does not include development of skills in diagnosing political forces within the firm. If these forces are understood, many firms may decide to withdraw from the exercise of making calls and submitting bids and save themselves and their company a great deal of time and money. This is another kind of market segmentation, once the politics and power structure within a buying organization are known.

Detailed flow diagrams of the streams of real-life activities, decisions, and interactions of people involved in planning and implementing industrial purchasing strategies are included in the chapters on our findings. Decision system analysis (DSA), including the triangulation of evidence from document analysis, personal interviews, and observations of actions (for example, meetings of persons involved in different phases of the purchasing decisions), was the research method used to collect data for the book. DSA is explained in detail in the appendix.

In summary, the purpose of the book is to provide knowledge and insight on how industrial purchasing strategies actually occur. Thus, a theory-in-use prospective is used to answer the question, "What really happens when industrial firms make purchasing decisions?"

Acknowledgements

Permission to observe, interview, and analyze the purchasing-related documents provided by executives in the firms studied is acknowledged with gratitude. Collecting data for inductive model building requires being present personally in the field for long periods of times. Participants spent substantially more time in answering multiple interviews than they would in completing a mail questionnaire. The researcher becomes a participant observer in the cooperating firm; the participants in the firms studies were generous and gracious in their cooperation. For competitive reasons and because of the substantial details reported on the communications among persons involved in the buying processes, the names and some of the organizational demographic profiles of the firms participating in the study have been changed. The activities, decisions, and interactions in the buying processes occurred as reported. Thus, the essential streams of industrial purchasing strategies are reported as found.

The National Association of Purchasing Management (NAPM) and its regional chapter, the Purchasing Management Association of the Carolinas and Virginia (PMA-CV), provided cooperation and introductions to executives in the firms participating in the study. Ervin Lewis, a past president of PMA-CV, provided substantial insights as a purchasing manager in designing the study and interpreting the findings; his help made the study possible.

We are grateful to our colleagues, Terence A. Shimp and William M. Morgenroth, for reading and providing detailed comments used in revising most of the chapters. Their comments made a difference.

The editorial work and typing of the complete manuscript by Deborah Byrum is acknowledged and appreciated. Much of the clarity of presentation is due to her review of the complete manuscript.

The authors are responsible for the remaining errors and omissions. Readers' comments and suggestions for future research would be appreciated. Please write to: Arch Woodside, Freeman School of Business, Tulane University, New Orleans, Louisiana, 70118.

1
The Nitty-Gritty of Industrial Purchasing Behavior

The central aim of this book is to provide buyers, purchasing managers, and marketers with deeper insights into how industrial purchasing strategies are decided and implemented. A basic premise used in doing the research reported in the book is that we can learn much by mapping the specific decisions, behaviors, and interactions of people in purchasing strategies as these strategies actually occur. Similar studies on purchasing strategies have been reported at the corporate level in large industrial firms (Corey 1978) and for international industrial purchasing (Hakansson 1982; Turnbull and Paliwoda 1986).

The focus in this book is on industrial purchasing strategies for manufacturing plants (plant-level buying). Industrial purchasing strategies for raw materials, component parts, and nonproduction items are described. Commentaries on the strengths and weaknesses of specific purchasing strategies are included.

This book helps provide answers to the continuing need of managers to know how industry buys. The effectiveness of industrial purchasers and marketers will increase if they have available accurate descriptions and commentaries of actual industrial buying behavior.

Detailed maps of the actual decisions and behaviors are included on plant-level buying behavior. The maps are presented as flow diagrams for each of the purchasing strategies reported in the book. Written descriptions and evaluations of the purchasing strategies are provided for each purchasing strategy described.

Industrial Purchasing Strategies

Industrial purchasing strategies can be defined from two perspectives: as a series of planned, deliberate decisions and as the series of actual decisions and behaviors that occur. Most decisions are not executed exactly as planned.

Purchasing and marketing managers are likely to increase their effectiveness in planning and executing future strategies by studying the actual series of decisions, behaviors, and outcomes that occur in industrial purchasing. This is the basic premise for this book: these managers can learn much and improve the effectiveness of their planned strategies by examining the nitty-gritty of recent realized strategies. Thus, the purchasing strategies in this book refer to the actual streams of buying-related decisions that occur among members of an organization.

Professional football players and coaches spend hours looking at the films of previous games to learn what decisions and executions worked and what did not. They observe, talk about, and evaluate what they see in the films and in the light of this information revise their planned strategies for the next game.

Industrial purchasing strategies are dynamic, just as football games are. Although we cannot film the action, we can learn the nitty-gritty of how decisions are made, and implemented, what persons and departments participate in the decisions and how they interact among themselves and with vendors, and the outcomes of their decisions and behaviors.

Learning such things requires many hours of observation, interviews, and analysis of written records. Thus, a triangulation of methods is used. The technique used is similar to investigative reporting: no one piece of information is taken to be factual until supported by at least one additional piece of information from a different source. At least two sources for the information are necessary before making the tentative conclusion that a single bit of information is part of the stream of decisions, behaviors, and interactions that occurred in the buying problem.

When bits of information received from two sources of information do not match, a third source of information is often necessary to resolve the difference. For example, in a study of how utility companies buy lighting poles for street and highway use, during an interview the purchasing manager (PM) of one utility reported that his firm purchased only aluminum standards (poles). In a separate interview, a buyer in the same firm stated that fiberglass lighting poles represented 20 percent of the firm's lighting pole purchases. The buyer's estimate was confirmed by examining the firm's written purchase requisitions. The PM was unaware of the development of new purchasing standards for lighting poles, but he was certain his information was correct when he reported initially that the company had purchased only aluminum poles (Wilson 1984).

The three methods used in combination to evaluate the actual purchasing strategies reported in this book are shown in figure 1–1. Since purchasing strategies are dynamic, the observations, interviews, and document analyses are made through several time periods.

Several weeks, months, or years may be necessary to apply the triangulation method to learn actual purchasing strategies. For example, in one of the earliest studies to use this research approach to learn what really occurs in

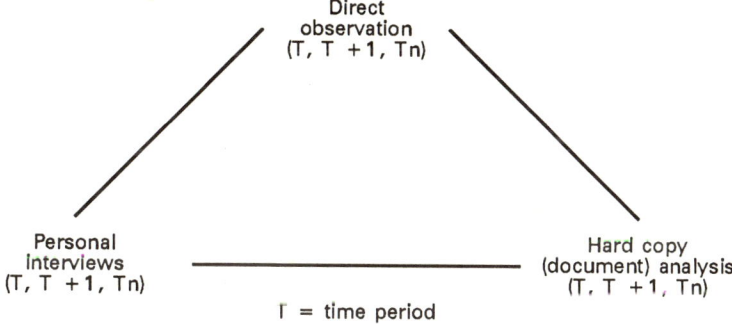

Figure 1-1. Research Method: Triangulation

planning and executing industrial purchasing strategies, three researchers (Cyert, Simon, and Trow 1956) observed the purchasing strategy of capital equipment, a main-frame computer, over a two-year period. A key finding was that the economic theory of choice processes does not capture how people actually go about making choices and that the theory needs to be modified substantially before it will be useful.

A major tenet of the economic theory of choice processes is that decisions are made rationally by moving through specific decision phases in a specific sequence, a process known as the phase theorem. The following steps, listed according to how they are prescribed to occur by the economic theory of choice processes, make up this theorem:

1. Problem definition
2. Search for solutions
3. Data collection, analysis, and use
4. Information exchange
5. Individual preferences
6. Evaluation criteria
7. Choice
8. Implementation

The phase theorem is the proposition that decisions should occur in the exact order shown according to the economic theory of choice processes. In real life, the phase theorem and other propositions of the economic theory of choice processes have not been found to occur. For example, individual preferences of participants may be formed before data are collected or the problem is defined. Evaluation criteria and decision rules often change after implementation. Problems are defined and redefined at different times; decision processes tend to loop back several times to phases thought to occur only initially in decision making. Important decisions are messy, and they appear to be unstructured (Mintzberg and Waters 1985).

Research on actual industrial purchasing strategies has resulted in a number of key findings. First, buyers, specifiers, users, and other participants in the decision process usually make judgments and have specific preferences during, before, and after search; in other words, few decision-makers can withhold judgment or prevent their biases from affecting vendor search and immediate evaluation. Second, the participants usually do not discuss methods of how to combine their individual views and ways of making choices; that is, the informal rules of making decisions (known as heuristics or choice rules) being applied by the different participants are not discussed. Conflicts sometimes occur due to differences in the choice rules being applied by the participants. Third, the participants in the buying decision are able to articulate what criteria they use in making choices and the specific decision rules they apply. One heuristic decision rule is never to award a new vendor the largest share of the total requirements no matter how attractive the new vendor's prices are relative to current suppliers' prices. Fourth, the search for vendors and materials to evaluate is limited; it rarely extends to include most viable candidate solutions, and it ends when a limited number (three to seven) of candidate solutions has been found. Fifth, specific decisions and the rationales for these decisions are linked together. Such links often result in a creeping or galloping commitment to a specific action; for example, many approved new vendors do not receive a share of the available requirements because the current vendors are often given the opportunity to revise their bids. Finally, detailed maps, or descriptions, of purchasing strategies can be constructed for production and nonproduction materials. These maps show the complete linkages of the decision rules, rationales for applying these rules, and the behaviors following each decision (for example, vendor approvals, purchase requisitions, written reports). Many specific decisions are followed by other specific decisions.

Revising the Phase Theorem

A revised phase theorem has been developed by Witte (1972) based on field research of actual decision processes. The revised theorem states that problem definition, the search for and gathering of information, the evaluation of alternatives, and choice making occur in all time intervals during a decision process, but the proportions of occurrence of each phase change for each time period. Thus, in one month of a five-month decision process, different vendors are likely to be added and eliminated from consideration, the problem may be redefined several times, and the rules for making choices may change two or three times. However, new vendors are not considered for adding to the approved vendor list during each week or month of the buying process; most new vendor evaluations occur during the first half of the purchasing strategies.

Other Theories of Management Strategies

Three other theories of management strategies have been proposed in attempts to predict and explain decisions rather than the propositions of the economic theory choice processes: the bounded rationality model (Cyert and March 1963), the political model (Pettigrew 1975; Pfeffer 1981), and the garbage can model (March and Olsen 1986).

The basic tenets of the bounded rationality model are that decision makers intend to be rational but are constrained by cognitive limitations, habits, and biases. They simplify problem definitions and limit the sequential search to familiar areas. They express the evaluation criteria applied to decisions in terms of cutoff levels derived from past experience, and they select the first alternative (for example, a vendor) that exceeds the cutoff levels.

According to the political model, organizational decisions are arenas in which individuals compete to satisfy their own interests. Thus, they establish preferences for material specifications and approved vendors early, usually on the basis of departmental goals, and these seldom change as new information is accumulated. Problem definitions, search, data collection, and evaluation criteria are merely weapons used to tilt the decision outcome in one's favor. Information exchange is biased toward the same end. Choice is a function of the distribution of power in the organization and the effectiveness of the tactics used by the participants in the decision process (Dean 1987).

In the garbage can model, decisions are seen as garbage cans into which problems, solutions, choice opportunities, and people are dumped. Problem definitions change as the strategy occurs and new problems and new people enter into the stream of decisions. Search is multifaceted according to this model: problems and solutions are looking for one another, problems are looking for choices, and decision makers are looking for work. In the garbage can model, data are often collected and not used. Preferences are unclear, and often have little impact on choice. Evaluation criteria for making decisions are discovered during and after the process, and choices are mostly made when problems are either not noticed or are attached to other choices.

Elements of the bounded rationality, political, and garbage models occur in each of the purchasing strategies described in the following chapters. No one model dominates reality.

Some researchers have attempted to report the structure that emerges during the course of actual industrial purchasing strategies without following a preconceived model of what should be included in the realized structure. This general research approach is applicable to studies on theory in use (Zaltman,

LeMasters, and Heffring 1982), inductive model building (Vyas and Woodside 1986), direct research (Mintzberg 1979), phenomenology (Denzin 1983), humanistic inquiry (Hirschman 1986), and decision systems analysis (DSA). All studies on strategies and behaviors identified by these names have one thing in common: they are attempts to describe and explain the structures of actual decision processes with as little preconceived theory as possible. Thus, the studies are inductive, attempting to reach general conclusions from studying specific decisions and behaviors, rather than being deductive.

Hulbert (1981) provides a review of this inductive research approach applied to marketing and purchasing strategies; he refers to the research method as DSA. Unique to DSA as an inductive research method is the construction of flow diagrams showing the decisions, behaviors, and interactions (meetings) of participants in the decision process through time. DSA has been applied successfully to model industrial purchasing processes in international settings by Moller (1986) and in corporate purchasing strategies by Woodside and Samuel (1981).

DSA includes the use of several rounds of interviews for constructing initial flow diagrams and revising these diagrams. The diagrams are shown to the participants in the purchasing strategies and revised to include changes they recommend. Documents are analyzed to verify the occurrence of events and decisions included in the diagrams. Researchers keep diaries of observations to record key events, dates, and times to verify the series of behaviors and decisions occurring in the buying process. Descriptive commentaries followed by written evaluations of the strengths and weaknesses of each decision process complement the flow diagrams. This DSA approach was the method used to collect the data reported in this book. Definitions and descriptions of terms have been included as an appendix to this chapter.

Applying Decision Systems Analysis

Decision systems analysis was used to describe and evaluate the purchasing strategies for eighteen long-term contracts (usually one year or longer) in six manufacturing plants in the United States. Such long-term industrial purchasing contracts are often referred to as plant purchasing agreements (PPAs). In essence, these are open-ended, blanket-type purchase orders for high-volume, repetitive, sometimes off-the-shelf standard products. PPAs were selected for research since such contracts covered the majority of the dollar purchasing requirements for each of the six manufacturing plants.

The six plants were selected based on the following criteria: the presence of plant-level purchasing, the use of long-term contracts with suppliers, and the manufacture of noncompeting products compared to the other firms in the study. The last criteria was necessary to help eliminate the perception among managers that the study might compromise competitively sensitive information.

The names of the companies and participants in the buying centers have been disguised. *Buying center* refers to all the members of an organization involved directly in the buying process for a particular product or service; the buying center often includes persons from several departments for PPAs (for example, purchasing, engineering, production, and inventory). People enter and leave the buying center at different phases in the buying process. Thus, the size of the buying center may expand and contract based on the phase in the buying process.

The face-to-face interactions of persons in the buying centers, their decisions, and the outcomes of their behaviors are described in the study for six manufacturing plants: (1) Apex Products, a plant of a large conglomerate, manufacturing staple textile fiber; (2) Chapman Machines, a division of a large international heavy railway equipment manufacturer; (3) Regal Technologies, a division of a large, high-technology manufacturer of sophisticated engineering products (Regal manufactures a range of portable electric and compressed air tools, high-speed drills, and heavy-duty rotary hammers); (4) the Evans Corporation, a chemical firm manufacturing aldehydes, acids, dyes, polyolefins, and polyesters; (5) Diamond International, one of the largest manufacturers of synthetic fibers in the United States; and (6) Southeast Electric Company, a medium-sized utility company.

The Products

The primary management contacts in the six firms were asked to identify important items purchased under PPAs for which requirements or requests for quotations (RFQs) were currently being prepared. To sharpen the research focus, items having annual purchase volumes of more than $100,000 were selected. Based on these guidelines, eighteen items, three from each firm, were selected for the study: corrugated boxes, bale ties, metal bars, bale caps, wooden pallets, rubber gaskets, investments castings, axles, batch mix tanks, hydraulic drive motors, fuel oil, parts for lift trucks, acids, electric cables, coal, purging gases, woodhog blades, and hydraulic valve castings.

Identifying Buying Centers

Initial interviews with purchasing managers and buyers responsible for completing PPAs revealed that individuals from other departments were active in the buying processes for all eighteen PPAs. These other people were interviewed separately and asked who else was involved in the decision process, which led to the identification of and subsequent interviews with still others. The interview process was terminated when no new individuals were identified who had taken part in the decision process. This interview technique, known as snowball interviewing, has been used successfully in research on industrial purchasing strategies (Johnston and Bonoma 1981; Spekman and Stern 1979).

Observation and Document Analysis

Several observations of meetings of buyers, users, and engineers with vendors, meetings of members of the buying centers with each other, and the actual use of the products covered by the PPAs were made during the buying processes. Written copies of forecasts of annual requirements, RFQs, internal memoranda, reports on evaluations of vendors' production facilities, correspondence with vendors, and purchase orders of related PPAs from prior years were read. Written diaries were kept of meetings, key events, decisions, rationales for decisions, and the interpretations by the participants of the buying centers of recent events.

For each product included in the study, the data collected from the personal interviews, observations, and document analyses were compared. Discrepancies in the data were resolved by additional interviews and observations.

Flowchart Development

The results of the initial interviews and observations were a series of descriptions and protocols of ongoing decisions. These protocols were then converted into flowcharts to summarize the roles and tasks of persons, events, problems, and decisions in the choice processes.

These initial flowcharts were integrated into one combined flowchart for each product studied and revised several times over periods of one to three months. Each integrated flowchart was shown to each person initially interviewed and modified as recommended during the reinterviews.

Major Phases in Industrial Purchasing Strategies

As the research progressed, a definite pattern of behavior emerged across the buying processes for the eighteen sets of PPAs studied. The participants in the buying centers were observed to use similar procedures for reducing the number of alternatives (for example, materials, specification choices, vendors) to be considered. This procedure, similar to heuristic programming, consists of successive applications of rules deemed to be appropriate, so that the number of alternatives is reduced to sufficiently few as to be manageable by the decision makers.

The supplier choice decision seemed to become a case of heuristic programming in a broad sense, consisting of five critical phases, each one narrowing the list of candidates. Each of the five phases comprised several subprocesses. The details of each of the five phases and subprocesses for the eighteen sets of PPAs are presented in the following chapters.

A summary of the five stages or phases is presented in figure 1–2. The revised phase theorem should be kept in mind while looking at figure 1–2. For simplicity, the arrows in the figure show a flow of decisions and behaviors from left to right. In practice, several feedback loops occurred during the decision process for each of the eighteen products purchased.

The key behavior occurring in each of the five phases serves to summarize and name the phase:

1. Prepare RFQ.
2. Search for potential suppliers.
3. Evaluate and select approved vendors for bidding product.
4. Analyze quotes received.
5. Evaluate and select suppliers.

Two observations are clear from figure 1–2. First, a limited number of criteria for making choices occur within each phase of the buying process. For example, usually five criteria were used for reviewing purchase requisitions in preparation of RFQs. To understand the reasons for specific decisions requires understanding the choice criteria used by the buying center and how these criteria are applied.

Second, simple heuristics appear in figure 1–2. For example, in the second stage, the search for potential vendors continues until at least three viable vendors are located. A complete search of all vendors that might realistically receive a share of the requirements called for in the RFQ was never made in the eighteen case studies. Thus, satisfactory solutions were sought by the decision makers. The buying processes may best be described as attempts to achieve rational decisions within certain bounds.

Not all the behavior and decisions appearing in figure 1–2 occurred in each of the eighteen buying processes. The figure serves only as a frame of reference for examining the details of the individual buying processes.

Recommendations for Purchasing Managers

Several specific recommendations for purchasing managers, buyers, and senior management are made following the descriptions of the buying behavior of the six manufacturing plants participating in the study. Three are noted here.

First, purchase requisitions and RFQs need to be prepared to encourage the use of value analysis, noticeably absent in the observed buying processes. (A

10 • *Industrial Purchasing Strategies*

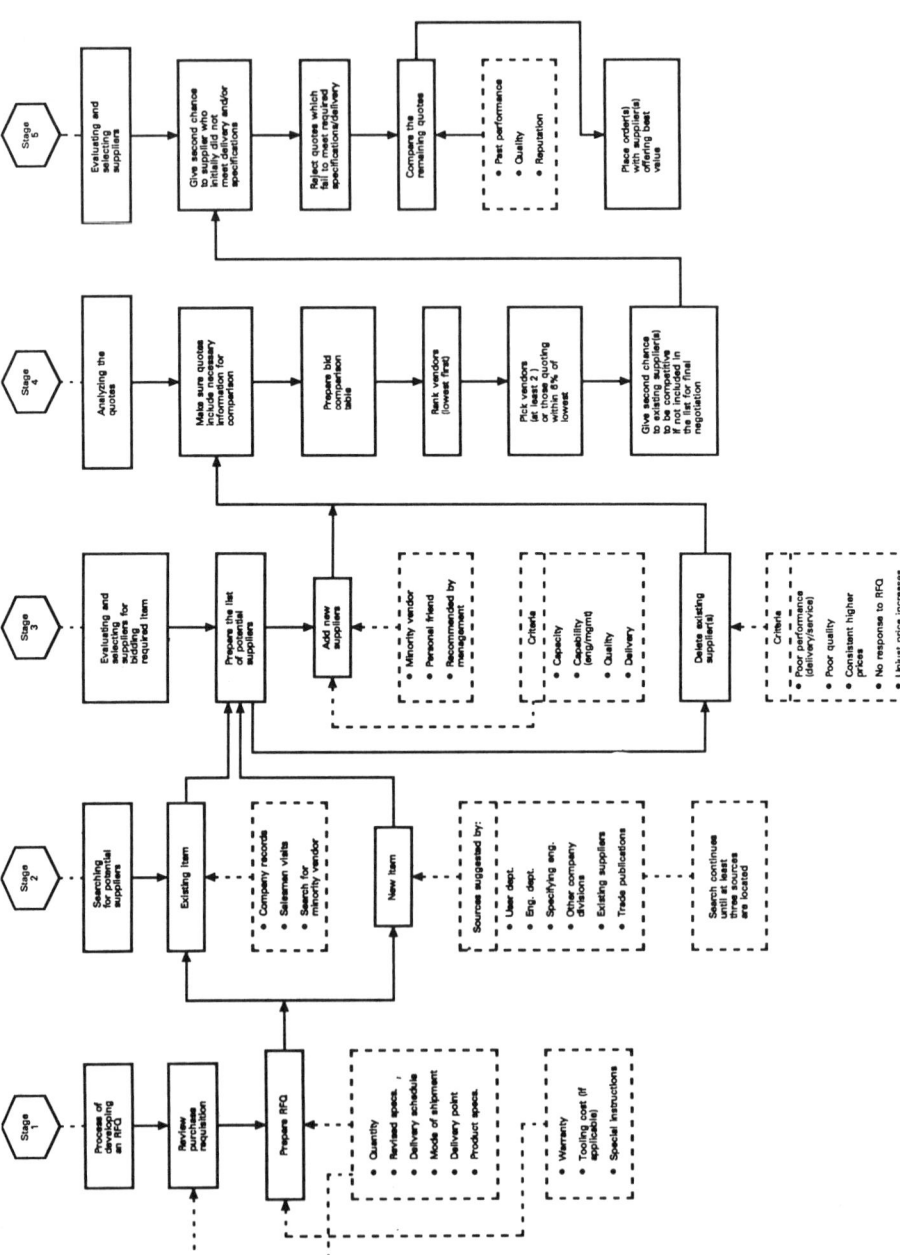

Figure 1–2. Major Steps Observed in the Purchase Decision Process

value analysis includes a review of the performance capabilities of alternative materials that might be purchased.) Purchase requisitions and RFQs usually were written narrowly and called for specific product materials (for example, "wood" pallets) instead of focusing on the function performed. Such narrow specifications restricted the possibilities for considering alternative materials and the use of value analysis to improve the effectiveness of purchasing.

Second, new vendors that have been tested and approved need to be awarded larger shares of purchase orders than the shares commonly awarded. The general tendency of favoring existing vendors over new ("out") suppliers, even when the out suppliers offer favorable prices and past strict tests of passing material specifications, often decreases the effectiveness of purchasing. Too often current vendors are given second and third chances to change their bids—both prices and bid specifications—to meet the competing bids of out suppliers. Ultimately, effective competition is eliminated by the current, widespread use of the informal second bid opportunity provided to current suppliers.

Third, purchasing would benefit by the use of formal supplier performance reviews. Reviews of the effectiveness of the purchasing function are performed by some manufacturing firms in the United States. These purchasing audits should be complemented by supplier audits. No formal annual reviews of current suppliers were performed by the firms participating in the study. Such formal reviews will help increase the professional stature of purchasing and the respect of members of the buying center from other departments in the manufacturing organizations and from vendors.

The Good News about Industrial Purchasing Strategies

A central finding should be kept in mind when reading the detailed industrial purchasing strategies in this book. The buyers, purchasing managers, user departments, engineers, and others involved in industrial buying processes thought actively about using a rational approach to buying. Most of the decision makers were trying to improve the effectiveness and efficiency of purchasing strategies. This is the good news about industrial purchasing strategies.

This central tendency to attempt to use a rational approach should not be taken lightly. As one plant purchasing manager explained, "Before we sat down and actually looked at how and why we were making purchasing decisions, our suppliers often said that we were a friendly place to do business with. Now that we have thought out the purchasing process and introduced a more formal approach to buying, our suppliers view us as being more professional, not as friendly. The change has done us a lot of good, I think."

Appendix 1A
Definitions and
Descriptions of Terms

Approved bidders list (Bidders list, Bid list)   These are used to refer to the list of suppliers selected for bidding on the required item. In other words, these are the suppliers qualified to receive RFQs.

Attribute (Factor)   These terms are used to refer to a characteristic by which the expected performance of a potential vendor is evaluated. This may be a characteristic of the vendor, or of the vendor's product. Examples of attributes include the ability to meet delivery schedules, ability to meet quality specifications, and the ability to offer technical assistance.

Bidder (Sources of supply, Supplier, Vendor)   These terms are used to refer to the outside companies from which purchases are made. In general, the terms refer to a company that sells or offers to sell.

Bid (Quotation)   This is the offer from the supplier, usually in writing, which includes prices and terms under which the seller is willing to meet the buyer's requirements.

Bidders list   See **Approved bidders list.**

Bid list   See **Approved bidders list.**

Buyer (Purchasing agent)   This is a member of the company's purchasing department who is responsible for purchasing specific items. Various titles are assigned to purchasing department employees, depending on their experience, educational background, and responsibility shared. Such titles include junior buyer, senior purchasing agent, purchasing supervisor, or purchasing manager.

CPA   See **Corporate purchase agreement.**

Corporate purchase agreement (CPA)   This contract is negotiated at some central point in the organization for a particular class of products at specified prices for a fixed time period, on which user locations may draw to meet their needs.

Deterministic model   A deterministic model is a representation of a process in which the manipulation of given information will invariably yield a certain outcome. That is, given exogenous information, the outcome predicted by the model is certain.

Factor   See **Attribute.**

FOB destination/job site   Freight and insurance charges are paid by the supplier. Supplier delivers the items to the purchaser at the location where they are needed.

FOB shipping point   Free on board at point of shipment. In this situation, the purchaser is responsible for paying the freight and insurance charges from the point of shipment to the destination where the item is required.

Level   A level is a quantitative (or, in some cases, qualitative) measure of a state in which an attribute may exist.

Long-term contracts   These contracts are agreements between the selling and buying organizations for a specific product, for a specific period of time, under mutually acceptable terms. The delivery of the item is usually spread over a specified time period, and the price may be subject to escalation based upon a certain formula, or subject to negotiations after a specified time period during the life of the contract.

Model   According to Miller and Starr (1967), a model is "a representation of reality that attempts to explain the behavior or some aspect of it." More generally, a model is a physical or logical representation (usually in simplified form) of a system, process, or object that is used in place of the original for the purpose of experimentation and study.

MRO items   These are nonproduct, maintenance, repair, and operating supplies.

Normative model   A normative model describes what the nature of a system or process ought to be in order to satisfy a predetermined objective function.

Payment terms 1% 10, net 30 days   The purchaser can deduct one percent of the invoice price if payment is made within ten days of item delivery. Failing this, the purchaser must pay the full invoice amount within thirty days of delivery.

Predictive model   A predictive model describes a system or process to the degree that—given the input to that system or process—it is able to determine what the output of that system will be.

Purchase   A purchase is any material to be used by an organization that must be bought from an external source. The word is intended to be used as a noun, rather than as a verb.

Purchase agent   See **Buyer**.

Purchase requisition   User departments develop needs for products; these needs are translated into requisitions. These are formal, usually written, requests to the purchasing department to buy specific items. Requisitions contain the necessary details, such as quantity, description and specification of the required items, and delivery schedules.

Quotation   See **Bid**.

Request for quotation (RFQ)   The RFQ requests a supplier to respond with a sales offer, and describes the particular product specifications, delivery requirements, quantity, and contract terms relating to a proposed purchase.

RFQ   See **Request for quotation**.

Sources of supply   See **Bidder**.

Stochastic model   A stochastic model is a representation of a process in which the manipulation of given information will yield a probability distribution of outcomes. In general, probability statements are attached to the workings of the process with the result that, given exogenous information, there is uncertainty as to the outcome predicted by the model.

Supplier   See **Bidder**.

Supplier choice   See **Vendor selection**.

Vendor   See **Bidder**.

Vendor analysis   Given a specific set of vendors whose characteristics are known, vendor analysis is the process by which alternative vendors are compared with each other. This is part of the vendor selection process.

Vendor rating system   A vendor rating system is one method of analyzing vendors. It is usually a fixed system, in which the potential vendor is quantitatively assessed in terms of past performance, or expected future performance.

Vendor selection (Supplier choice)   This is the process of deciding with which vendor or vendors to place an order, given a specific purchase to be made.

Weight   This is a quantitative measure of the importance of various attributes or factors compared to one another.

2
Buying Tanks, Ties, and Boxes at Apex Products

Apex Products is a diversified company that produces a broad range of products. It was incorporated on 20 December 1918, under a perpetual contract in New Jersey, as Apex Industries. Its present name was adopted on 26 April 1955. The company's 1979 sales were $4.88 billion; the total number of employees was fifty-nine thousand.

The company's operations are carried out by four divisions, described briefly below.

1. *Oil and gas*: Principal products include crude oil and condensate; produced and purchased natural gas; liquified natural gas; liquified petroleum gases; and natural gasoline, residue gas, and ethylene.

2. *Chemicals*: These include process chemicals such as sulphuric, hydrochloric, and nitric acids, soda ash, coal tar pitch, and tar acids. This division also manufactures agricultural chemicals for mixed and direct application as fertilizers.

3. *Fibers and plastics*: Apex Products is one of the largest producers of nylon in the United States, and is also a large producer of caprolactam, which is the primary intermediate of type-6 nylon. These products have applications in textiles, carpets, industrial fabrics, automotive belting, and tire cord.

4. *Electrical and other operations*: Products in this division include batteries, motors, ignition systems, alternators, generators, wires, and cables. These are used in automotive, truck, marine, farm, aviation and recreational vehicles, material handling equipment, and telecommunications.

Other operations include industrial products such as refractory bricks, zinc and aluminum die castings, fittings, and industrial measuring devices. Consumer products include athletic footwear.

As is evident from these descriptions, Apex Products is a truly diversified organization. The company's products are used in agriculture, and by almost all major industries including the steel, textile, construction, petroleum, plastics, automotive, chemical, paper, soap, glass, paint, leather, and aluminum industries.

The fibers and plastics division operates five plants, with total sales close to $1 billion. Research was conducted at one of the plants operating under the fibers and plastics division. This plant produces staple and filament nylon fibers, employs about twenty-five hundred people, and operates three shifts per day, seven days a week, continuously. The plant has been in operation since 1955.

The plant has its own purchasing department, which buys most items needed for the plant's operation. The company's basic philosophy is to allow the local purchasing department to operate independently, but within company guidelines. There is little centralized purchasing. Corporate contracts are available for common items used by all of the company's plants, but if the local purchasing department is able to get better prices elsewhere, it is not required to purchase through corporate contracts.

Because the company is so diversified, each plant has special needs and its own purchasing department. If this department is located at the plant, communications between the purchasing and the manufacturing departments are more effective, requirements of the plant are better understood, and the response time from purchasing is reduced considerably. The purchasing manager indicated that local purchasing helps in developing better contracts with local suppliers, thereby attaining better service from them. Overall, it gives a boost to the local economy, encouraging community development.

The purchasing department at plant level consists of a purchasing manager, three senior buyers and three buyers who handle approximately fifty-four thousand items used by the plant. Total plant purchase amounts to $35 million, which is close to 50 percent of the cost of finished products manufactured at this location. The purchasing manager pointed out that 80 percent of dollar volume is spent on 20 percent of items purchased.

Production items used continuously by the plant are purchased on long-term contracts to assure continuity of supply, to obtain better prices with volume buying, and to reduce the time spent by purchasing. The organization chart for the purchasing department is shown in figure 2–1.

The purchasing manager and materials manager report directly to the manager of the plant. However, the vice president of Purchasing is responsible for directing improvements to the company's purchasing policy. Corporate headquarters also monitors the activities of plant purchasing to ensure that corporate guidelines for purchasing departments are followed.

The following items purchased on long-term contracts by the company were selected to be researched: batch mix tanks, bale ties, and corrugated boxes.

Batch mix tanks are highly engineered items. Their purchase decision process is complex, and requires input from many departments. In contrast, bale tie is a relatively simple item that requires minimum input from other

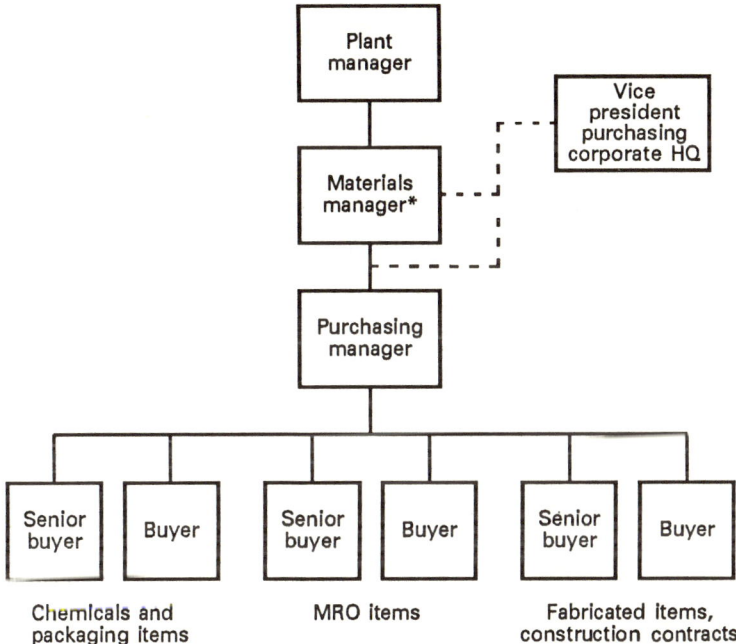

*Includes responsibility for inventory control and transportation (shipping and receiving departments).

Figure 2–1. Apex Products' Purchasing Department: Organizational Chart

departments. These two items were selected in order to compare differences in the decision process.

Competition in the corrugated box market is intense, and many suppliers are willing to place bids. This item was selected in order to gain a better understanding of the supplier evaluation process.

Purchase of Batch Mix Tanks

Batch mix tanks are used for mixing chemicals to produce nylon. There are nineteen such tanks in operation. Because of year-round nonstop usage and continuous handling of strong acids and chemicals, these tanks have an average life span of eight to ten years. The nineteen tanks in operation at this time were purchased in groups of four of five, as gradual plant expansion was carried out. The long-range forecast for the next ten years shows a strong demand for nylon. The manufacturing department, therefore, feels that at least one batch mix tank should be added each year for the next five years. After five years, this decision will be reviewed. In addition, at least one batch mix tank per year will be needed to replace worn-out tanks for the next eight to ten years. Thus, the company needs to buy at least two tanks per year; these tanks will be purchased on long-term annual contracts.

The purchasing agent was questioned about why contracts were not negotiated for longer time periods. He responded that past experience had revealed that technology in this field changes rapidly. The materials used in fabricating might change, the process might be improved and modified as openings and nozzles on tanks are changed, and instrumentation might also change. For this reason, the same manufacturer might not remain competitive over a longer period of time.

Tank specifications are continually reviewed by design engineering. The tank design is so important in the entire production process that it can increase or decrease the company's competitive edge.

This is a highly complex technical item, and therefore design engineers and production engineers play key roles in its purchase. They are involved in writing specifications, contacting potential vendors, conducting technical discussions with them, visiting manufacturing facilities, and even talking with suppliers' customers who have purchased similar items.

Each tank costs about $50,000 FOB job site. Installation is carried out by the design engineering department once the vendor delivers the tank. Thus, the total value of the annual contract with the vendor is approximately $100,000.

Selecting Suppliers to Submit Bids

Although the long-range decision to buy two batch mix tanks per year had been made by management, a formal appropriations request for funds had to be made by production engineering. This request then had to be approved at various levels of management. These included the safety, environmental, and process control departments. Whenever an item related to chemical processes was to be added to the facility, the state Environmental Protection Agency had to be contacted for their approval. This was coordinated through the environmental department. Once the EPA gave its approval, the design engineering and production departments finalized specifications, and made a detailed drawing of the tank. The specifications and drawings are sent to various departments for comments. Also, design engineering discusses the documents with potential vendors.

When a purchase requisition is sent to purchasing, a list of potential vendors to be contacted is also sent by the design engineering department. Purchasing may decide to add its own supplier to the list, but it usually does not delete suppliers listed by design engineering without a strong reason and an explanation.

In this case, the design engineering department submitted the names of four suppliers. All of these had supplied tanks in the past, and the company had satisfactory experiences with each of them. Because this item was very specialized, few suppliers in the area were capable of producing it. The location of suppliers was important, because the tanks were large—about five feet in diameter and ten feet high—and they require special transportation, which added to the cost of the item.

The purchasing department did not add or delete suppliers; they knew of no new suppliers, nor had they had bad experiences with any of the suppliers recommended by design engineering. Therefore, the specifications were sent to four vendors, who were given two weeks to submit quotations.

Evaluating and Selecting Suppliers

Two suppliers responded in two weeks; the other two responded after one reminder. Only one supplier quoted a price; the others responded with no bids. The purchasing agent explained that this situation was not unusual. Because other companies were buying many fabricated items, suppliers were fairly busy, and unable to quote. There was no point in repeating a request for quotation, because the delivery time of these suppliers was probably over a year. This was not a good time to search for new sources, as it takes four weeks to six months to develop and approve a new source; it is an expensive and time-consuming process. The decision had to be made quickly; otherwise, the only supplier quoting might also receive a large order for fabricated items from other customers, and might not be able to keep the offer open for longer than the thirty days indicated in the offer.

The purchasing department sent the quotation to design engineering and production engineering for evaluation. The quotation was acceptable to both, and the order was placed with this supplier.

An important question was raised by this process. How did purchasing know if the price quoted was competitive? And, what about the company policy of requiring at least three quotations? The purchasing agent explained the situation as follows:

> The price quoted by the supplier is checked with the price paid by the company last year for this item. If it is within 6 to 8 percent of last year's price, then it is reasonable. Further, the supplier who submitted the price this year does not know that he is the only one quoting. He always thinks that there is competition, and hence he will give best price.

Concerning the company policy requiring three quotes, the purchasing agent indicated that "no bid" is considered for auditing purposes to be a quote, and is therefore acceptable.

The Buying Center

The following people who influenced the supplier choice decision process were interviewed: John Davis, purchasing supervisor; Dot Sims, purchasing agent; Julian Tanner, design engineer; and Mac Gable, production engineer.

Mr. Tanner, of design engineering, is responsible for preparing specifications for the tanks. He also works closely with Mr. Gable of the production engineering department to finalize specifications. According to Mr. Tanner, "Mac is responsible for the operation of the tanks. He knows what he wants and, therefore, I try to understand his needs and respect his opinion."

Mr. Gable and Mr. Tanner are also responsible for approving potential vendors before adding them to the bidders list. Mr. Tanner conducts all technical discussions with suppliers, visits them (accompanied by Mr. Davis), and evaluates their manufacturing facilities and capabilities. The final technical evaluation of the bids is carried out jointly by Mr. Gable and Mr. Tanner. According to Mr. Davis, "This is a common practice for technically complex items. Mac and Julian should know best if the tanks offered by the vendor will do the job."

Ms. Sims and Mr. Davis, of purchasing, are responsible for commercial evaluation of bids.

The decision process as described is depicted in the flow diagram, figure 2–2.

Evaluation

Members of the buying center seemed to work together very well. They accepted the expertise of different people in their fields. Because only one bid was received, the negotiating power of the purchasing agent was severely curtailed. The agent could have avoided this situation by keeping in touch with vendors and monitoring their work loads. Planning ahead, he could have sent the request for quotation (RFQ) at a time when the work loads of the other three vendors were light, thereby improving the chances of receiving more than one bid.

The order was placed with the vendor without negotiating price or other commercial terms. The supplier did not know that his was the only bid received, so it is likely that negotiations for a better price and delivery schedule would have proven successful.

No attempt was made by purchasing to develop new sources in order to avoid similar situations in the future.

Purchase of Bale Ties

The company uses heavy nylon yarn in the manufacturing of carpet. Unlike fine nylon yarn, which is wound on pirns and shipped in corrugated boxes, heavy nylon is shipped in bales. Each bale weighs approximately four hundred pounds. The nylon yarn is compressed in machines, with heavy-duty cloth wrapped around it. While the nylon is still under pressure in the machine, it is tied with four steel wires that keep the nylon inside the cloth in the form of a bale. These steel wires are one quarter inch in diameter, and are under tremendous pressure as they hold the nylon in compressed form during transportation. The steel wires are called bale ties. Approximately two million of them are used by the company annually at a cost of about $350,000.

Because bale ties are required continuously for producing bales, the company buys them on long-term contracts, usually for a one-year period. The company has been using bale ties since 1969, when production of heavy nylon began in the plant. The industrial engineering department prepared specifications after extensive testing in 1969, and this item is currently standardized. Over the past eleven years, the industrial department has tried several times to use something else in the place of wires, such as steel straps, in order to save money. However, other items have all failed. Steel straps of the required strength are unavailable in the market. Special straps can be manufactured to meet specifications, but they are more expensive than bale ties.

Production control prepared estimates of the annual usage of bale ties, and informed the purchasing department to buy them on annual contracts. Once suppliers are selected, production control remains in close contact with vendors to ensure delivery of the required quantity, and keeps purchasing informed about vendor performance.

The Buying Center

The following people involved in the purchasing process were interviewed: Marion Baker, purchasing supervisor; Helen Lee, production control supervisor; and Robert Kaiser, industrial engineer.

This case served as an excellent example of fine teamwork between departments, specifically purchasing, industrial engineering, and production control. The responsibility of each department was clearly defined, and the order execution was very smooth. Mr. Kaiser, the industrial engineer, explained: "The purchasing department does not specify bale ties, and I do not order them." Ms. Lee of production control remarked: "As long as the supplier delivers on time and as per specifications, I don't care where purchasing buys from."

Selecting Suppliers to Submit Bids

Over the past eleven years, the company has developed reliable sources for the supply of bale ties. These were originally the suppliers of steel straps used by the company for other applications. When the steel straps did not work as bale ties,

24 • *Industrial Purchasing Strategies*

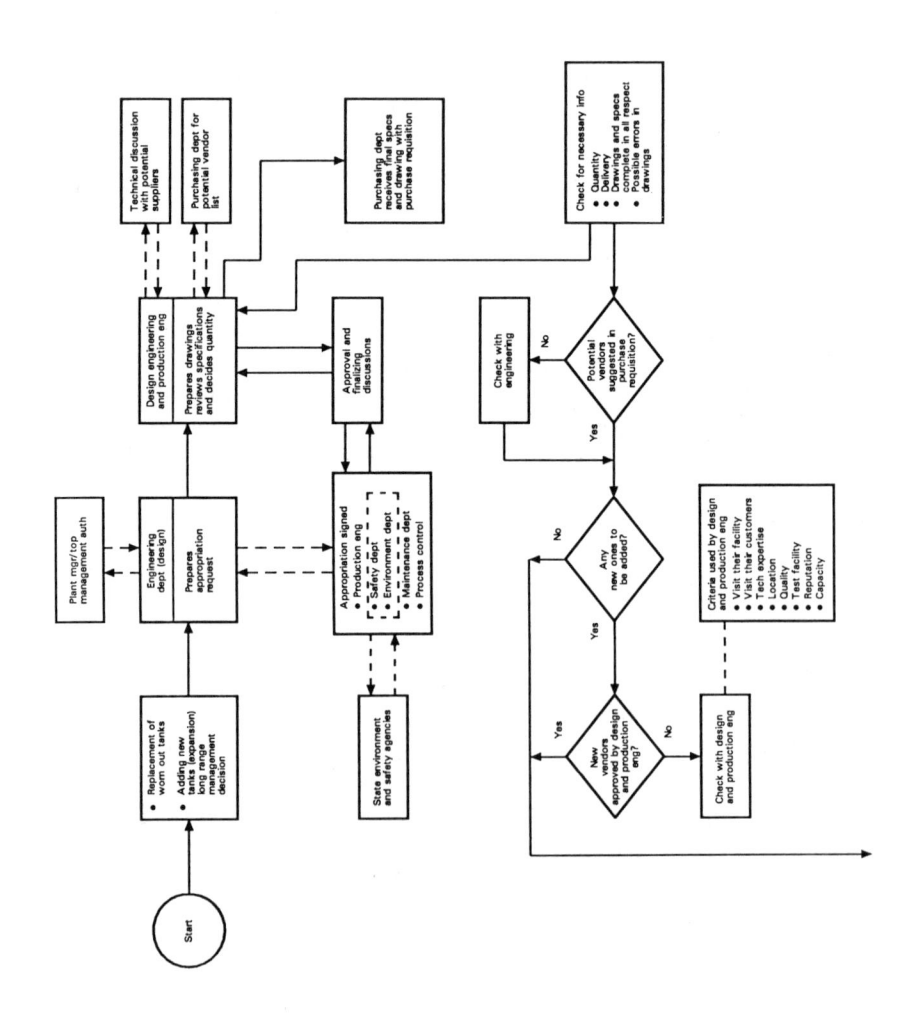

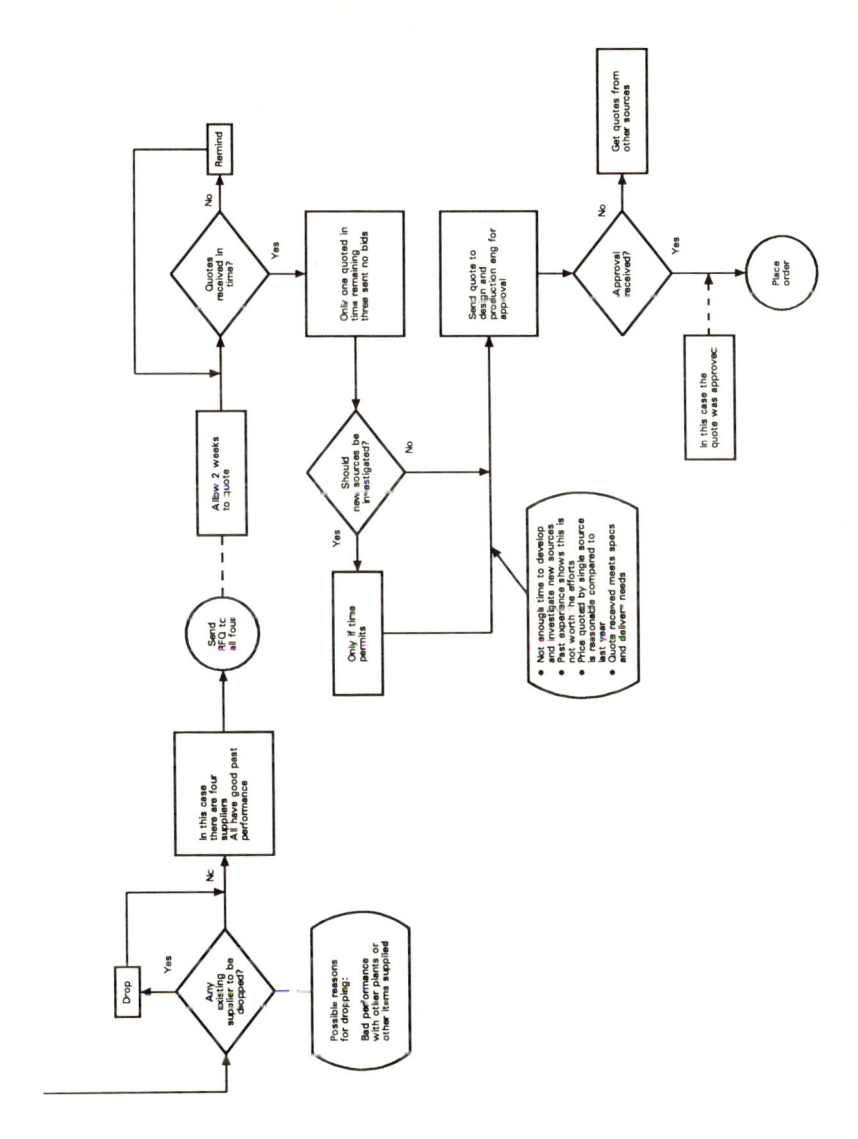

Figure 2-2. Purchase Decision Process: Batch Mix Tanks

some suppliers suggested the use of steel wires. When these worked, other suppliers were also asked to quote for steel wires. It is a company policy to give any new supplier a chance to quote if the supplier is willing to understand the company's needs. Such suppliers must also have the capacity to delivery the required quantity, and meet specifications.

There were five established suppliers in this case. No new supplier had shown interest in the bale tie business recently. However, the purchasing department dropped one supplier from its 1980 list, because he had tried to increase his price immediately after the order was placed. The purchasing department felt that his price increases were unreasonable, and out of line with other suppliers. The remaining four suppliers had supplied bale ties in the past, and their quality and delivery performances had been satisfactory. RFQs were sent to these four suppliers. This met the company requirement to have at least three suppliers bid on an item. All of the suppliers submitted quotations within two weeks.

Evaluating and Selecting Suppliers

When the quotes were analyzed, the following characteristics were common:

All suppliers quoted prices FOB destination.

Terms were net 30 days.

Delivery was as required.

All suppliers met specifications.

The bid comparison table is shown below.

Supplier	Price per 100-Wire Bundle	Remarks
Eastern Strapping	$18.25	Price not firm. Had a few bale ties broken in past. Luckily, no one was hurt.
Belton Bagging	$18.34	Price firm for six months.
Gargill-Tennants	$18.48	Price firm for one year.
A. G. Whaley	$18.52	Price firm for six months.

The supplier who quoted the lowest price did not quote a firm price, and had experienced problems with quality. A few of his bale ties broke, and the bales opened up. Bale ties are under tremendous pressure and when they break, they fly open like a whip. Someone could easily be hurt in such a situation, although this had not happened yet. However, for these reasons, this supplier's bid was rejected.

When possible, the purchasing department prefers to avoid single-source situations. According to the purchasing agent: "Having more than one source is the cheapest way of buying insurance. If one source fails, you can fall back on the other."

Having more than two suppliers is also undesirable, as there would be too little volume for each supplier. A. G. Whaley was therefore dropped, because of his high price, and the two remaining suppliers were selected. Because the price difference between these suppliers was less than 1 percent, the volume was split fifty-fifty. This made it easy for production control to divide the quantity between the two suppliers.

The flow diagram showing the purchase decision process described is shown in figure 2–3.

Evaluation

The bid analysis was carried out strictly by the purchasing department. Formal technical evaluation by industrial engineering was not necessary because of the simple application of the item.

No attempt was made to negotiate better prices or commercial terms with the vendors. The purchasing manager's argument against negotiations was as follows:

> If vendors know they will not be given a second chance to revise their bids, they are likely to give their best offer to start with. On the other hand, if they know you are going to negotiate, they may not give their best offer. You end up spending too much time negotiating without achieving much.

The absence of a formal vendor rating system for evaluating bids was pointed out to the purchasing manager. He did not favor such a system because, in his opinion,

> it needs continuous updating which is time-consuming and expensive. The ratings are subjective and therefore may vary from one purchasing agent to the other. Overall, we do not see any improvement in the decision of selecting suppliers and therefore, the system is not worth our extra effort and time.

Purchase of Corrugated Boxes

Corrugated boxes are used to pack nylon bobbins, or pirns, as they are called in the fiber industry. Pirns are produced in two sizes; therefore, there are two sizes of corrugated boxes. The company spends approximately $250,000 annually to purchase these boxes. To take advantage of volume buying, the

28 • *Industrial Purchasing Strategies*

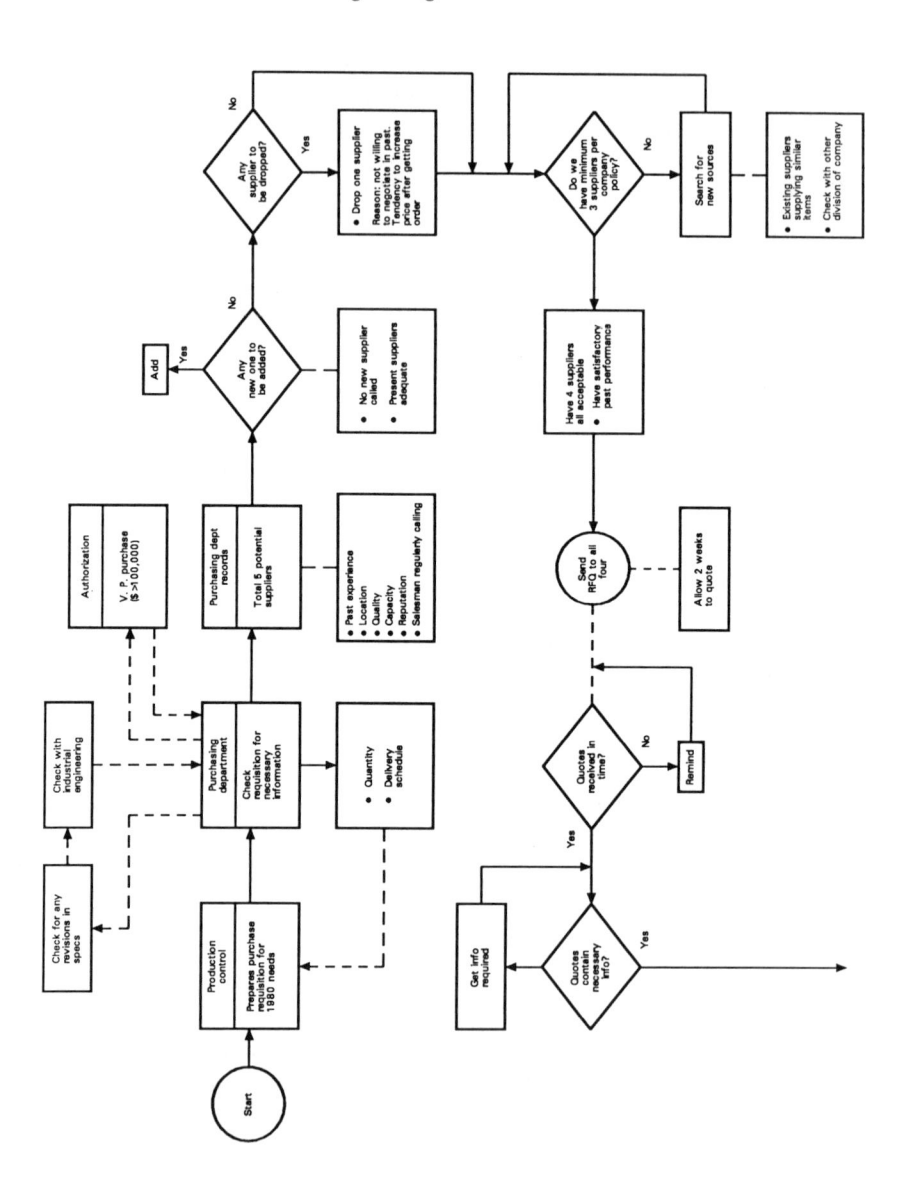

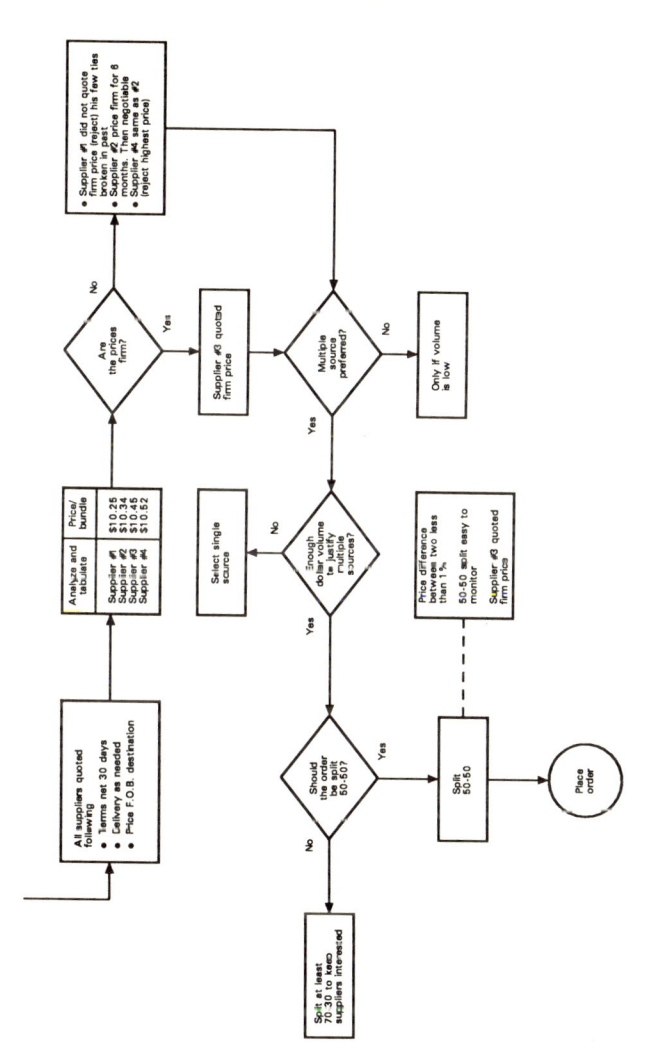

Figure 2-3. Purchase Decision Process: Bale Ties

company purchases corrugated boxes on a long-term contract. The policy is not to extend the contract period beyond one year. Changing economy and supplier unwillingness were the two main reasons cited by the purchasing agent for this policy.

The industrial engineering department is responsible for preparing specifications for this item. In addition, industrial engineering is involved in the actual design of the box. This department relies heavily on vendors for assistance in design. Once the box's design is finalized, it is tested on the vibration table to check the design's integrity. The box may appear to be simple; however, if it is not designed and specified correctly, it can cause the pirns inside the box to rub against each other, and damage the nylon yarn. The boxes may break open in shipping, causing the nylon to become unusable. The design should be such that boxes can be stored safely at the customer's location without being affected by heat and moisture. Other considerations in designing the boxes include ease of recycling after use, and box dimensions such that the maximum number can be fitted into a standard truck without wasting space. Therefore, specifications are quite important when purchasing corrugated boxes.

Once boxes are ordered, the company's production control department deals directly with the supplier's employees at the manufacturing location to schedule delivery of the boxes. Due to space restrictions, the company keeps two weeks' inventory of corrugated boxes in storage. When boxes are received, quality control inspects them, and contacts production control if problems arise, such as boxes of the wrong size, or damaged boxes delivered. Production control, in cooperation with purchasing, resolves these problems promptly with the supplier.

Supplier representatives regularly visit the purchasing department to discuss commercial aspects of the business; technical discussions are carried out with the industrial engineering department. Industrial engineering relies heavily on suppliers to suggest improvements in packaging to lower costs. The production control department is also regularly visited by supplier representatives to ensure that delivery from their manufacturing plant is punctual, and to see if large fluctuations in requirements are anticipated in the near future.

The Buying Center

Discussions with the purchasing agent indicated that the industrial engineering and production control departments have maximum input in the purchasing decision process for corrugated boxes. The following people were interviewed to study the purchasing process: James Walker, senior buyer (purchases packaging materials); Helen Lee, production control supervisor; and Robert Kaiser, industrial buyer (prepares specifications).

Ms. Lee schedules weekly delivery directly with suppliers and monitors delivery performance. Mr. Kaiser conducts all technical discussions with vendors.

The industrial buyer pointed out some very interesting facts about his department's efforts to control the cost of corrugated boxes. Over the past fifteen years, the cost of box paper has more than doubled. However, during that time, the price of the corrugated boxes has remained practically unchanged. He explained that initially heavy boxes were used, but as experience was gained and better testing methods were developed, design changes were introduced continuously to reduce the cost of the boxes. This was the main factor in offsetting the increase in cost of box paper.

Whenever industrial engineering initiates a change in design, it takes six weeks to six months to implement that change. Before the change is implemented, a thousand pieces of corrugated box of the new design are purchased, and shipped to various customers. Their performance in the field is closely monitored. If this performance is satisfactory, the new design is standardized.

Selecting Suppliers to Submit Bids

The company does not have a formal rating system for vendors. However, the purchasing agent who was responsible for purchasing boxes informally rated various vendors on their performance. Over the past years, the company has done business with different suppliers, and has developed histories on their performances. Further, only a few reputable suppliers in the United States can meet the volume of boxes required by the company. This eliminates small manufacturers. According to the purchasing agent, sales representatives from box manufacturers visit the purchasing department once every three months; they constitute the bidders list.

Those suppliers who were reputable, whose products were used by the company's other divisions, and who had the capacity to supply the required quantity of boxes were included on the bidders list. Those who had not supplied this specific type of box previously were required to submit samples before the order for the large quantity could be placed with them.

The company went to the trouble of getting samples and testing them only if the new perspective supplier quoted an attractive price. Otherwise, samples were not required, because testing and monitoring performance is expensive for the company and supplier alike. Past experience had revealed that it is difficult to simulate all of the conditions of handling the box in actual shipping. According to the purchasing agent,

> if the boxes pass the laboratory test, they are then subjected to the actual field test. This becomes a special project since many departments get involved in monitoring the performance of the boxes in the field.

The boxes have to be marked specially for identification, they require special handling in the receiving department, quality control has to make sure the markings are proper, and industrial engineering has to keep records of all the sample boxes. The shipping department has to be notified to ship these boxes out to different locations in the country using different means of transportation (usually truck or railroad). Customers who receive these boxes must be notified through the marketing department so they can check the final condition and give necessary feedback. In case any boxes fail, the industrial engineering department has to investigate the failure, which involves individuals from the transportation companies, from the customer's receiving and inspection departments, and from our own marketing department. The supplier in the meantime is constantly asking for feedback since he is eager to know how the sample boxes performed in the field. As you can see, this is an expensive project.

According to the purchasing agent, there were eighteen suppliers on the bid list. All were capable, reputable suppliers. There was no adverse feedback from production control on any of these suppliers; therefore, none of them were dropped. RFQs were sent to all eighteen suppliers, and they were given two weeks to quote.

What factors determine minimum or maximum numbers of suppliers on the bidders list? The purchasing agent said that

company policy requires a minimum of three suppliers on the bidders list. The rationale is that two suppliers can get together and may decide to fix a price—it is difficult for three suppliers to do the same. There are no restrictions on the maximum number of suppliers which can be on the bid list. However, this usually depends on the amount of work one is willing to put in, the dollar volume, and the item purchased. The higher the dollar volume and the more important the item, the larger the number of suppliers preferred on the bid list.

In this case, ten suppliers submitted bids within two weeks, two additional suppliers quoted after a reminder, and one indicated no bid; the remaining suppliers did not quote. The purchasing agent indicated that those who did not quote would be dropped from the bidders list for the following year.

Evaluating and Selecting Suppliers

Once quotations are received, the first question asked is: Do they meet all of the specifications? In this case, they all did. The next step is to check the suppliers' responses to the delivery requirement. All suppliers quoted delivery as needed. The purchasing department then tabulated bids. All suppliers quoted prices FOB destination, and offered terms of 1 percent 10, net 30 days.

The next step was to rank vendors using price for each size of box as the ranking factor. The only other factor to be evaluated was the time period for which prices remained firm. Except for two vendors, all quoted a price firm for ninety days, after which the price was subject to negotiation, depending upon the price of raw materials. Two suppliers quoted a price firm for six months. Crown Zellerbach quoted the lowest price for one size of box; Container Corporation quoted the lowest price for another size.

The final decision was made to place an order for the entire quantity of size A boxes with Crown Zellerbach, who quoted the lowest price for size A boxes. Container Corporation received the order for size B boxes, as their price was lowest for this item. Both suppliers had supplied boxes in the past; thus, there was no need to request samples. The orders were not split further between suppliers for each size of box, because the selected suppliers had reliable delivery records. It was not worth paying the higher price required to split the volume between a supplier quoting the lowest price and one who quoted the second lowest price. The entire purchase decision process is shown in figure 2–4.

Evaluation

The company policy is not to negotiate prices once bids are submitted. The company also does not use a formal vendor rating system. In these two areas, the company could reassess existing policy to improve supplier choice decisions.

The supplier selection decision was simple and straightforward when existing suppliers performed satisfactorily, and quoted the lowest prices.

34 • *Industrial Purchasing Strategies*

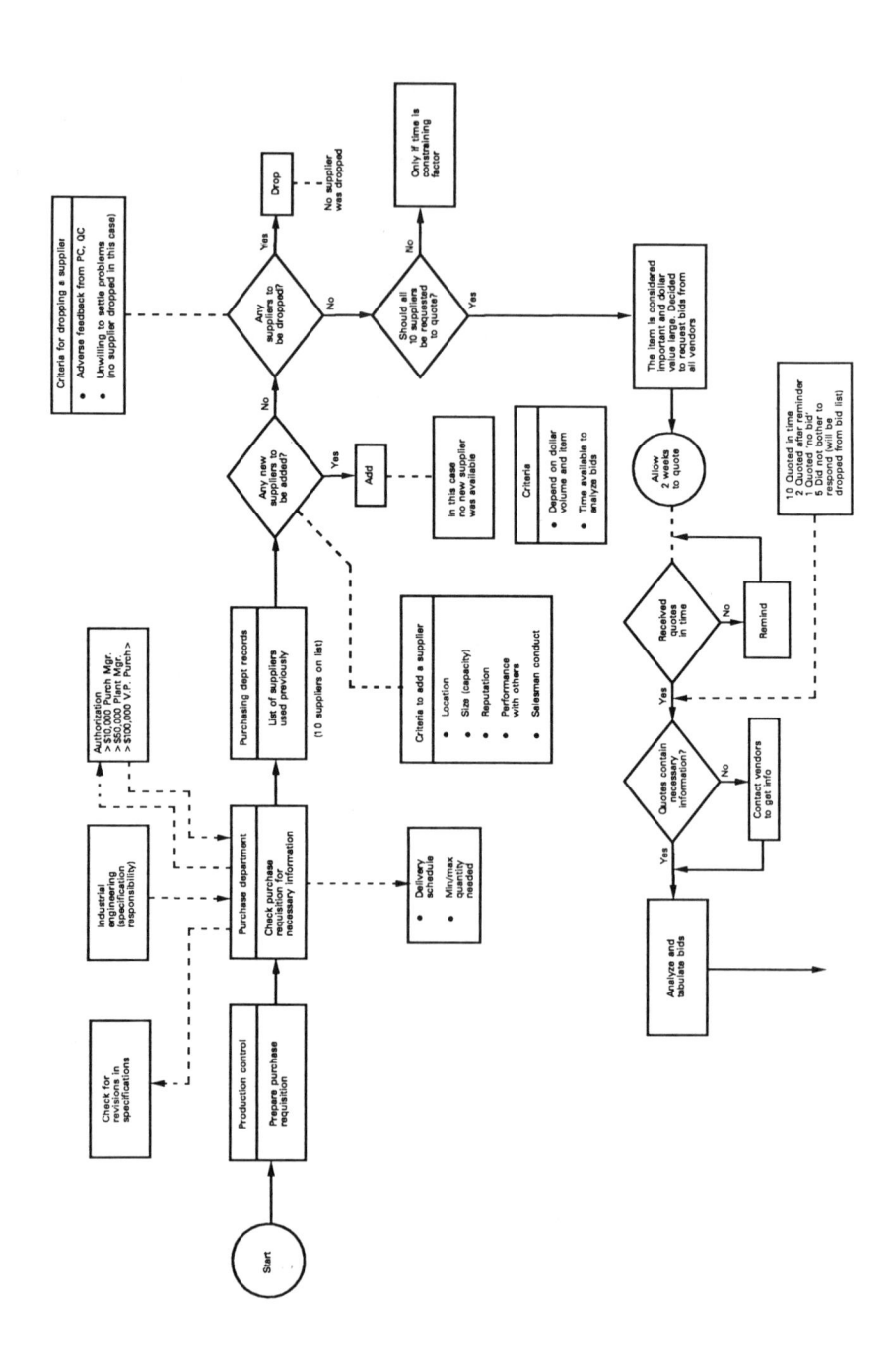

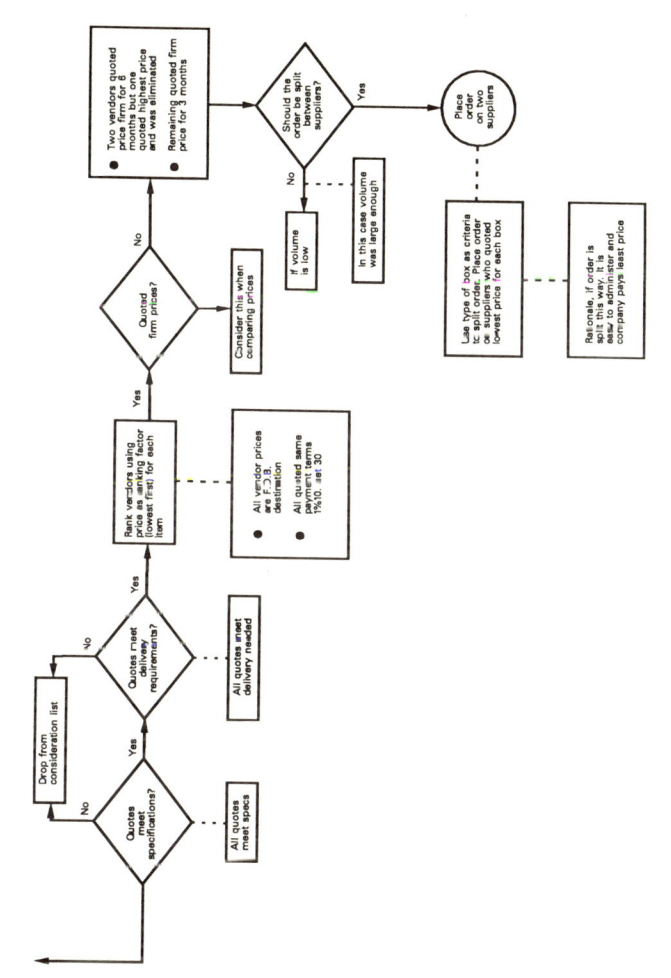

Figure 2–4. Purchase Decision Process: Corrugated Boxes

3
Buying Axles, Motors, and Valves at Chapman Machines

Chapman Machines is a British-owned and -managed corporation, with headquarters in London. The company makes products and equipment for heavy industry throughout the world. Total sales in 1979 were about $500 million, including $15 million profit.

The corporation at the time of the study employed approximately seven thousand people in plants and offices in Austria, Britain, Canada, France, Italy, Japan, Spain, Switzerland, the United States, and West Germany.

Because of the corporation's diversified product line and widely dispersed operations, a decentralized divisional type of organization was used. The corporation's business strategy was to maximize use of existing manufacturing and marketing expertise, and to seek opportunities for profitable growth. Thus, along with internal expansion and product development, the corporation pursued acquisition opportunities.

The company has several divisions that manufacture diversified products. The research for this study was conducted at one of the railroad divisions. The railroad division specialized in the manufacture of tamping equipment and truck equipment, such as track renewal trains, car movers, rail-laying machines, automatic spike drivers, rail gauging machines and rail lubricators. Also included were ballasting equipment, and power tools for railroads such as tie renewers, rail saws, tie drills, spike pullers, rail bolters, drills, and grinders.

Each division functioned as an independent entity with profit center responsibility. This particular division had total annual sales of about $70 million in 1979, and at the time of the study employed about 1,250 people. The total dollar volume of all items purchased in 1979 at this location was $42 million.

The purchasing function was decentralized. This division had its own purchasing department on location. This department consisted of a purchasing manager, two supervisors, and seven purchasing agents. (The organizational chart for the purchasing department is shown in figure 3–1.) The purchasing

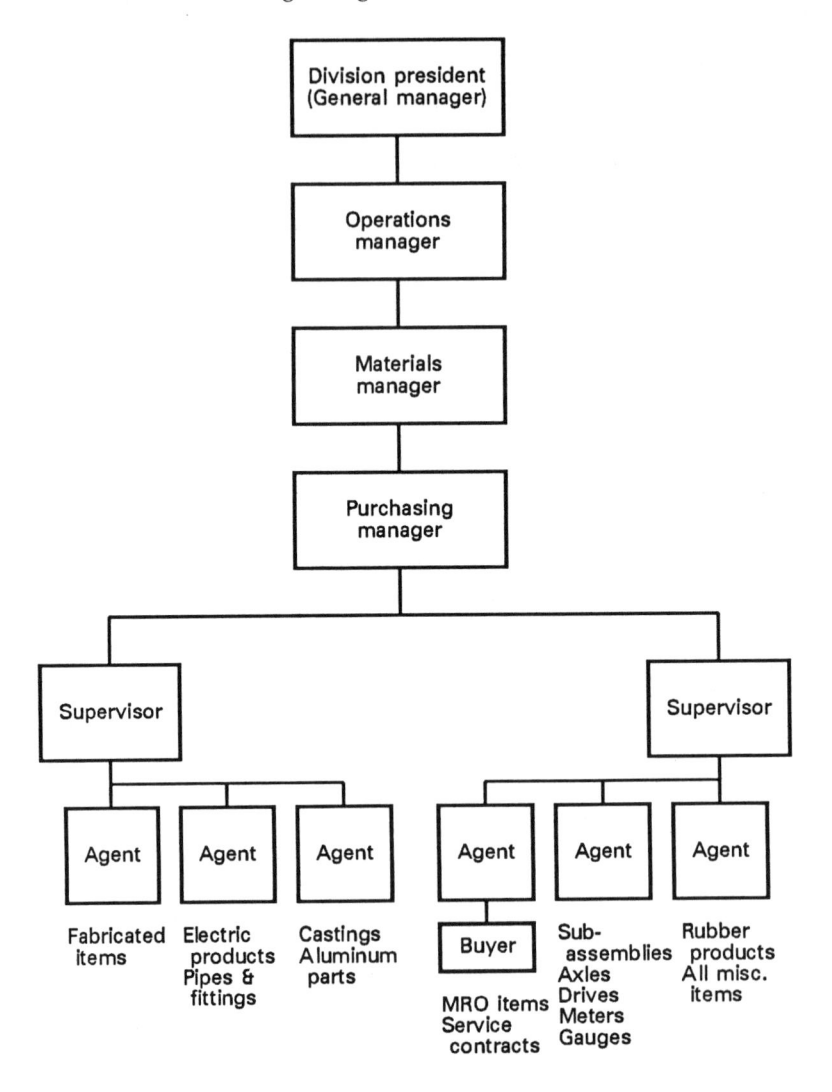

Figure 3–1. Chapman Machines' Purchasing Department: Organization Chart

department annually bought twenty-eight thousand items required for the operation of the plant. Except for the general guidelines set by the corporation regarding purchasing policy, the purchasing departments of each division functioned independently.

The following items purchased by the company through long-term contracts were studied in detail: front axle assemblies, hydraulic motors, and directional valve castings.

These items were selected because they each represent a different buying situation. Single situations for front axle assemblies required tactful negotiations with the supplier. Hydraulic motors were critical for the operation of $300,000 machines manufactured by the company. The special design of the motor restricted the number of suppliers on the bid list. Directional valve castings were being purchased for the first time. This item was of special interest in understanding how the purchasing agent screened potential suppliers for a new item.

Purchase of Front Axle Assemblies

Chapman Machines produced approximately three hundred heavy tamper machines annually. Each machine required a front axle assembly. The axle assembly was purchased through long-term "evergreen" contracts. Evergreen contracts have no limit on the time period of the contract. The buyer or seller can terminate the contract by giving notice in writing and allowing sufficient time to complete the "in-process" work.

The purchase history of this item dates back to the late 1950s, when Chapman Machines first began development work on large tamper machines. At that time Napco Industries, located in Minneapolis, had purchased a large fleet of old army trucks. They repaired these trucks, and sold them to industrial users. The trucks that could not be repaired were disassembled, and usable components were sold to customers who needed them. The old army trucks were known for the sturdy design of their front axles. Chapman Machines decided to use these axles in their tamper machines because of their ruggedness, reliability, and price advantage. Napco Industries fully cooperated with Chapman in modifying the design of these axles to suit the special needs of tamper machines.

Later, Napco Industries opened a repair shop for these axle assemblies, and started producing some of the axle components needed for repairs. In the late 1960s, Napco began the full manufacturing of front axle assemblies, and sold them to Chapman Machines. Napco and Chapman have worked together since then in developing the axle assembly currently used in tamper machines. Napco has always responded to the changing needs of the railroad industry, and modified the design of the front axle assembly when needed.

Chapman Machines had a blanket order for this item with Napco. Each year, Chapman would instruct Napco as to the annual requirements of front axle assemblies. Forecasts were updated every three months. Napco had been very fair in offering good prices for axle assemblies. They knew the company's needs, and their service was excellent, in spite of the fact that they were Chapman's only known source for this item.

Two years ago, Napco was bought out by Spicer Industries. The new management took a hard look at the axle assembly line, and felt that the profit margin on this item was too small. During the last two years, the price of the axle had increased from $1,480 to $1,850. This represented a 25 percent increase. The purchasing department was uneasy about the single-source situation for front axle assemblies. Claude Green (purchasing) and Warren Cole (engineering) visited several axle manufacturers. These manufacturers included Chrysler Corporation, Rockwell Industries, White Motors, General Motors, and General Dynamics. Because of the special design needed, and relatively small volume required, Rockwell, General Motors, and General Dynamics refused to quote. White Motors indicated a price of about $3,900 per axle assembly. Chrysler Corporation did not respond, even after several reminders.

The Buying Center

The following individuals were interviewed to study the decision process: Claude Green, purchasing supervisor; Warren Cole, product engineering manager; and Sarah Reese, inventory control supervisor.

Mr. Green was responsible for buying the front axle assemblies. He was working to develop new sources to end the current single-source situation.

Mr. Cole had the responsibility of specifying the axle assembly. He was also involved in approving new suppliers to submit bids. According to Mr. Cole, "No other supplier is interested because of the special design of the axle and the huge cost of development. Napco is fair, knows exactly what we need, responds to our changing requirements, and the relationship which has developed over many years is mutually beneficial."

Ms. Reese dealt directly with the supplier concerning shipment of the axle assembly when stock went below the required level. Ms. Reese observed, "Napco is extremely reliable for their delivery. They always do what they say. If they run into any problem, they immediately inform us. This has always helped to reschedule the production."

The purchasing agent sent a requisition to Spicer Industries for the 1980 requirement (three hundred) of front axle assemblies. With this, he included a detailed delivery schedule.

Spicer Industries responded after three weeks. They indicated that the price of the front axle assemblies would go up 11 percent in 1980. They explained in detail how the increase in material and labor costs were responsible for the price increase.

The purchasing agent discussed the 11-percent price increase with his purchasing manager. They decided to discuss this increase with Spicer Industries. A meeting was arranged with Spicer management in Minneapolis. The meeting was cordial and informative, but Spicer indicated that they could not roll back the price increase. The purchasing manager had no options. The price increase was confirmed by Chapman Machines. However, the purchasing agent resumed his search for new suppliers.

The purchase decision process as described above is shown in figure 3–2.

Evaluation

This is an excellent example of a single-source situation. Due to the enormous development costs, no other manufacturers were willing to submit offers. The current supplier had good quality, and reliable service and delivery. Therefore, the engineering, quality control, and product engineering departments were reluctant to switch to a new supplier.

Purchase of Hydraulic Motors

The large rail-laying machines produced by this division were an assembly of complex mechanical systems. The rail-laying machine used hydraulic systems for a variety of drives. The hydraulic system was operated by direct current electrical motors.

The company used about three hundred motors annually in the assembly of rail-laying machines. Each machine required one hydraulic motor. The cost of the motor ranged from $125 to $150. The company purchased these motors as a subassembly, to be mounted as part of the main hydraulic system of the machine.

Specifications for this item were prepared by the hydraulic systems engineering group. Because the motor was a component of a hydraulic system, the motor capacity, physical size, and operating duty cycle were determined as part of the complete system.

The company's policy was to buy the motors through annual contracts, directly from the motor manufacturer. Chapman Machines, in this case, was an original equipment manufacturer (OEM) for motor producers; therefore, they received special prices. Motor manufacturers prefer OEM business because it helps them to fill their basic production capacity. They can schedule production runs in advance, and thus increase efficiency. Thus, there is no build-up of excessive inventory of either the finished products or raw materials.

The Buying Center

The following individuals were interviewed to study the decision process: Sonny Harman, senior purchasing agent; John Cooper, hydraulic engineering manager; Bill Palmer, quality control manager; and Pat Roberts, materials manager.

Mr. Harman was in charge of buying hydraulic motors. He remained in

42 • *Industrial Purchasing Strategies*

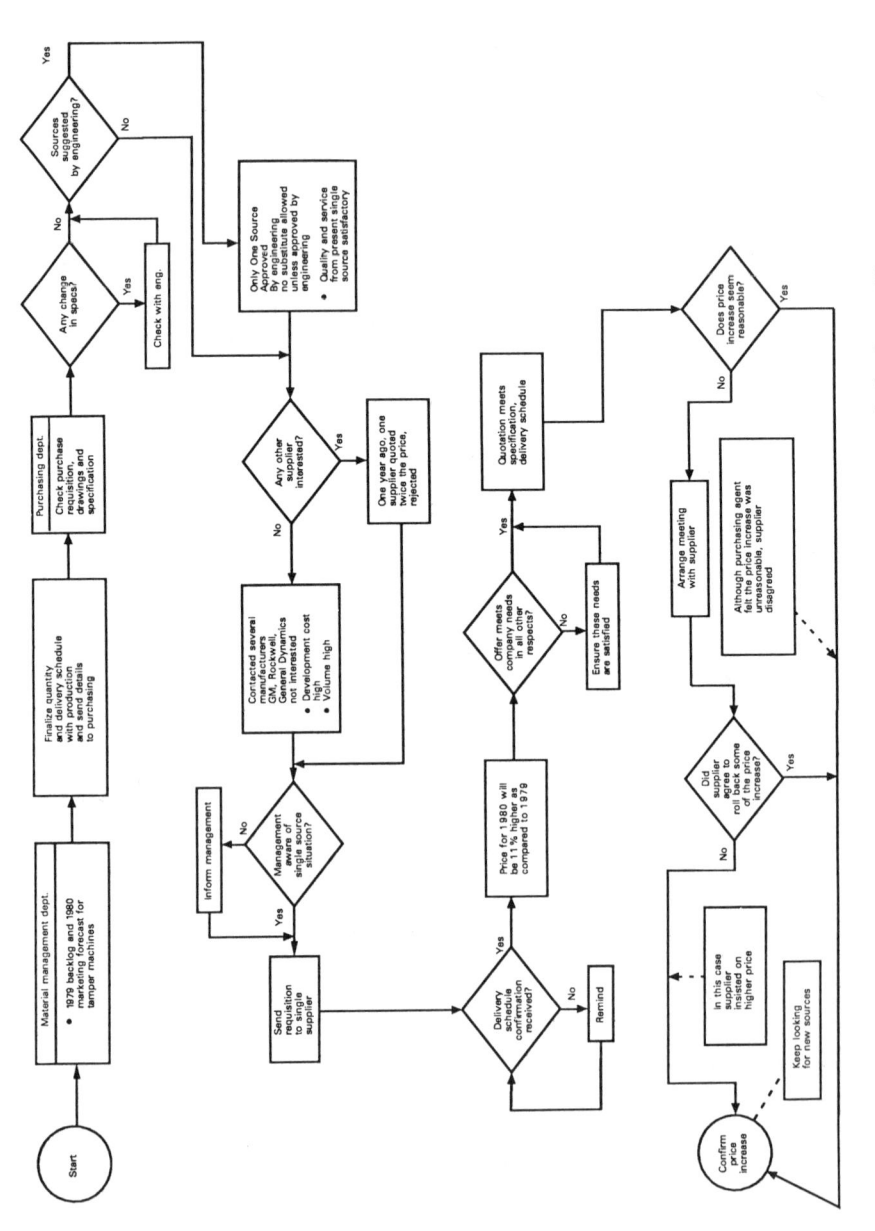

Figure 3–2. Purchase Decision Process: Front Axle Assembly

contact with the price-economic editor of *Purchasing World* magazine to keep abreast of price changes in the market for basic raw materials which might affect the cost of the items purchased by the company. "You must constantly stay abreast of market conditions; otherwise the vendor will snow you," argued Mr. Harman.

Mr. Roberts became involved when multiple sources were chosen to purchase an item such as hydraulic motors. He usually approved the purchasing department's decision to split the volume of the business among suppliers. However, he preferred to be kept informed.

Mr. Cooper specified motors. Vendors had to receive his approval, even in the case of minor deviations from the specifications. Mr. Palmer and Mr. Cooper were responsible for approving the vendors for hydraulic motors before bids were submitted.

Selecting Suppliers to Submit Bids

Motor specifications were determined at the time of the design of the hydraulic system. The design engineer, Mr. Cooper, pointed out, "We design around the equipment we know, and vendors we are familiar with." The design engineers, based on their past experience and familiarity with certain manufacturers' equipment, used their items as components of the system they were designing. Usually the engineer got technical assistance from the manufacturer during the design stage. The supplier's engineering department could design equipment specifically to meet the needs of the designer. They could also do this in the case of hydraulic motors. The design engineer worked closely with three or four motor manufacturers, who agreed to meet the special dimensional needs of the system. Once the system was designed, it was tested extensively within the company plant, and then in the field. Based on the results of this testing, the design was modified until it worked satisfactorily.

The hydraulic motors were required to meet certain mounting details, dimensions, pressures, duty cycles, vibration resistance, and temperature cycles. Those manufacturers whose motors were tested and approved by the hydraulic engineering department as part of the system were the only approved suppliers.

Four manufacturers were on the engineering-approved list. Any new supplier had to be approved by engineering. Before approval, the engineers conducted extensive evaluation and testing programs within the plant and in the field. This was expensive and time consuming. Therefore, without compelling reasons, engineering was reluctant to approve additional suppliers. They had other priorities. Approving new suppliers for components of existing systems that were working just fine was a very low priority. Therefore, when the purchase requisition was received from production control, the purchasing department compiled a list of approved vendors from engineering. Then they quickly checked with other departments to determine if any of the approved suppliers' past performances were unsatisfactory; if they were, they were dropped.

In this case, there were four manufacturers on the approved list. Two of these were existing suppliers, whose performances had been satisfactory. The purchasing agent decided to send RFQ's to all four suppliers. They were given two weeks to submit quotations.

Evaluating and Selecting Suppliers

All four suppliers sent in their bids on time. The motors were offered according to company specifications by all of them. The delivery schedule given by each vendor was also acceptable. The prices were FOB shipping point, and the purchasing department converted them to FOB destination by adding freight and insurance charges. All suppliers offered a firm price for six months. The prices were subject to negotiation thereafter. Terms of payment were identical for all—net 30 days.

The next step was to analyze the prices. The two existing "in" suppliers quoted lower prices than the other "out" suppliers. Because their prices were about 8 to 10 percent higher, the two "out" suppliers were rejected.

Of the remaining suppliers, one quoted $130 per motor, and the other quoted $147. Because the purchasing agent wanted to have two sources, the order was split between the suppliers. Price was used as a basis for dividing the volume of available business. The purchasing agent decided on a seventy-thirty split. He explained, "This will save the company the maximum amount and at the same time keeps the second source interested in the company's business." (Interestingly, the purchasing agent indicated that the supplier who quoted $147 was the primary supplier in 1979, with 60 percent of the company's business. Last year their price was $117; the other supplier had quoted $122.)

Three months into the contract period, the primary supplier for 1980 ran into delivery problems. Because of a huge backlog of orders from other customers, it would be six weeks before he could deliver any motors to Chapman Machines. The purchasing agent cancelled the order. Additional business was given to the second supplier. Fresh quotes were obtained from the other two suppliers.

Figure 3–3 gives the flowchart for the purchase decision process.

Evaluation

The policy of having multiple sources paid off in this case. The delivery of hydraulic motors was not adversely affected by the primary supplier's inability to deliver.

"When the company designs a system around an item which is specially developed to meet the specific requirements, it takes a long time to develop a new source. Therefore, one must develop as many sources as possible during the design stage," the materials manager said. The purchasing agent felt that, taking into account the increase in prices of copper and steel, the prices quoted by the two existing suppliers were reasonable. Company policy was not to negotiate prices with suppliers. "If you push them too far, they will drop you like a hot potato in the time of shortages. You can't afford to stop the production of a $300,000 machine for the lack of a $150 hydraulic motor. We expect our suppliers to quote the best price to start with. It saves their time and our time in unnecessary negotiations," argued Mr. Harman, the senior purchasing agent.

Purchase of Directional Valve Castings

The railroad division of Chapman Machines was renowned for manufacturing railroad track equipment. One of the largest machines produced here was a rail-laying machine. The company produced about three hundred rail-laying machines per year. Each machine used seven highly specialized hydraulic valves, which the company purchased from a hydraulic valve manufacturer.

For the past several years, hydraulic valve failures were a major problem. The company worked with the supplier, but was unable to completely eliminate the quality control problem that seemed to be causing the failure. Hydraulic valves are highly engineered items, requiring close tolerances in machining. The design of the valve at that time required castings to age for a certain length of time to relieve stresses in the metal. If this was not done carefully, the valve might lose the specified tolerances after a certain length of service.

The supplier at this time was the only manufacturer for this item. Other suppliers consistently quoted higher prices, and were unwilling to quote acceptable delivery schedules. In addition, this supplier had been raising the prices of hydraulic valves an average of 10 percent each year for the past two years. The company felt that this was unreasonable, but because of the single-source situation, were unable to do anything about it.

About four years ago, the company hired one of the top hydraulic engineers in the country to develop and redesign the entire hydraulic system in the rail-laying machines. He was respected in the industry for his knowledge in the design of hydraulic systems. Because the problem of valve failure was urgent, he was assigned to solve this problem. After intensive analysis, he submitted a proposal to the company. He suggested the development of an entirely new design of hydraulic valves. The highlights of his report to management included the following:

1. The present design of the hydraulic valve was outdated, expensive, and required castings that must be allowed to age. The present supplier's expert and

46 • *Industrial Purchasing Strategies*

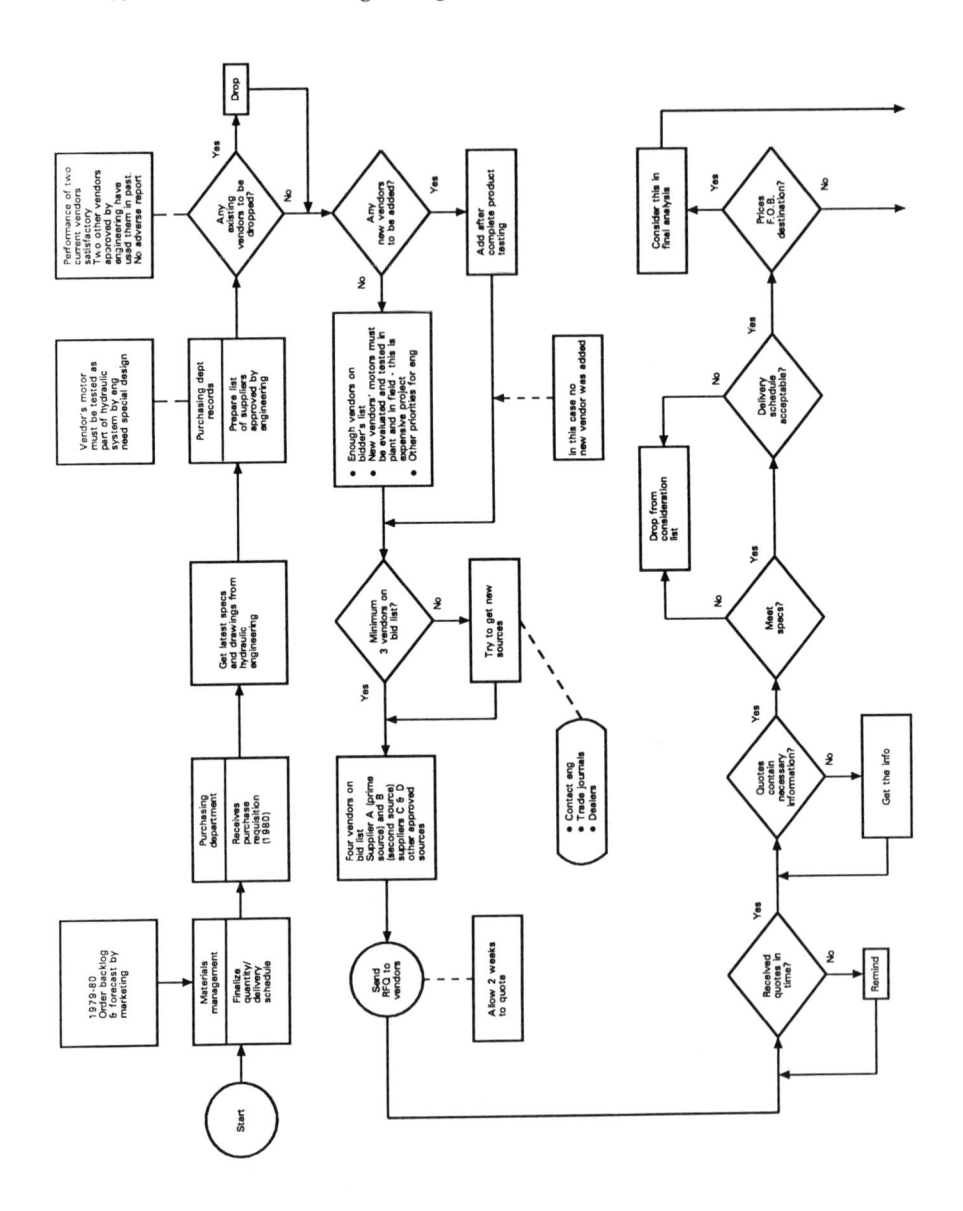

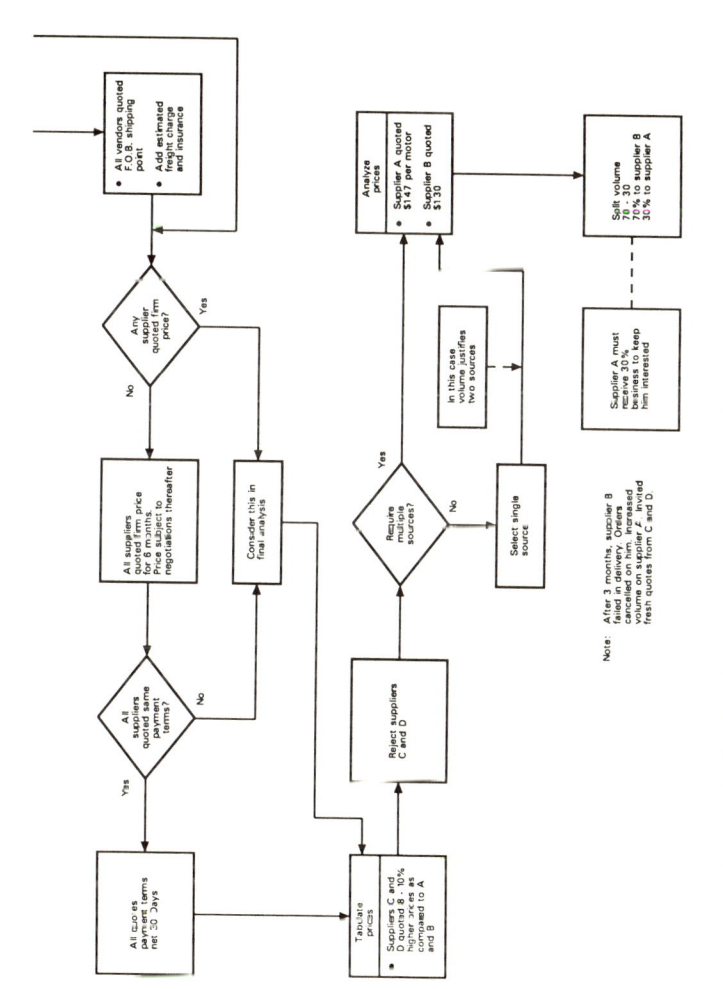

Figure 3–3. Purchase Decision Process: Hydraulic Motors

experienced machinists have retired, and this supplier constantly had quality control problems.

2. The company is currently paying $338 for each valve. The new design suggested by the hydraulic engineer would cost the company only $52, if manufactured by this division of the company. This would save about $600,000 every year.

3. If the project were approved, there would be a possibility of the company selling these valves to other railroad manufacturers, including the company's other division in Switzerland. The Swiss division was currently using more expensive valves, which it bought from a European supplier.

Two years ago, management approved the proposal, after analyzing the development cost, the market potential, and the time required to complete the project. In late 1979, the design work was completed. The prototype was successfully tested by the hydraulic laboratory at the University of Wisconsin. The division then ran a pilot production of two thousand valves.

The company was in the market for two thousand castings for the body of the new directional valve. The complete valve system consisted of several components that were assembled within the casting of the valve. The market potential for the new valve was estimated to be about ten thousand per year for the next three years.

The pilot production for 1980 was the responsibility of the hydraulic engineering department. Therefore, the purchase requisition for two thousand directional valve castings was sent to purchasing from this department.

The Buying Center

The following people were interviewed who were involved in the decision process: Art Sims, purchasing supervisor; Pat Keenan, purchasing manager; Bill Page, quality control manager; Harry Mann, chief hydraulic engineer; and Warren Cole, product engineering manager.

Mr. Sims was responsible for purchasing all types of castings for the company. He was familiar with the foundries in the southeastern United States. He coordinated the entire decision process in the purchase of castings for the hydraulic valve.

Mr. Keenan asked Mr. Sims to keep him informed of the decision process, because the castings were being purchased for an item to be produced in the plant for the first time. "I would like to make sure the purchase order is placed without losing too much time. We have schedule dates to meet. The top management is watching us because of their keen interest in this new product," Mr. Keenan said.

Mr. Page and Mr. Mann were responsible for approving potential suppliers. They visited the suppliers' facilities when necessary, and tested the samples.

Mr. Cole was involved in reviewing specifications. He also held discussions with suppliers' representatives. They talked about machining operations to be carried out on the castings after they had been delivered to Chapman Machines.

Selecting Suppliers to Submit Bids

The company decided to purchase the castings on an annual contract. The quantity of two thousand would be required over several months. The company did not want to have a contract period longer than one year for several reasons. This was a new product, and the quantity required in the following year was dependent on the results of the pilot production. Also, after suppliers had produced several castings, they would get a better feel for the cost. They would then be willing to quote for a contract period longer than one year.

The hydraulic engineering department developed specifications for castings in consultation with production engineering, industrial engineering, quality control, the University of Wisconsin, and several suppliers of castings. The hydraulic engineer, from his experience in the industry, knew several reputable castings manufacturers and was in contact with them during the development of the prototype units. Two suppliers submitted samples for testing. One supplier had trouble attaining the proper strength, and decided to reevaluate the process. The hydraulic engineer and the quality control manager visited the suppliers' facilities and discussed technical concerns with their engineering personnel. They were satisfied with the suppliers' quality, inspection procedures, and capacity to produce the required number of castings.

The hydraulic engineer had recommended these two vendors in his purchase requisition. The purchasing agent prepared a list of several existing suppliers in the area. Two of these supplied other types of castings to the company. The purchasing agent saw two advertisements in the foundry magazine specifically for hydraulic valve castings. He requested that these companies send their sales representatives for discussions. Both new suppliers were interested in submitting bids after receiving specifications. The purchasing agent thus had six suppliers on the bidders list.

The purchasing agent had formally collected information on the financial status of the new suppliers. He also examined their production capacities, names of current customers, number of employees, and the experience and qualifications of their engineering and quality control personnel. Technical brochures, along with the above information, were submitted to the hydraulic engineering department for their approval. The purchasing agent explained that such approval was not required. However, because this was a new product, it was good to consult them, and to gain approval. Approval was given by the hydraulic engineering department; they commented that they would prefer to see the samples of castings for similar products.

The purchasing agent sent RFQ's to the six suppliers. All of them were asked to quote the cost of tooling separately, in this case, the cost of molds and patterns. They were also requested to quote in quantities of five hundred pieces. They were given four weeks to submit the quotations.

What is the maximum number of suppliers allowable on the bidders list? What is the minimum number? These questions were asked of the purchasing agent. He responded, "The minimum number is three according to company policy. There is no restriction on the maximum number of vendors you can have, but for a new item like this, it is good to have more than three. The goal is to make sure there is enough competition."

Evaluating and Selecting Suppliers

All of the suppliers responded on time. The two suppliers who had worked with the hydraulic engineer submitted bids. The remaining four suppliers declined to quote, explaining that the castings were too intricate for their facilities to make.

Both suppliers complied with company specifications, quoted acceptable delivery schedules, and indicated payment terms of net 30 days. Both suppliers also quoted prices FOB destination. Each indicated a firm price for ninety days, and price escalation based on the price of scrap metal thereafter. The scrap metal prices were published weekly in the foundry magazine.

Supplier A was successful in submitting a sample of the required quality during the development stage. Supplier B had problems producing castings that were strong enough. It submitted several samples before one passed the pressure tests.

The price analysis is shown below.

Supplier	Price
A	$5,950 (tooling)
	$15.75 each (1,000 pcs.)
B	$7,300 (tooling)
	$25.45 each (1,000 pcs.)

Because the tooling cost was high, the order for the entire quantity was placed with one supplier. Supplier B experienced failures of some castings submitted earlier. It may have quoted casting prices almost 50 percent higher because of the failure rate anticipated in the earlier production. Based on the prices quoted, the order was placed with Supplier A. Supplier B was retained as a back-up source, and was told to reevaluate its tooling and casting costs for the following year. In the meantime, the purchasing agent decided to search for additional sources.

The entire decision process as described is depicted in figure 3–4.

Evaluation

Supplier A was associated with the development project from a very early stage. It established contact with the hydraulic engineer, understood his requirements, and developed castings to meet the specifications. These factors facilitated Supplier A's success.

This is an excellent example showing the importance of understanding the customer's needs at an early stage in the development process for a new item. The suppliers involved at a later stage may not fully understand the specifications, and may decide not to quote, thereby losing an important new customer.

The engineering department played a decisive role in developing and approving the sources, because this was a new item.

52 • Industrial Purchasing Strategies

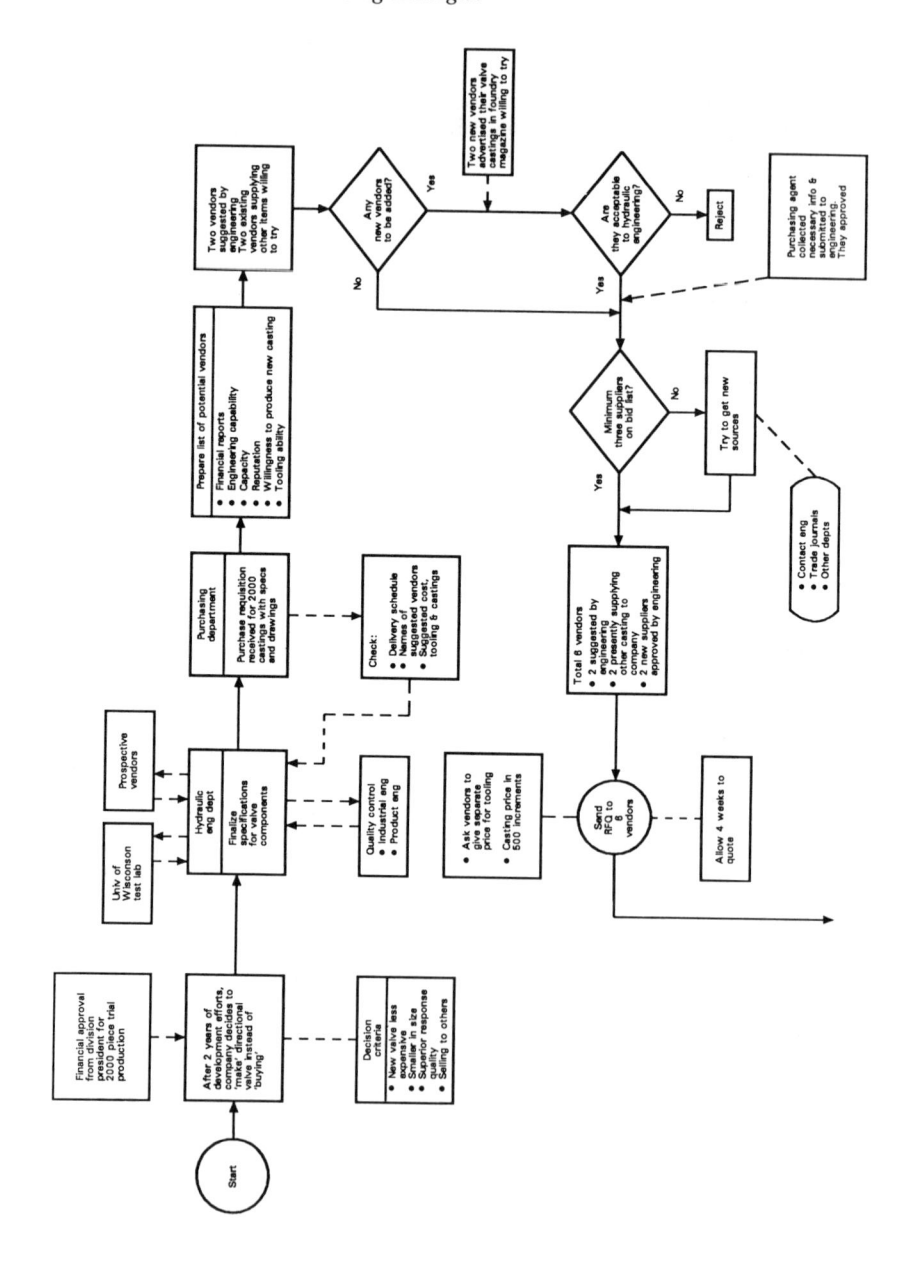

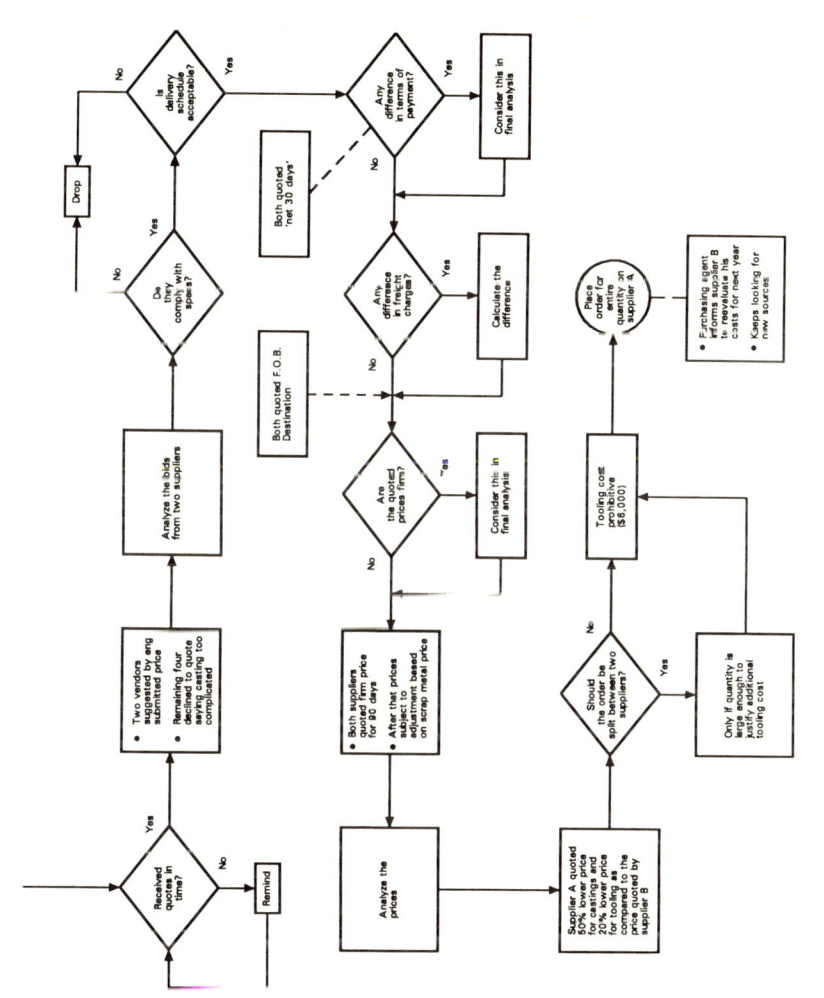

Figure 3-4. Purchase Decision Process: Casting for Directional Valve

4
Buying Castings, Bars, and Blades at Regal Technologies

Regal Technologies is a Chicago-based corporation that employs about 120,000 people worldwide. Of these, twenty-one thousand are located outside the United States. Approximately 16 percent of the employees are professional engineers, scientists, or supporting technical staff. The company had worldwide sales of $8 billion in fiscal year 1979, which was 16 percent higher than sales in 1978. Pretax earnings for 1979 reached $550 million, a new record, up 17 percent from the previous year's level.

The company was founded in 1915 as a manufacturer of truck axles and brakes. It was incorporated in 1929 in New York. In 1961, the company was merged with North Atlantic Corporation, a leading supplier of armored vehicles and railroad equipment. In 1971, Clark Radio, a well-known supplier of communications electronics, was added.

Regal Technologies currently has four business segments, each headed by a corporate vice president who is the president of that particular segment. Each corporate vice president also serves as a board member. The four segments, from largest to smallest, are automotive, aerospace, electronics, and general industries.

Automotive components, which are primarily heavy-duty truck axles and brakes, comprise the company's largest and most profitable business. The firm supplies OEM (original equipment manufacturer) components to the domestic industry. It has begun to enlarge its overseas role through joint ventures and acquisitions, primarily in Europe.

Regal is the primary defense contractor for nuclear ships, and is also a major supplier of satellite systems, components for the MX missile, and business aircraft.

The electronics segment supplies a large variety of aircraft and missile guidance and communications systems. These include the digital flight instrumentation for Boeing's 757 and 767 transports, as well as commercial telecommunications equipment and specialized electronic components. Electronics is Regal's fastest growing segment.

General industries is a catch-all category. It includes a very large energy-related segment, primarily manufacturing valves and meters. This segment also receives considerable government funding for research on nuclear- and coal-related power plants and conversion systems. This division is also the leading supplier of large newspaper presses, industrial sewing machines, U.S. loom components, and woodworking tools.

In 1979, about 40 percent of Regal's sales were to the U.S. government, primarily for aerospace and electronics; this was an increase from 36 percent in 1978. International sales accounted for 25 percent of the total revenue.

Management Structure

Regal's management structure is an orthodox hierarchy. There are 150 separate profit centers, consolidated into fifty-two divisions. Most of these are associated with twelve groups, which are divided among the four operations of the firm, described earlier. The presidents of these operations are corporate vice presidents; they report to the chairman and chief executive officer of Regal.

Complementing this operating hierarchy is the financial control network. The controllers, down to the profit center level, report directly to the firm's chief financial officer. They also report to their operating segment's president. Though this dual reporting system is difficult to maintain, it does minimize the risk of surprises.

The firm's planning cycle is for five years, and includes a more detailed one-year operating forecast. Planning begins at the profit center level; it is then consolidated into a corporate forecast. This from-the-bottom-up approach ensures greater realism as well as more effective employee involvement.

Over the next five years, the firm projects sales growth of 14 percent with earnings rising more rapidly at 17 percent. This reflects improving operating margins. Management believes that this growth can be funded internally, provided that the current 18 percent ROE (return on earnings) is maintained.

Industrial Tool and Railroad Division

The research for this study was conducted at one of the seven plants of Regal that manufactures industrial tools. The industrial tool division contributed $300 million to the company's total revenue of $8 billion.

The products marketed by this division include a comprehensive range of portable electric and compressed-air tools for professionals; high-speed drills for aerospace and automotive markets; heavy-duty rotary hammers; and special dry-wall fasteners used in construction. For the do-it-yourself consumer, various types of portable electric, stationary, and automotive air tools are manufactured.

The plant where the research was conducted manufactures only industrial air tools. This plant was built about fifteen years ago, and presently employs six hundred people. Regal industrial air tools are respected throughout the industry for their quality and engineering standards. More than forty years of air tool engineering expertise, research experience, and assembly techniques are incorporated into the Regal comprehensive line of air tools. At this plant, the product line in the woodwork area is currently being expanded.

Purchasing Organization

This plant uses more than eighty-thousand components in the assembly of air tools. About half of these components are purchased from outside vendors. The total value of the items purchased is approximately $15 million. This constitutes 34 percent of the total value of tools manufactured at this location.

This plant has its own purchasing department; it buys the items required for regular production. There is little central purchasing at Regal because each plant produces specific products, and uses a different manufacturing process. The company has corporate purchasing guidelines and policies, which each purchasing department follows.

There are five buyers at this location, who report directly to the purchasing manager. The purchasing manager reports to the materials manager, who is supervised by the plant manager. In addition, there is a value engineer, who reports directly to the materials department. His main function is to reduce the cost of purchased components used in the assembly of air tools. He develops good sources of supply and evaluates their capabilities, and suggests "make" or "buy" alternatives to management. He also prepares a budget for components purchased for the newly manufactured items. He has direct contact with vendors, and has the authority to conduct technical discussions with suppliers on behalf of the purchasing department; he also visits vendor facilities when necessary. When an item is technically complex, he acts as a coordinator with design engineering, production engineering, and quality control. He assesses their needs and helps the purchasing department evaluate the items offered by suppliers.

The responsibility for purchasing is divided among buyers, as shown in figure 4–1.

The following items purchased through long-term contracts were selected for study: investment castings, steel rods (bar stock), and woodhog blades. Investment castings represent a typical item purchased through a long-term contract. The steel rods were purchased as needed in the past, but the company decided to buy them through a long-term contract in 1980. Woodhog blades

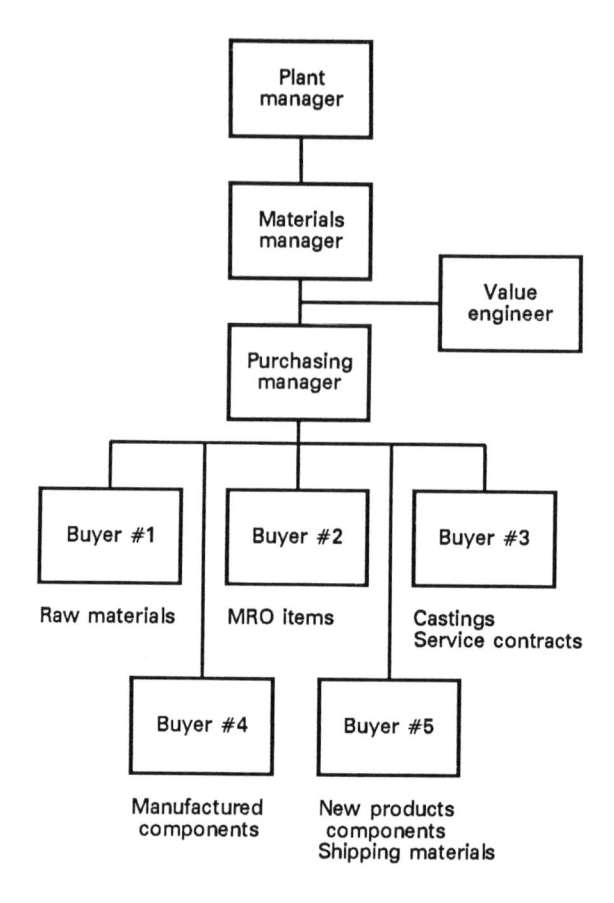

```
                    Plant
                    manager
                       |
                    Materials ———— Value
                    manager        engineer
                       |
                    Purchasing
                    manager
        ┌──────────────┼──────────────┐
     Buyer #1       Buyer #2       Buyer #3
     Raw materials  MRO items      Castings
                                   Service contracts
              ┌──────────┴──────────┐
           Buyer #4              Buyer #5
           Manufactured          New products
           components            components
                                 Shipping materials
```

Figure 4–1. Regal Technologies' Purchasing Department: Organizational Chart

were manufactured by Regal, but the company decided to buy them from an outside source in 1980, to see if "buying" would be less expensive than "making" them.

Purchase of Investment Castings

The company purchases investment castings, which constitute the main body of compressed-air tools. The term "investment" is used to identify a type of casting that is precise in maintaining specified dimensions. Because of this precision, a minimum of machining is required during tool assembly.

The total value of investment castings purchased by the company is approximately $500,000 annually. There are about 120 varieties of investment castings used to produce various models of air tools. According to the purchasing agent, "These castings are needed on a continuous basis to keep the production going. The company policy is to buy the castings on long-term contract to assure continuity of supply and to get better prices because of volume buying."

The specifications for investment castings are prepared by the engineering department in consultation with value engineering, industrial engineering, and vendors. Engineering strives to specify castings that apply the latest technology and materials. This saves money without sacrificing quality and requires minimum machining when castings are received. This necessitates the preparation of detailed drawings, which indicate precise dimensions needed, including acceptable deviations. These drawings are crucial for the vendors. The purchasing agents pointed out that "engineering has a habit of revising the drawing continuously and they forget to keep us informed of these changes. If we are not careful, the vendor will produce castings based on earlier drawings and when the castings are delivered, quality control will reject them since they are not per the latest revisions. This type of error can cost the company large amounts of money and lost production time."

The Buying Center

The following people were interviewed to study the purchase decision process: Marvin Benton, purchasing agent; Daniel Williams, design engineer; and Harry Bailey, value engineer.

Mr. Benton is responsible for buying all types of castings for the company, including investment castings for the air tools. He remains aware of market trends by reading commodity price reports from *The Wall Street Journal*, and various purchasing magazines. From his reading, Mr. Benton realized that "the slowdown in the auto industry has caused a slowdown in the demand for aluminum parts including aluminum castings. The prices for these items should go down. I will watch the prices very closely when we get the bids from suppliers for aluminum castings."

Mr. Williams and Mr. Bailey are responsible for providing specifications for the investment castings. They also perform technical evaluations of the bids received from suppliers.

Selecting Suppliers to Submit Bids

The purchasing agent indicated that "the manufacture of investment castings requires special skills and only a few foundries have the facilities to do the job well." Most of the suppliers are aware of the company's needs, and their sales representatives visit regularly. The most common way of getting acquainted with a new supplier is through the visiting salesman. The purchasing department also receives suggestions from value engineering and design engineering, who read technical magazines and attend trade shows.

In this case, there were four established suppliers. One of these had been extremely busy lately, with a large backlog of orders. Deliveries had therefore taken too long. The other supplier had consistently quoted high prices in the past. For these reasons, these suppliers were dropped. One new supplier was added this year, after its sales representative had called the company. According to the value engineer, "Further investigation into this supplier indicated that they have a good engineering and management staff, ample capacity, and a fine reputation for tooling facility. The samples of similar items produced for their other customers indicated quality workmanship."

Thus, three suppliers were included on the final bidders list. Two of these sources had performed satisfactorily in past business; one new source seemed to have acceptable quality and was willing to do business with the company.

The purchasing agent explained his philosophy of selecting vendors for bids as follows. "It is always a good policy to drop one supplier from last year's bidder list and add a new source to this year's list if possible. You penalize the supplier who quoted consistently higher prices by dropping him and telling him so. Simultaneously you are giving a chance to a new source who may quote very competitive prices and save you some money, and in the process you have developed a new source for the company which assures good competition in the future for the company's business." The purchasing agent explained that in this way the bidders list remains manageable. The agent's work load does not increase, and supplier prices remain competitive. Suppliers realize that quoting high prices may lead to their being dropped. The purchasing agent further indicated that the time and effort spent developing and analyzing more than six good suppliers is not justified by improvements gained. Company policy required a minimum of three suppliers on the bidders list. The maximum number was restricted to six, in order to increase efficiency in the purchasing department. The agent stressed that an average purchasing agent buys from five to six thousand items per year, and time is an important factor to consider.

The company sent RFQs to three suppliers, to meet the company's requirement for 1980 investment castings. Suppliers were given two weeks to submit quotations. Each supplier was requested to quote a price supplying the basic price of the casting, as well as the total cost of tooling. The cost of tooling was required because a slight change in the drawings of castings would result in a need for new moldings and tooling. After a couple of reminders, all three suppliers submitted their prices within four weeks.

Evaluating and Selecting Suppliers

Because the tooling cost is about $12,000, it is not advisable to have more than one supplier. Having more than one supplier would require having a second set of molds, doubling the tooling cost. When the company pays for molds and tooling, these belong to Regal. If the performance of the existing supplier is not satisfactory, the company may ask for the molds to be returned, and may give them to another supplier.

The purchasing agent analyzed the quotes. The deliveries quoted by all three suppliers were acceptable, meeting company specifications. The prices quoted were FOB destination, and terms of payment given by all three suppliers were 2% 10, net 30 days. None of the suppliers quoted a firm price. The price adjustment quoted was based on variations in the price of metal. However, each supplier indicated that before increasing prices, they would give ninety days' notice. The three quotations were very similar in these aspects. The company next compared the price of tooling to the number of castings to be supplied annually. They added this cost to the cost of each casting. Each supplier's price was thus converted for comparison.

The new supplier's price quoted was 7 percent higher than the lowest price. Because this supplier was a new source, and also quoted the highest price, it was dropped. The price difference between the other suppliers was 4.5 percent. The purchasing agent considered the following. Does the second lowest bidder have any specific strong points that would justify the price difference? Strong points could include reliability in delivery, better service, and better quality. Because the price difference could not be justified, the agent placed his order with the supplier quoting the lowest price. As explained earlier, the order was not divided between two suppliers because of the extra tooling cost involved.

The purchasing decision process is depicted in figure 4–2.

Evaluation

The purchasing agent was effective in updating the bidders list. He stated, "You add one supplier and drop one if possible at the time of inviting fresh bids. This keeps the suppliers on their toes."

Because of the supplier choice process, a new supplier quoting higher prices was dropped from consideration early in the decision process. During the final evaluation, price differences between the two acceptable suppliers were weighed against their attributes. These included past performance, quality, service, and delivery reliability. Thus, price became the determining factor only when the suppliers possessed similar attributes.

The company does not negotiate prices with the vendors unless collusion is detected among vendors submitting bids. "If the vendors know we are going to negotiate, they will hesitate to quote their best price to begin with. Then you spend too much time negotiating with each vendor, and in the end you are still not sure if you negotiated enough," argued the purchasing agent.

62 • *Industrial Purchasing Strategies*

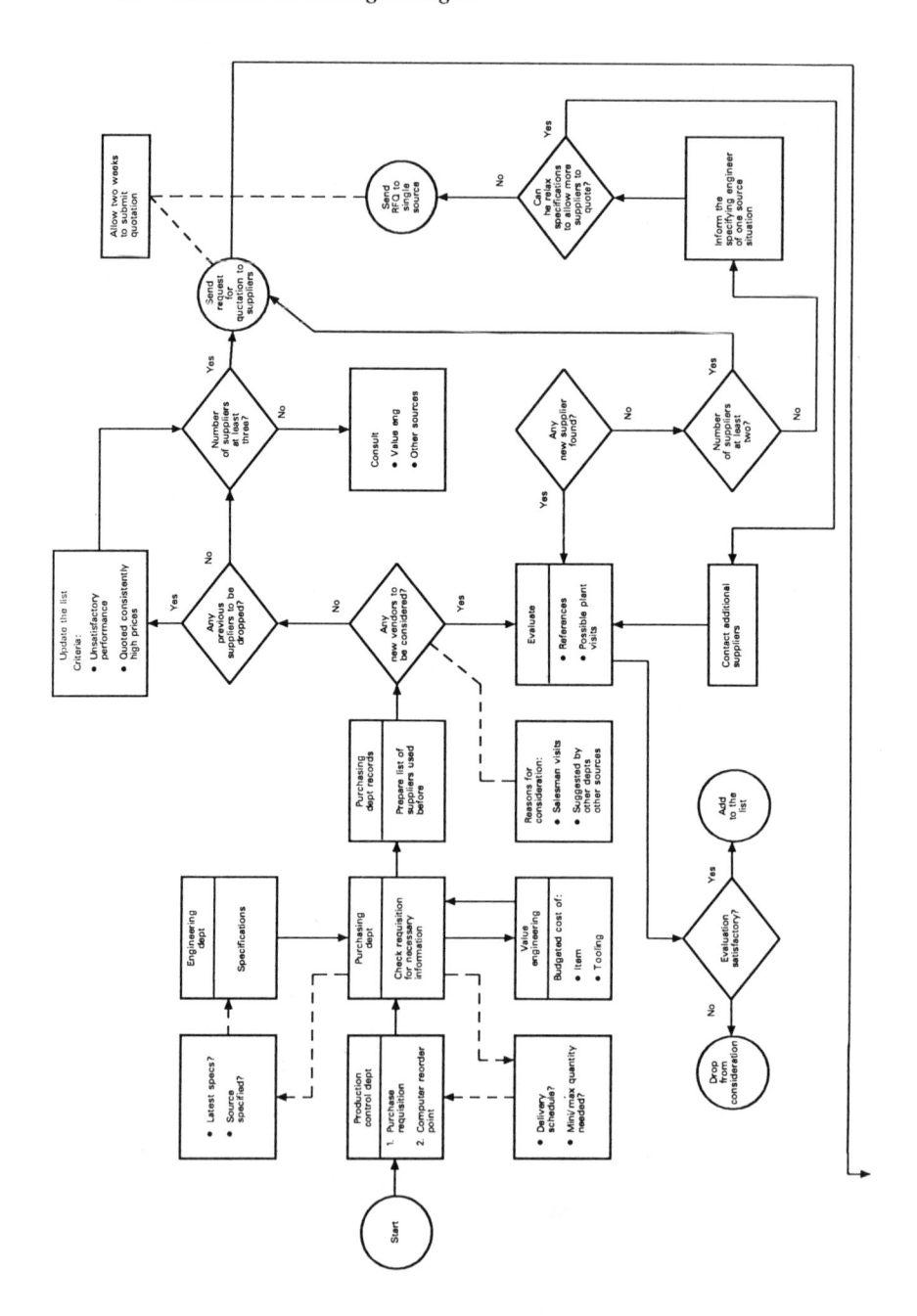

Regal Technologies • 63

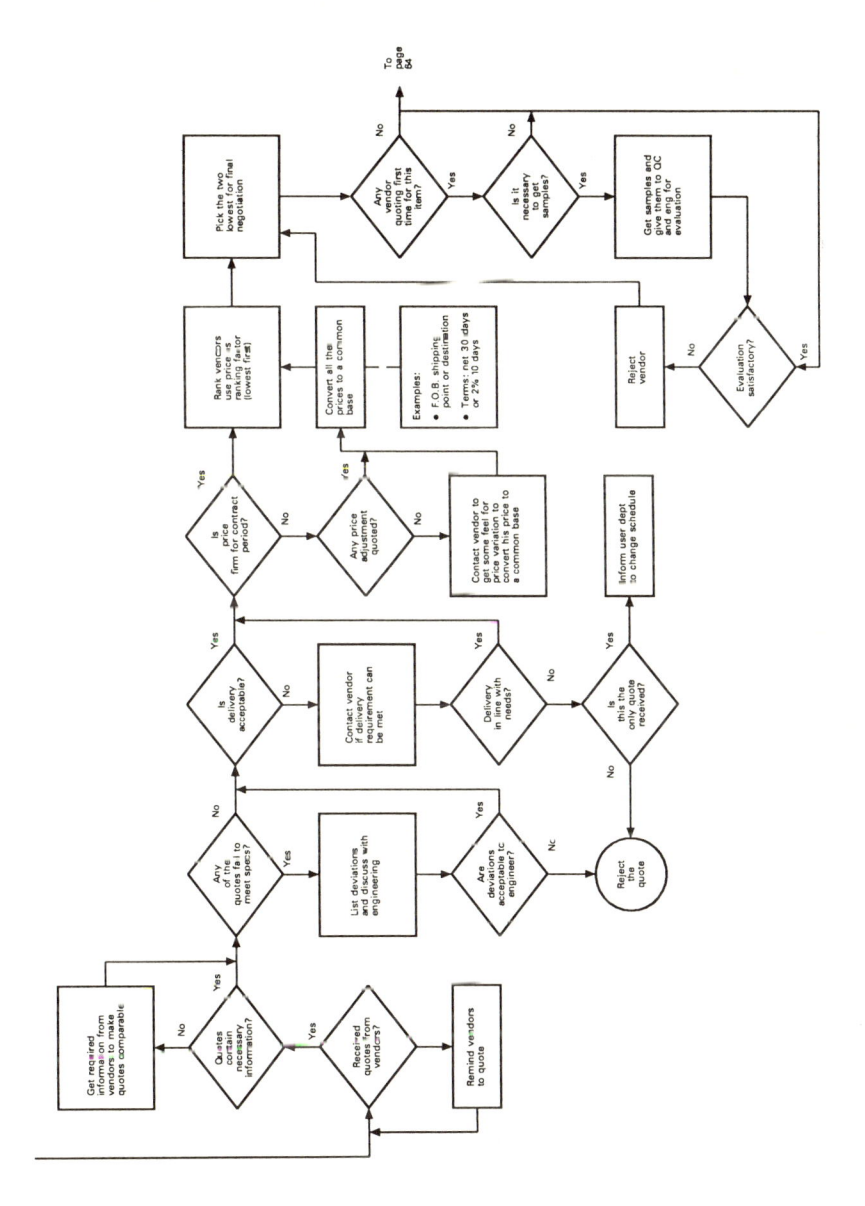

Figure 4–2. Purchase Decision Process: Casting for Pneumatic Tool (continued)

64 • *Industrial Purchasing Strategies*

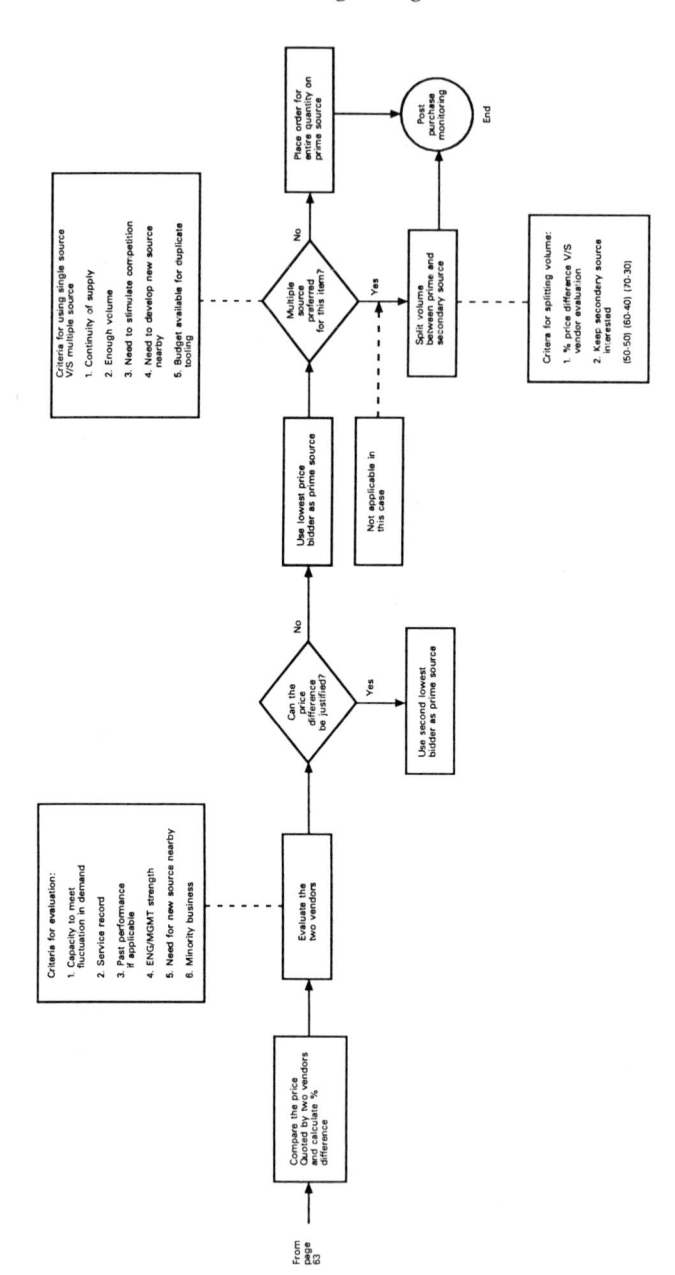

Figure 4–2. Purchase Decision Process: Casting for Pneumatic Tool (continued)

Purchase of Steel Rods (Bar Stock)

Regal purchases steel rods or bar stock (in technical terms) to manufacture a variety of items. These include spindles, pinion shafts, extension attachments, and many other components needed to produce compressed-air tools. Approximately four hundred different sizes and grades of steel rods are purchased at a total cost of $120,000.

Bar stock can be purchased directly from steel mills, but the minimum quantity of each size and grade ordered would have to be ten thousand pounds. Delivery from the mills varies from three to four months. The quantity of bar stock Regal needs is not large enough to justify buying directly from the mills; therefore, they purchase bar stock from distributors. Although their prices are 30 to 35 percent higher than those quoted by the mills, there are several advantages to buying from distributors. First, in buying the variety of bar stock needed, the company would have to go to several different mills, as most mills specialize in certain sizes and grades of steel rods. However, distributors stock items from several mills, and most of the company's needs can be met by two or three distributors. Secondly, the distributors can usually ship items within a week, or twenty-four hours when urgently needed. This reduces both the company's inventory of bar stock and the space used to store it. Third, the service given by the distributors is better than that of the mills.

The company prefers to buy these rods on an annual contract from distributors for several reasons. The company gets better prices from distributors when purchasing a greater quantity. Annual contracts also allow distributors to plan their stocking schedules, and when to order from the mills. However, because of fluctuations in steel prices, the distributors are not willing to enter into a contract agreement for more than a year.

In the past, the company has been purchasing bar stock from distributors on the spot market. The new purchasing manager, who joined the company about a year ago, analyzed bar stock purchasing processes. He determined that the items needed could be purchased on long-term annual contracts, with substantial cost savings. He also felt that annual contracts would save the purchasing department the time and effort required in buying continuously from the market. Purchasing through annual contracts would also force production control to predict their needs more accurately, and avoid urgent shipments from distributors.

The bar stock is purchased according to ASII (American Steel and Iron Institute) specifications, which are well known and accepted by the industry. The company simply specifies the size and grade of the bars required. They need not specify the name of the mill that manufactures these rods, as all of them are manufactured to meet ASII standards.

The Buying Center

The following individuals were interviewed: Wesley Derrick, purchasing agent, Bill Wilson, purchasing manager; Harry Bailey, value engineer; and Vincent Kimble, administrative engineer.

Mr. Derrick is responsible for purchasing bar stock. Mr. Wilson initiated the idea of purchasing bar stock on an annual contract; he delegated this project to Mr. Derrick. Mr. Wilson wanted to make the final decision on vendors selected, as this was the first time bar stock was purchased through an annual contract.

Mr. Bailey and Mr. Derrick visited various distributors of bar stock on the original bid list and analyzed the strengths and weaknesses of each in meeting Regal's needs.

The purchasing department asked Mr. Kimble if the variety of steel rods currently used could be reduced. In other words, Mr. Kimble was asked to investigate the possibility of using a common size and grade of steel rod to make as many different parts as possible. Mr. Kimble and individuals from local distributors were involved in technical discussions with the representatives of steel mills.

Selecting Suppliers to Submit Bids

Because the company was buying bar stock on an annual contract for the first time, the purchasing department initiated discussions with existing distributors. These distributors supply bar stock to the company on a spot purchase basis. There are currently twelve suppliers who supply Regal with bar stock through individual purchase orders. The sales representatives from all of these suppliers expressed a willingness to participate in the annual contract bids. The purchasing department collected the following information on each supplier to qualify them to bid on annual contracts.

1. *Ability to carry a large inventory of bar stock.* This is a primary requirement for any supplier in meeting the company's demand. This includes warehouse facilities, method of maintaining inventory of items in stock, variety of size and grade of steel rods in stock, and financial strength. Financial strength is important for suppliers to get credit from steel mills, and to simultaneously offer credit to Regal for the items supplied.

2. *Contact with mills.* This is another important factor to consider. The supply of steel rods from mills fluctuates with demand. When demand is high, mill deliveries increase, and suppliers who have good contact with mills get better service from them. A supplier having good contact with several mills is also in a much better position to meet the company's demands when shortage situations develop.

3. *Location.* Steel rods are heavy and therefore, transportation cost is high, and is likely to continue rising in the future. Therefore, distributors with warehouse facilities close by are preferred. In an emergency, it would be easy for the company to send its own truck to pick up required items if the warehouse was nearby.
4. *Past performance.* Service quality and delivery reliability are important. This is judged from the past performance of the vendor. Because these suppliers have supplied bar stock on individual orders, the company has records of past performance, and the ability and knowledge of their salesforce and management.

The value engineer and purchasing agent visited most of the suppliers. After applying the above criteria, five suppliers remained on the bid list. The other suppliers were dropped. The criteria applied were developed by the purchasing department, from past experience in buying steel rods.

The management of each supplier was asked if they could satisfy the company's needs for bar stock. All five suppliers expressed a willingness and desire to work with Regal. All of them were sent RFQs.

The purchase requisition covered some four hundred items. It contained a detailed delivery schedule along with the quantity required in 1980. The entire requisition was in the form of a computer printout. This requisition was based on annual forecasts prepared by the marketing department and approved by the corporate planning division.

The purchasing department allowed the suppliers two weeks to submit bids. However, because they were quoting for the first time and there were so many items to cover, most of them asked for a four-week extension in submitting the bids. This was granted in writing by the purchasing department. After several reminders and clarifications, all five suppliers sent quotations.

Evaluating and Selecting Suppliers

None of the suppliers quoted on all of the items. Most of them specialized in certain grades of materials, and each one submitted bids for specific grades. Each item was quoted on by at least one supplier. Each item was offered from stock and met the ASII specifications. None of the suppliers quoted a firm price, but each indicated that prices would vary according to price revisions by the mills. However, each supplier indicated that they would give thirty days' notice before revised prices become effective. All prices were FOB destination, and the terms of payment were 1% 10, net 30 days, which is standard for all bar stock suppliers.

The purchasing department next analyzed the quotes. They first grouped all the items by size and grade. This was time-consuming; when it was finished, all items fell into one of four basic groups. A combination of three suppliers emerged, who quoted the lowest price for the total package. This avoided the single-source situation. One supplier quoted one group of items that covered 45 percent of the total dollar volume. A second supplier quoted two groups of items with 35 percent of the dollar volume. The third supplier quoted the remaining items covering 20 percent of the dollar volume.

As a quick check, the value engineer calculated the total price of the package if the items were purchased on an individual order basis. It revealed a 12 percent savings on the cost of materials. This did not include the savings in time and effort by the purchasing department. These savings resulted from handling one single annual contract with three suppliers, instead of hundreds of orders with twelve suppliers through spot purchases.

The complete analysis of the three recommended suppliers was submitted to the purchasing manager for his final approval. When the researcher left Regal, the purchasing manager had not yet made the final decision.

After three weeks, the researcher contacted Regal to find out if the decision had been made. It had been delayed, as the forecast for air tools was being drastically revised by the marketing department. These air tools were used primarily by the automotive and aircraft industries; these had just cancelled orders to Regal for their 1980 requirements.

After several visits, the researcher was informed by Regal's purchasing manager that in early 1980, the management had decided not to buy bar stock through an annual contract. Because demand was so uncertain, and so low, bar stock would be purchased according to individual requirements.

Regal does not have a formal system for vendors, but general company policy requires three suppliers on the bid list.

The internal purchasing decision process is depicted in figure 4–3.

Evaluation

The entire decision process was well coordinated by the purchasing agent. Individuals from different departments worked well as a team.

The purchasing manager recognized the advantage of consolidating requirements for steel rods, and decided to purchase them on an annual contract. The resulting savings represented 12 percent of the total cost of bar stock from the spot market. Unfortunately, the savings could not be realized because of uncertain conditions in the market.

Purchase of Woodhog Blades

In February 1979, Regal introduced wood-boring drills, used to drill large diameter holes in wood. The size of the hole varies from one-half inch to five inches in diameter. The company has given the trade name "woodhog" tools to these wood-boring drills. At the end of the long shaft of the drill are two blades made of special, tempered steel.

The company has been making these blades since February 1979. But the value engineering department indicated that if the company purchased these blades from outside suppliers, costs could be reduced by about 20 percent. The value engineer pointed out that "the Regal corporate office has a computer program which can analyze 'make/buy' decisions depending upon the cost of the item, quantity, lead time, future needs, interest on money, storage charge, machining capacity available, and the need to keep the existing labor force busy." Based on this analysis, management decided to buy the woodhog blades from outside vendors.

There were 230,000 blades required for 1980, based on the forecast given to production planning by marketing. Design engineering had also introduced some changes in the blade design that would require new tooling. The value engineer estimated the cost of the tooling to be around $30,000, and the total cost of 230,000 blades at about $138,000. There were seventeen different sizes of blades required for the woodhog drills.

The specifications were finalized by design engineering in consultation with potential vendors, value engineering, and industrial engineering. Detailed drawings of the blades were prepared illustrating dimensions required with maximum allowable tolerances.

The Buying Center

The following individuals were interviewed to study the purchase decision process: Bill Wilson, purchasing manager; Ron Ford, design engineer; and Tom Hopkins, materials manager. Mr. Wilson is the purchasing manager responsible for buying woodhog blades. He believes in strict personal ethics. "If I go out for lunch at all with vendor representatives, I pick up my own bill," he stated. "This is not the company policy—it is my personal philosophy. Wining and dining with vendor salesmen may cloud your vendor evaluation and the final choice."

Mr. Ford is responsible for providing specifications for the blades. He must approve any deviations from the specifications. He also carries out technical evaluations of bids received from vendors. If differences between engineering and purchasing arise in evaluating the vendors, Mr. Ford says, "I let them [purchasing] do their job and I do mine. Commercial evaluation of bids is the responsibility of the purchasing department. Technical evaluation is my job." Mr. Wilson's answer to the same question was a little different. "We have to deal with many departments within the company. If differences arise [in choice criteria, vendor selection, or in dealing with the vendors], I voice my opinion. We discuss it, see each other's point of view, and try to decide what is best for

70 • *Industrial Purchasing Strategies*

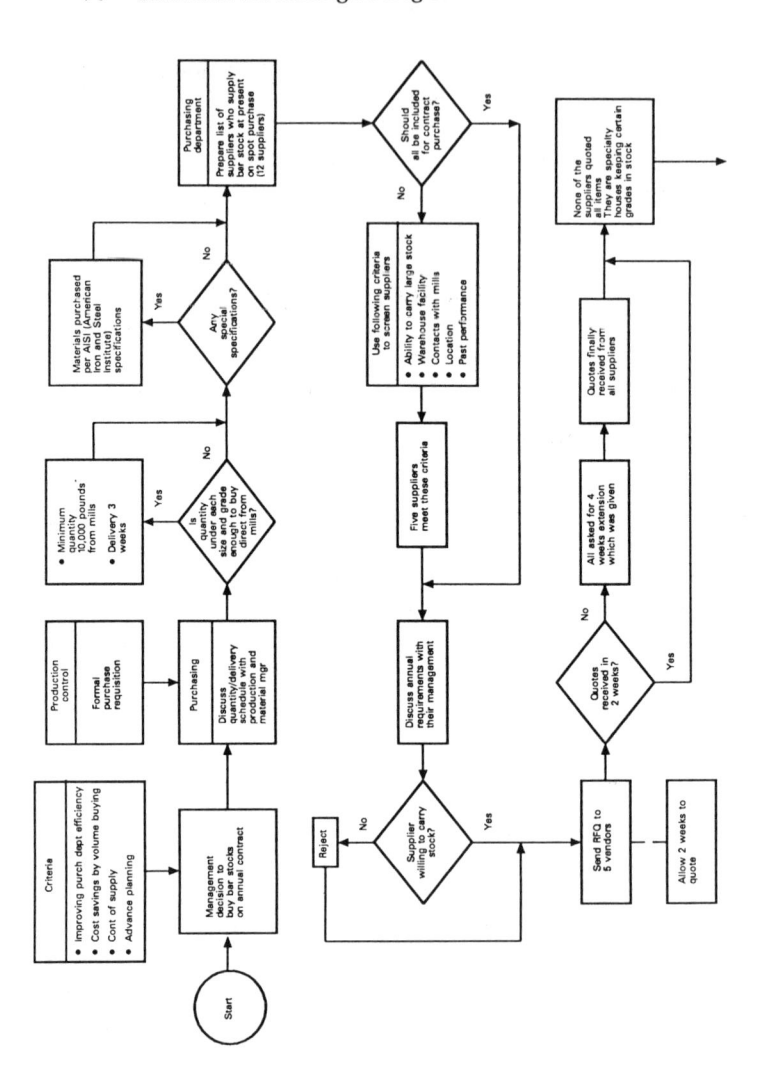

Regal Technologies • 71

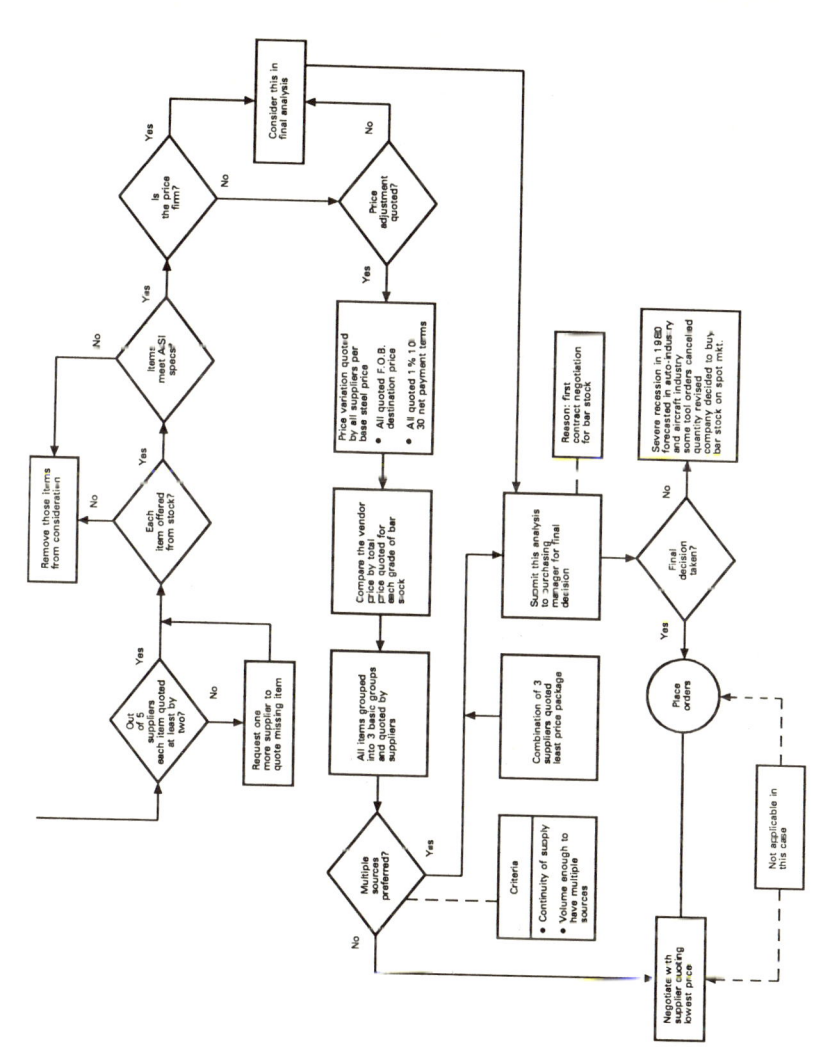

Figure 4-3. Purchase Decision Process: Bar Stock

the company. We try not to get personalities involved. I have been in purchasing for over twenty-five years and this approach has always worked."

Mr. Hopkins has direct contact with vendors once annual contracts are placed with them. The vendors contact Tom to find out what quantities they should ship each month. The purchasing manager gets feedback from Mr. Hopkins on the vendors' delivery performance.

Because this was a regular production item, the company decided to purchase it through a long-term annual contract. The reasons for this, cited by the purchasing manager, included continuity of supply and better prices due to quantity buying. A contract period longer than one year is not realistic, according to the purchasing agent, because of changing technology and volatile prices of material.

Selecting Suppliers to Submit Bids

When an item is to be purchased for the first time, the purchasing department usually obtains names of potential sources from value engineering. Value engineering and design engineering work closely with potential vendors. In this case, the potential vendors are those who supply the company with similar items; they must have the ability to manufacture this particular item. This is an effective way to search for potential vendors, because existing suppliers are known to the company, and they generally are aware of Regal's needs. According to the purchasing agent, "This is a special item and there are only a few suppliers who have the capacity and capability to meet the company's needs."

The value engineer played an important role in conducting technical discussions with potential vendors, and in explaining the company's needs to them. The vendors then made suggestions about the types of materials to be used, and the type of heat treatment the blades must receive to improve their life.

The value engineer suggested three suppliers to the purchasing department who were recognized leaders in the industry, and with whom Regal had done business in the past.

The purchasing department added no new names to the list. Therefore, the company sent RFQs to the three suppliers, allowing them four weeks to submit quotes. The purchasing agent explained, "This is a new item and they should be given enough time to work out the prices." All suppliers were asked to quote separate prices for each variety of blade as well as the cost of tooling. All suppliers submitted prices within four weeks.

Evaluating and Selecting Suppliers

The quotes were scrutinized by the purchasing agent to determine if they contained the necessary information. Two suppliers were not specific enough concerning alloy price adjustment. They were asked to clarify this. The next step was to determine if all the quotes met specifications. All of the suppliers explained the tolerances they could adhere to in general remarks. This was a technical matter, so it was discussed with design engineering. Design engineering determined that the remarks were in line with company requirements, and approved them. The purchasing agent noted that all three suppliers quoted acceptable delivery schedules.

When the purchasing agent began to analyze the quotations, he noted that the costs of tooling quoted by all three suppliers were within $50 of each other. When the tooling cost is about $30,000, it is difficult for three suppliers to quote a price within $50 of each other. The purchasing manager felt that this was very unusual, and decided to investigate the situation. He examined the budget cost worked out by value engineering, and it was $30,000. These three vendors had worked closely with the value engineer, and had tactfully obtained the information about the amount of money budgeted for the tooling and blades. Further analysis of the blade prices quoted by all three suppliers confirmed that the prices were very close to the budgeted price. The purchasing manager, who had experience in tooling costs, felt that the tooling price quoted by the vendors was very high. He had good contacts with independent tool makers in Chicago. He telephoned two of them and mailed them drawings, requesting estimated prices for tooling.

Within a few days, the Chicago tool makers quoted their prices, which were 40 percent lower than the prices quoted by the three suppliers on the bid list. There was a difference of about $400 between the prices quoted by the two Chicago tool makers. This seemed reasonable.

This is an excellent example of how suppliers can quote identical prices when they have inside information. The purchasing manager explained, "One must react strongly to a situation like this. I called all three vendor salesmen immediately and threatened to take them off Regal's bidders list, not only for this item but for all the items purchased by Regal plants at various locations, unless they submitted revised and realistic prices for blades and tooling. Within twenty-four hours the three vendors submitted their revised prices. They reduced tooling costs by almost 35 to 40 percent and blade cost by 10 to 15 percent."

The revised prices were then analyzed. All of them quoted delivery FOB destination, and the standard terms of payment offered by the industry (2% 10, net 30). The price adjustment quoted by all three vendors was subject to variations in alloy cost. Further, each supplier indicated that thirty days' notice would be given before price increases or decreases became effective.

The total price, including the tooling costs, was tabulated. This time the price difference between the two lowest bidders was about 7 percent; the difference between the highest and lowest bidder was about 12 percent. Because the tooling cost is high, it is not advisable to have more than one

74 • *Industrial Purchasing Strategies*

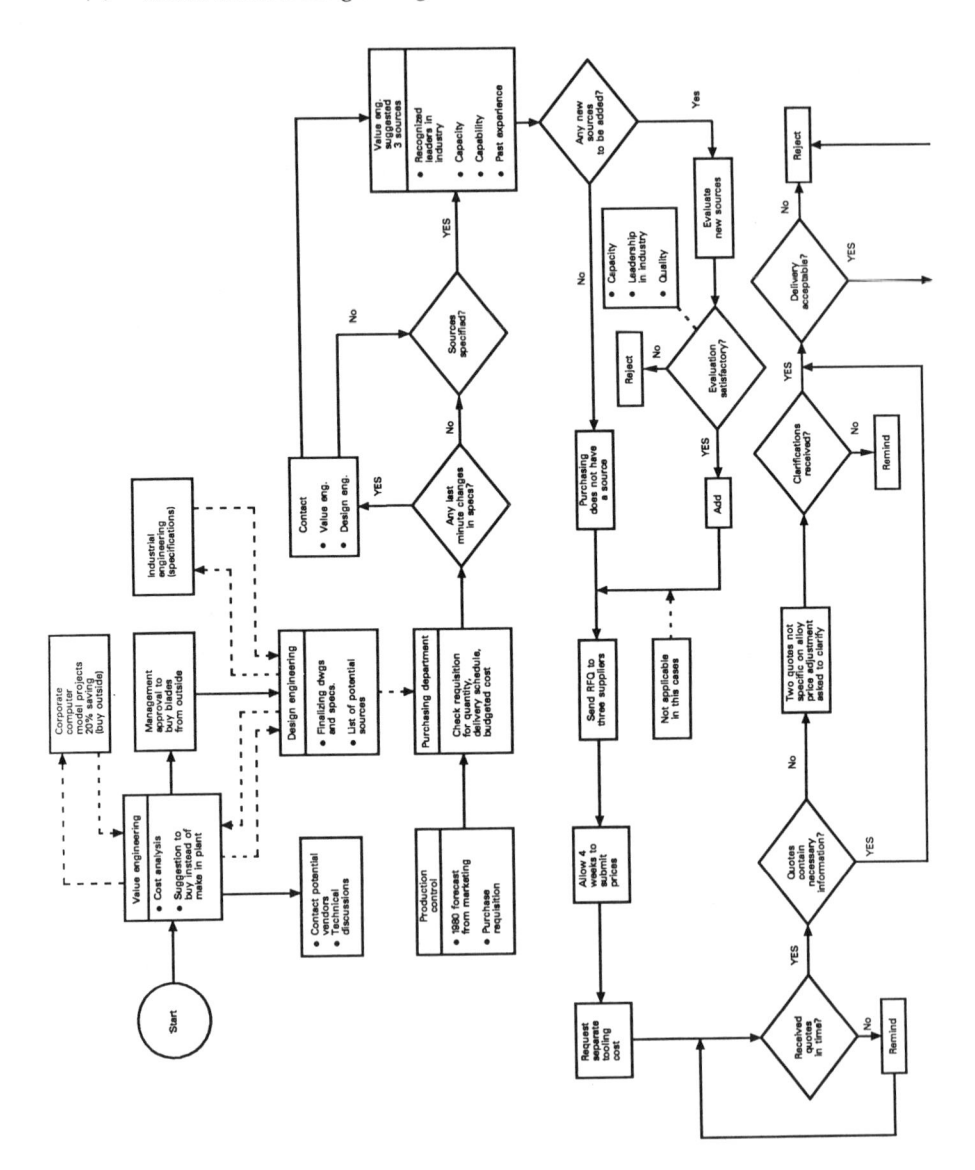

Regal Technologies • 75

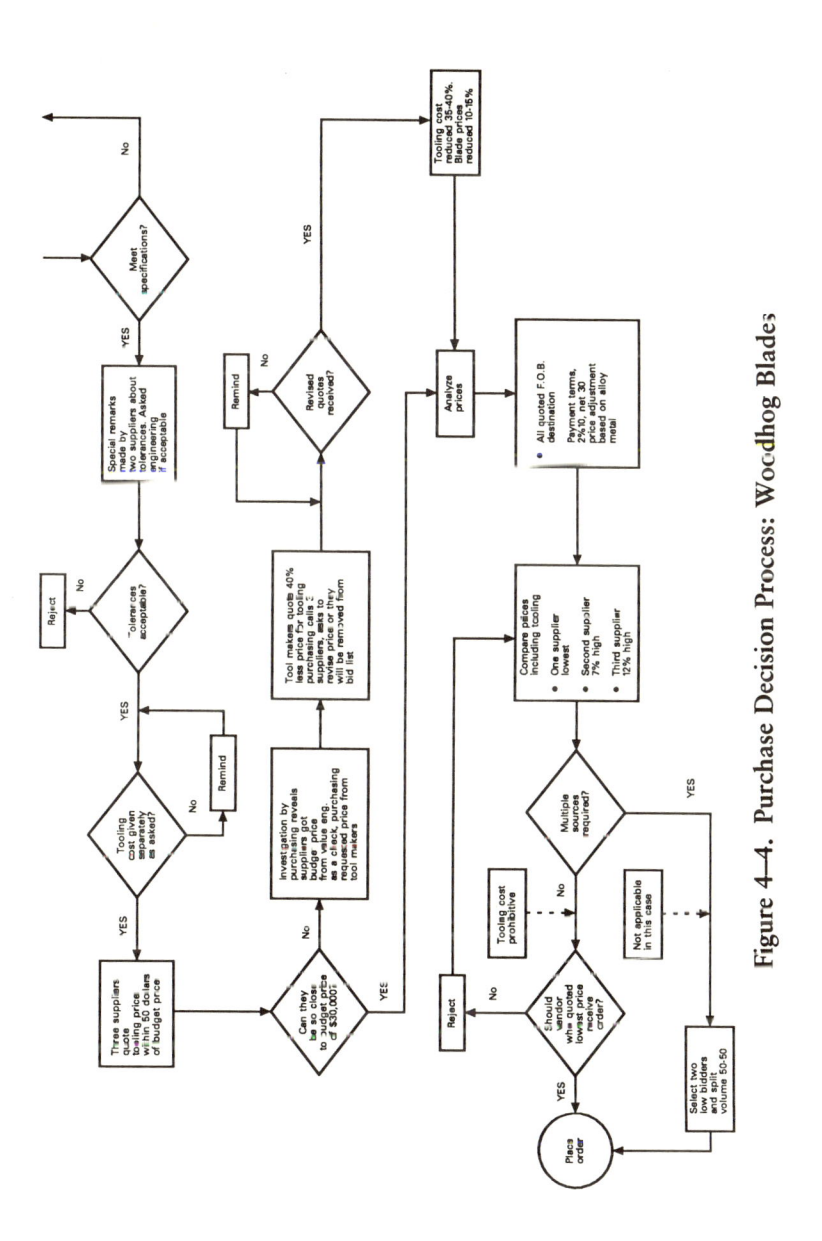

Figure 4-4. Purchase Decision Process: Woodhog Blades

source. Further, if there are problems with the selected vendor, the company can take possession of its tools, and give them to the next lowest bidder to produce the blades. This would maintain continuity of supply. In the worst possible case, the company could manufacture the blades itself.

The vendor who quoted the lowest price was a well-known source, and had had satisfactory performance in supplying other items to the company. Therefore, the company decided to place the order for the entire quantity of woodhog blades with the low bidder. The purchase decision process is depicted in figure 4–4.

Evaluation

The experience of the purchasing manager was of immense importance in detecting collusion among vendors. He knew how to be tough with the vendors when he needed to be. The purchasing manager did an excellent job saving the company a considerable amount of money.

When the tooling cost is high, it is not advisable to have annual contracts with more than one supplier. Price was again the deciding factor in selecting the supplier of woodhog blades, when the choice had been narrowed down to acceptable vendors.

Concerning the value engineer's mistake in revealing the budgeted cost for tooling to vendors, the purchasing manager advised him, "Don't go to pieces when you make a mistake. Learn from it."

The entire decision process was well coordinated by the purchasing manager.

5
Buying Caps, Parts, and Oil at Evans Products

Evans Products develops, manufactures, and markets photographic and related products, man-made fibers, plastics, and industrial and other chemicals. The market served by the company's photographic section can be divided into the following categories: amateur, audio-visual and entertainment; radiography; business systems; professional and photofinishing; U.S. government and defense contractors; and customer equipment services.

For the amateur market, the company produces a wide variety of films, papers, processing chemicals, and equipment. The company also maintains processing laboratories that serve amateur photographers in many parts of the world. In the area of audio-visual and entertainment, Evans Products produces films and photographic equipment for the motion picture and television industries, as well as audio-visual aids for education. For radiography, the company produces x-ray films, papers, chemicals, and processing equipment for medical, dental, and industrial use. In the area of business systems, Evans Products is involved in the development and manufacture of microfilm and related equipment. It also develops supplies used to photograph, display, store, and retrieve large quantities of information quickly, or to reproduce engineering drawings.

Evan Products supplies photographic paper and plates, chemicals and equipment to professional photographers. Products produced for the graphics industry include materials for photofabrication and lithographic plates. The company also operates equipment maintenance programs, repair services, and customer information services.

The chemical division's products include: polyester fiber; aldehydes, acids, and dyes; and cellulosics, polyolefins, and polyesters sold under the name Tenite.

The company's sales and earnings set new records in 1979; earnings were above $1 billion for the first time in the company's one-hundred-year history. Worldwide sales amounted to $9.5 billion, representing an increase of more than a billion dollars over sales in 1978. Higher volume contributed to much of the gain. The demand for the company's twenty-five thousand diversified products reached record levels in 1979, as the company entered its one-hundredth year. Worldwide sales of chemicals and plastics were strong; fiber sales experienced solid gains. The company employed 140,000 persons at the end of 1979. Evans Products' activities are classified according to two divisions. These are the photographic division and the chemicals division. This study was researched at one of the company's plants in the chemical division.

This plant has been operating in the southeast since 1967, and produces polyester staple fibers and continuous filament yarn. Plant capacity was expanded in 1973, so that it could manufacture chemicals such as terephthalic acid, dimethyl terephthalate, and polymer. Polymer, in the form of tiny white pellets, is the raw material used in the fiber and yard production processes. In 1977, work was completed on the expansion of plant services and environmental protection facilities; these included wastewater and water treatment facilities. Increases in staple fiber and continuous filament production capacity were also made.

Fibers and yarns are used in a variety of clothes, home furnishings, and industrial fabrics. The yarn is used extensively in knitted and woven fabrics. Staple fiber is usually blended with cotton for use in durable-press fabrics, lightweight fabrics such as broadcloth and batiste, and in sheets and pillowcases.

The plant is located on approximately three thousand acres of land, and employs about two thousand people. It has its own purchasing department, which purchases items necessary for the plant's operation. The purchasing department is administrated by the purchasing manager, who reports directly to the plant manager. Three senior purchasing engineers in supervisory capacities report to the purchasing manager. Each senior purchasing engineer supervises three to four purchasing agents. In addition, there are six clerical workers (see figure 5–1).

Company policy requires that purchasing agents must work at least five years in one of the company's other departments before joining the purchasing department. All of the supervisory persons in the purchasing department have degrees in engineering. The senior purchasing engineer, in charge of purchasing all electrical products, has a degree in electrical engineering. He worked in the marketing department for six years before joining purchasing.

More than thirty-six thousand items are bought annually by the purchasing department, amounting to approximately $60 million.

The purchasing department works closely with the purchasing departments of other chemical plants within the chemical division of the company. The headquarters of the chemical division is in Kingston, Texas. This division has five manufacturing units: (1) Texas Chemicals; (2) Florida Chemicals; (3) Arizona Chemicals; (4) Distillation Products Industries in Cleveland, Ohio;

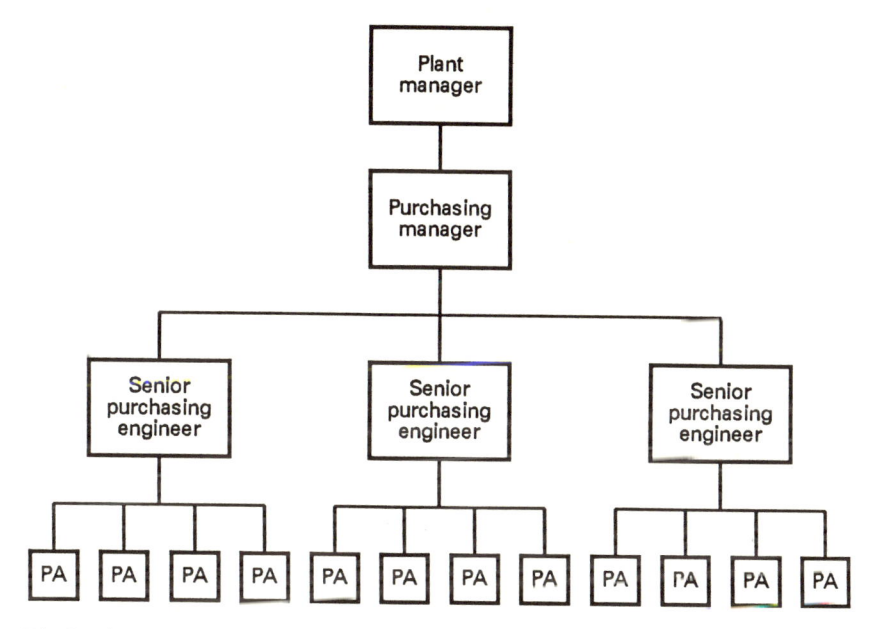

```
                    ┌─────────────┐
                    │   Plant     │
                    │  manager    │
                    └──────┬──────┘
                           │
                    ┌──────┴──────┐
                    │ Purchasing  │
                    │  manager    │
                    └──────┬──────┘
          ┌────────────────┼────────────────┐
    ┌─────┴─────┐    ┌─────┴─────┐    ┌─────┴─────┐
    │  Senior   │    │  Senior   │    │  Senior   │
    │purchasing │    │purchasing │    │purchasing │
    │ engineer  │    │ engineer  │    │ engineer  │
    └─────┬─────┘    └─────┬─────┘    └─────┬─────┘
```

PA: Purchasing agent.

Figure 5–1. Evans Products' Purchasing Department: Organizational Chart

and (5) Carolina Chemicals. If a product is needed by more than one plant, the possibility of a joint purchase is explored by the marketing department at Kingston. The department determines if there is a possibility of realizing substantial savings through such a purchase. At Kingston, the purchasing department has computerized records of all purchases made by these five chemical plants. The department analyzes the items purchased by all of the plants, the total quantity purchased, the price paid by each plant, and the suppliers and their locations. They finally decide, in consultation with the purchasing departments at each plant location, to make a joint purchase of a common item.

The following three items purchased through long-term contracts by the company were studied in detail: corrugated bale caps; parts for lift trucks; and #6 fuel oil.

All of these items are supplied by multiple sources. These items were selected to study the criteria the purchasing agent applies in dividing the available volume among various suppliers. New suppliers were added to the bid list for each item when purchasing the 1980 requirements; the reasons for adding new suppliers differed for each item. According to the purchasing manager, these three items represent a good cross section of the company's purchase decision processes.

Purchase of Corrugated Bale Caps

The company purchases corrugated bale caps worth $350,000 annually. The polyester fiber it manufactures is shipped to various mills as a compressed bale. Corrugated bale caps are used at the top and bottom of the bale to hold the fibers together.

The bale caps are manufactured out of heavy cardboard, according to company specifications prepared by the packaging department. The bale caps must withstand rough handling during transportation. If the caps burst, the fiber becomes damaged, resulting in customer complaints and loss of fiber.

The dimensions, type of cardboard used, and the minimum bursting strength of the caps are carefully specified. In order to make it possible to trace the caps in the field if failure occurs, specifications call for identification marks on each cap. These provide the name of the manufacturer, shipment date, manufacturing code indicating the day, month, and year of manufacture, and the purchase order number.

The bale caps are purchased through annual contracts. This is a company policy; as explained by the purchasing supervisor, "It is a good idea to evaluate suppliers every year. It tends to keep the prices down, and keeps the existing suppliers honest."

The Buying Center

The following individuals were interviewed in studying the decision process: Ron Taylor, senior purchasing engineer; Pat Kelly, packaging engineer (located in Kingston, Texas); and Bill Jackson, quality control staff engineer.

Mr. Taylor is responsible for purchasing packaging materials, including corrugated bale caps. He stated, "The company policy to deal with local suppliers makes sense. It gives a boost to local suppliers, helps develop better contacts with them, and in the end you get better services from them. In the long range, this is mutually beneficial."

Mr. Kelly is in Kingston, Texas. He was interviewed by telephone. Mr. Kelly is responsible for providing the specifications of the caps. He visits vendors and evaluates their manufacturing facilities, along with Mr. Jackson. Mr. Kelly indicated that "product specifications are extremely important in buying any item. One must specify the proper quality for the intended use. It is foolish to buy a higher quality than necessary." Regarding the changes in specifications, he observed, "Generally the companies change product specification to satisfy the changing needs of the customers, to satisfy government requirements, or to reduce cost. Otherwise, there is no need to tinker with product specifications."

Mr. Jackson is responsible for investigating failures of bale caps, and all other quality-related problems involving packaging materials. He visits vendors and customers to analyze and resolve packaging problems. According to Mr. Taylor, "Bill's feedback to the purchasing department is important in evaluating the quality of the caps."

Selecting Suppliers to Submit Bids

Over the years, the company has developed reliable sources for cardboard products. Because cardboard products are bulky and heavy, most large national producers have manufacturing facilities in various regions of the country. Each facility produces specific sizes of boxes and caps from basic cardboard sheets. Sales reps from these suppliers visit the company every three months in order to secure business. Regular visits from suppliers' also indicate the supplier's eagerness to do business with the company. As the purchasing supervisor stated, "This constitutes the group of your potential suppliers."

Thirteen suppliers currently manufacture cardboard products; their sales reps visit the purchasing department. These suppliers are in South Carolina, North Carolina, and Georgia. The company has done business with all of them at one time or another. The purchasing agent decided to add a new supplier to the list, because that company's sales rep and sales manager visited frequently in 1979. They exhibited keen interest in supplying cardboard products to the company. The supplier's brochures indicated that it had good machinery, test facilities, and the capacity to supply bale caps according to the required specifications. The purchasing agent requested the names of their current customers.

Because the performances of the four current suppliers were satisfactory, the company decided not to drop any of them. The purchasing agent sent RFQs to fourteen suppliers. He explained that "it is a good idea to give a chance to all the suppliers to quote whose sales reps visit regularly, who have the capacity to produce, and who can meet specifications of the required items." The request for quotations included fifteen cardboard items required for packaging the company's products, as well as bale caps. The purchasing agent felt that "some of the suppliers may not quote for bale caps depending upon the loading they have on certain types of machines that produce bale caps."

After allowing two weeks for the suppliers to respond, a couple of telephone reminders, most bids were received within four weeks. One supplier sent "no bid." Two suppliers did not respond. Four other suppliers did not send a quote for bale caps, but submitted bids for other cardboard items. The remaining seven suppliers quoted prices for bale caps.

Evaluating and Selecting Suppliers

The seven quotes were examined for the necessary information. No suppliers quoted a firm price for the entire contract period. All prices quoted were firm for ninety days, and subject to variation in cardboard prices thereafter. All suppliers confirmed that they would meet the required delivery schedule as well as the company's specifications for bale caps. The prices quoted by all vendors were FOB destination; terms of payment were 1% 10, net 30 days, which is an industry standard.

All of the quotes contained similar terms and conditions. The final step was to tabulate the quotes, using price as the ranking factor. The lowest quote was listed first.

A	$942.80
B	$973.00
C	$944.00
D	$1,023.00
E	$1,051.00
F	$1,138.00
G	$1,318.00

Supplier E is a new supplier. Because he quoted a price 11 percent higher than the lowest price, he was rejected. Suppliers F and G were also rejected because of high prices.

Suppliers A, B, C, and D are existing suppliers. Supplier B is the primary source, receiving 40 percent of the company's business. The remaining three suppliers receive 20 percent each.

The purchasing agent said, "I would prefer four sources for the 1980 requirement. I feel the quantity is large enough to justify four suppliers. The question now is: How should the business be split among the suppliers?" The purchasing agent awarded 40 percent of the business to Supplier B. Although Supplier A had quoted the lowest price, there had been quality problems with its caps in 1979. Several caps had burst during transportation. A bad batch of caps had been supplied, and the vendor immediately took action. The caps were recalled from the company's warehouse. Further, Supplier A's labor contract expired in 1980, and the purchasing agent hesitated to give A a major share of business. The price difference between A and B was 3 percent and B's quality and service were excellent.

The remaining business was divided equally among A, C, and D in order to simplify the execution of the contracts. "The price difference between C and D is 8 percent, while A's labor contract expires in 1980. It's not worth fooling around with splitting the volume differently among A, C, and D," said Ron.

The flow diagram of the decision process is shown in figure 5–2.

Evaluation

This case provides a good example of the fact that it is difficult to displace a primary supplier if its quality and service are excellent and its price is not appreciably higher than that of the competitor. In this case, the difference in price was less than 3 percent. If a supplier's price is attractive, and it responds promptly to quality problems, it can retain its share of the business (in this case, Supplier B).

The purchasing agent stated, "I will not consider a new vendor unless he quoted 10 percent lower prices as compared to the prices quoted by the established prime source. This is because the product from the new vendor requires special monitoring for a few months, which is time consuming and expensive."

According to Ron, "How the volume should be split among the suppliers and how many suppliers to have for a specific contract is strictly a purchasing decision."

Purchase of Parts for Lift Trucks

The company operates a fleet of lift trucks within this plant to transport materials from one department to another. The plant operates twenty-four hours a day, 365 days a year, so these trucks are in continuous operation. A sufficient number of trucks must be in operating condition at all times to keep production running without interruptions. Therefore, trucks are scheduled regularly for periodic maintenance. After three months of continuous usage, the trucks are checked thoroughly, and worn parts are replaced.

The maintenance department establishes the annual budget for parts required to keep the lift trucks operating. The company spends approximately $100,000 every year to purchase lift truck parts. The lift trucks currently used are from two major manufacturers. The companies are Caterpillar Company and Hyster Truck Company. The parts required for the lift trucks the companies manufacture are not interchangeable. The maintenance department identifies the parts to be ordered according to the manufacturer's part numbers. "There is one Caterpillar dealer and one Hyster dealer in the area, and these parts are purchased from them on an annual contract," according to the purchasing engineer, Mr. Martin.

The reason for purchasing lift truck parts through an annual contract is to

84 • *Industrial Purchasing Strategies*

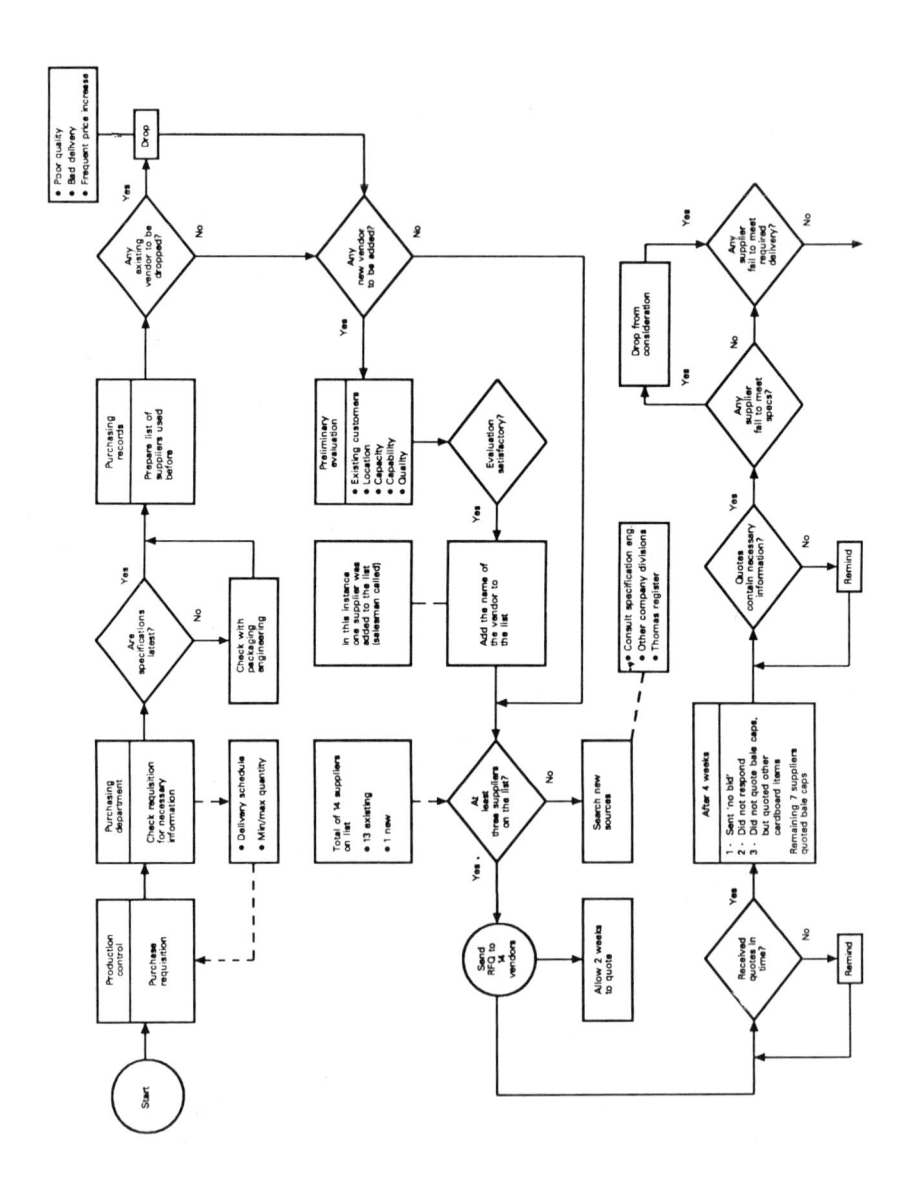

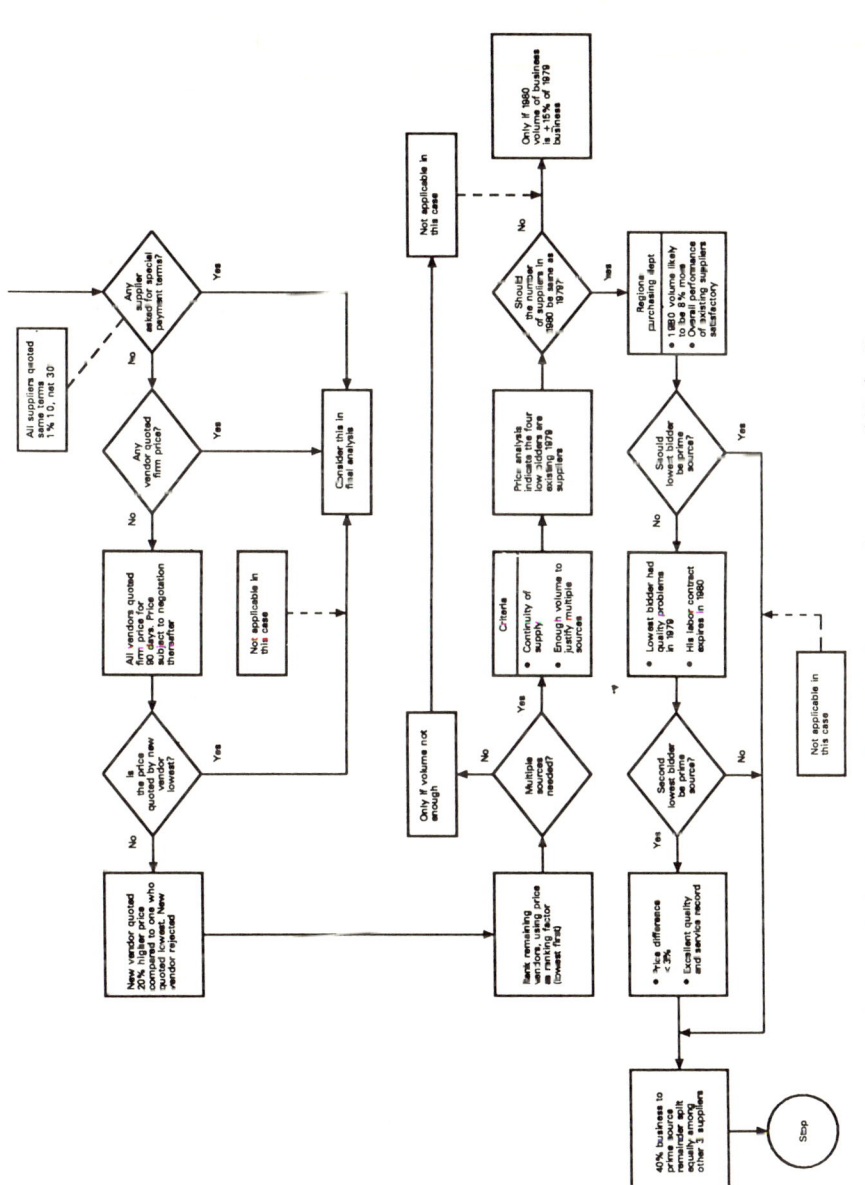

Figure 5-2. Purchase Decision Process: Corrugated Bale Caps

ensure the continuity of supply of parts and to obtain better prices. Also, when the dealers are aware of the company's requirements in advance, they are able to stock the necessary parts. "The dealers know that the company has to buy these parts from them for the trucks manufactured by the manufacturers they represent. This is a captive situation that removes competition. The manufacturers have a tendency to increase prices for the parts more often than the complete trucks. The service from the dealers sometimes is also not the best," Mr. Martin complained.

In 1978, a sales rep from an independent dealer in Charleston, S.C., contacted the company's purchasing department. He represented a quality manufacturer specializing in lift truck parts for renowned U.S. manufacturers. He also indicated that his prices would be an average of 25 percent lower than those quoted by dealers of lift truck manufacturers. The purchasing agent welcomed this development; competition had been lacking in this market for a long time. It was a very important business for the company, which spent almost $100,000 annually on truck parts. The maintenance department was contacted to see if they could use the parts manufactured by an independent manufacturer. According to the purchasing agent, "The maintenance department refused to use these parts because they were skeptical about the quality of parts and service from this new source."

In late 1978, the representative of this independent manufacturer and his dealer in Charleston, S.C., visited the company. They brought samples along, and met with the maintenance supervisor and the purchasing agent. They explained that their company was similar to NAPA, the independent manufacturer of auto spare parts; NAPA supplies spares for any car manufactured in the United States. The quality of their company's parts is even higher than that of the original parts supplied. The representative suggested that the company test these samples on a few trucks to determine how long they lasted. This information could then be compared to the lifetime of parts supplied by the lift truck manufacturers. The maintenance department discussed their annual requirements for lift truck parts at length. They also talked about the service these parts require, and the warehouse facility available with the dealer in Charleston.

In mid-1979, the maintenance department completed a study of the samples from the new supplier. The quality of parts was satisfactory. The purchasing department added the name of this supplier to the bidders list. A few weeks after this, another dealer from Columbia, S.C., approached the purchasing department. He indicated that he represented the same independent manufacturer of lift truck parts and would be willing to do business with the company. The purchasing agent said, "I was already working with a dealer in Charleston and told the Columbia dealer that he would get a chance to quote if he had the capacity to stock the required parts locally."

Selecting Suppliers to Submit Bids

When the annual requirements for lift truck parts for 1980 were received by the purchasing agent from the maintenance department, the single-source situation for these parts was eliminated. There were now four suppliers on the bidders list. Two dealers represent lift truck manufacturers (Caterpillar and Hyster), and two represent independent manufacturers of lift truck parts.

The purchasing agent decided not to drop any existing suppliers from the bid list in order to gain competitive prices. The RFQs were sent to these dealers, allowing them two weeks to submit quotes. There are no set company specifications for lift truck parts, as they are identified by the truck manufacturer's part number.

Evaluating and Selecting Suppliers

After two weeks, quotes were received from all four dealers. All of them confirmed that they could meet the delivery schedule, and quoted the same terms of payment—net 30 days. Each price quoted was FOB company plant location. None of the dealers quoted a firm price for the entire contract period. However, the prices quoted by the two current suppliers were firm for ninety days; thereafter, prices were subject to change as prices of the lift truck manufacturers changed. The two new dealers quoted a price firm for 120 days, and subject to change thereafter. When prices were tabulated, the two new dealers' quotes were an average of 30 percent lower than prices quoted by the existing suppliers. Because of this large difference in price, the two current suppliers were rejected. The order for 1980 truck parts was placed with the two new dealers. However, the order was divided seventy-thirty between the dealer in Charleston and the one in Columbia. The purchasing agent explained this as follows. "Both new dealers quoted prices within 1.5 percent of each other, the Charleston dealer quoting the lower price. However, in addition to the lower price, the Charleston dealer has spent a lot of time working with the company's maintenance department, submitting samples, and convincing them of the quality of the parts to be supplied by him. He should be rewarded for his efforts by giving him an additional share of the available business."

The Buying Center

The following individuals were interviewed in studying the decision process: G. R. Martin, senior purchasing engineer; L. S. Stewart, maintenance supervisor; and E. L. Harris, purchasing manager.

Mr. Martin is responsible for purchasing parts for lift trucks. He was aware of the company's captive situation with the two existing suppliers representing the lift truck manufacturers in South Carolina. He was happy to receive the independent dealer's representative from Charleston.

Mr. Harris supported Mr. Martin in developing new sources and creating competition between suppliers of lift truck parts. "The higher the dollar volume and the more critical an item, the easier it is to get attention from the plant manager," Mr. Harris explained. "In this instance, the dollar volume was not that high and the item was not critical, because it was not directly a production item."

Mr. Harris continued, "For the existing equipment, the maintenance department insists on parts from the same manufacturer. Therefore, we expected resistance from the maintenance department against the new dealer. Martin and I had several meetings with Stewart and persuaded him to at least try the samples. This is an inside selling job. You have to be persistent, but patient."

Mr. Stewart was responsible for testing the samples. He held a series of discussions with the Charleston dealer's representative, and was impressed with his technical knowledge and familiarity with the operation of lift trucks. Mr. Stewart stated, "You always value a sales rep who is willing to solve your problems and knows the equipment."

The purchase decision process is shown in figure 5–3.

Evaluation

This case illustrates the fact that persistent efforts by the purchasing supervisor can lead to a change in the captive single-source situation. It can become a competitive bidding situation, without the sacrifice of quality. Other companies can learn from this case, and should implement the policy to develop new sources for the purchase of replacement parts. There is potential for considerable savings.

The differences between the maintenance department and the purchasing department were resolved in a problem-solving manner.

The two existing suppliers were not aware that two new dealers were added to the bid list. When they did not get any business for 1980, they reacted, according to Mr. Martin, by saying, "We will inform the manufacturers (Caterpillar and Hyster) that we have lost this business for 1980 and tell them to be less greedy in 1981 so that we can beat the competition."

Purchase of #6 Fuel Oil

Evans uses a great deal of steam in manufacturing chemicals and staple fibers. This steam is generated by boilers that are oil fired; these burn #6 fuel oil. The boiler manufacturers specify the type of oil to be burned in the boiler, because the type of fuel to be burned varies with boiler design. All of the boilers in this plant use #6 fuel oil.

The company has been buying #6 fuel oil since 1969; the annual quantity purchased is about twenty-five million gallons. The price of fuel has increased drastically over the last ten years. For example, in 1969, the company paid 3.5¢ per gallon for #6 fuel oil; in 1979, the price was 38¢ per gallon. The projected average price for 1980 was approximately 48¢ per gallon.

In November 1979, the company converted two of the oil-fired boilers into coal-fired boilers. This was expected to lower the quantity of #6 fuel oil required in 1980 from twenty-five million gallons to approximately ten million gallons. Thus, the dollar value of fuel oil to be purchased in 1980 was projected to be approximately $4.8 million.

The company does not have specifications for the fuel oil, because it is labeled as #6 type, and is defined by the petroleum industry's standard, based on BTU content. In order to meet the local environmental agency's standards, the company specifies only the allowable sulphur content. For example, in the state of New York, the maximum allowable sulphur content in fuel oil is 1.5 percent; in South Carolina, it is 2.9 percent. To meet this requirement, the company specifies that the sulphur content of the oil to be delivered in South Carolina should not exceed 2.5 percent.

The company purchases fuel oil through long-term contracts. The purchasing agent indicated that long-term contracts assure continuity of supply, especially when shortages occur. Fuel oil is critical because without it, the plant shuts down. The price of #6 fuel oil is regulated by the government; therefore, there is no price advantage gained by contract volume buying. The major advantage in contract buying is in having an assured supply of #6 fuel oil during shortages. The purchasing agent indicated that during a shortage, suppliers give preference to customers purchasing through contracts. The long-term contracts also enable suppliers to plan ahead for storage, as well as shipping schedules.

The Buying Center

The following individuals were interviewed in studying the purchase decision process: Charlie Barnes, senior purchasing engineer; E. L. Harris, purchasing manager; and Rosco Carter, power and service department senior engineer.

Mr. Barnes is responsible for purchasing #6 fuel oil. Mr. Harris asked him to develop additional sources for oil supplies. He also told Mr. Barnes to get authorization from him before giving contracts for #6 oil to the suppliers, because the order amounted to approximately $5 million.

Mr. Carter has direct contact with the suppliers in coordinating the delivery of the oil, metering the quantity received, and analyzing its quality.

90 • *Industrial Purchasing Strategies*

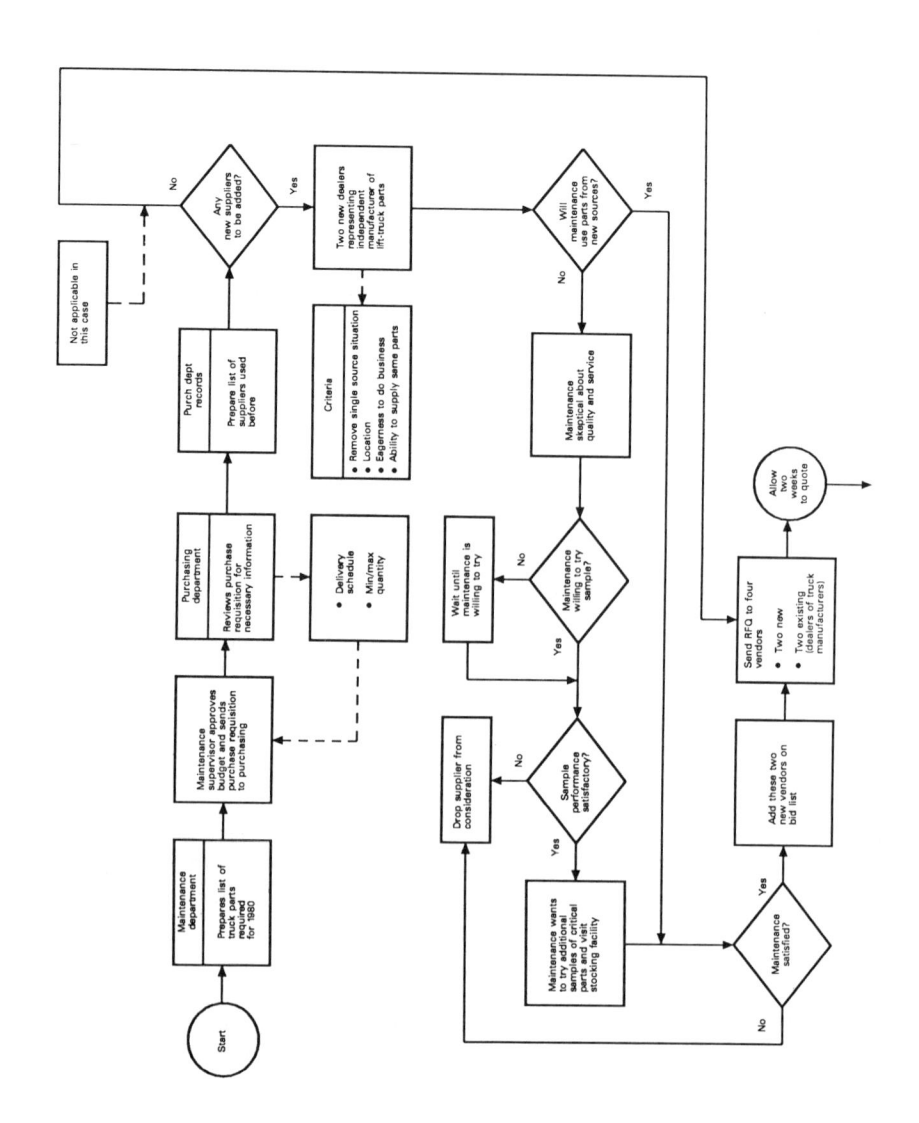

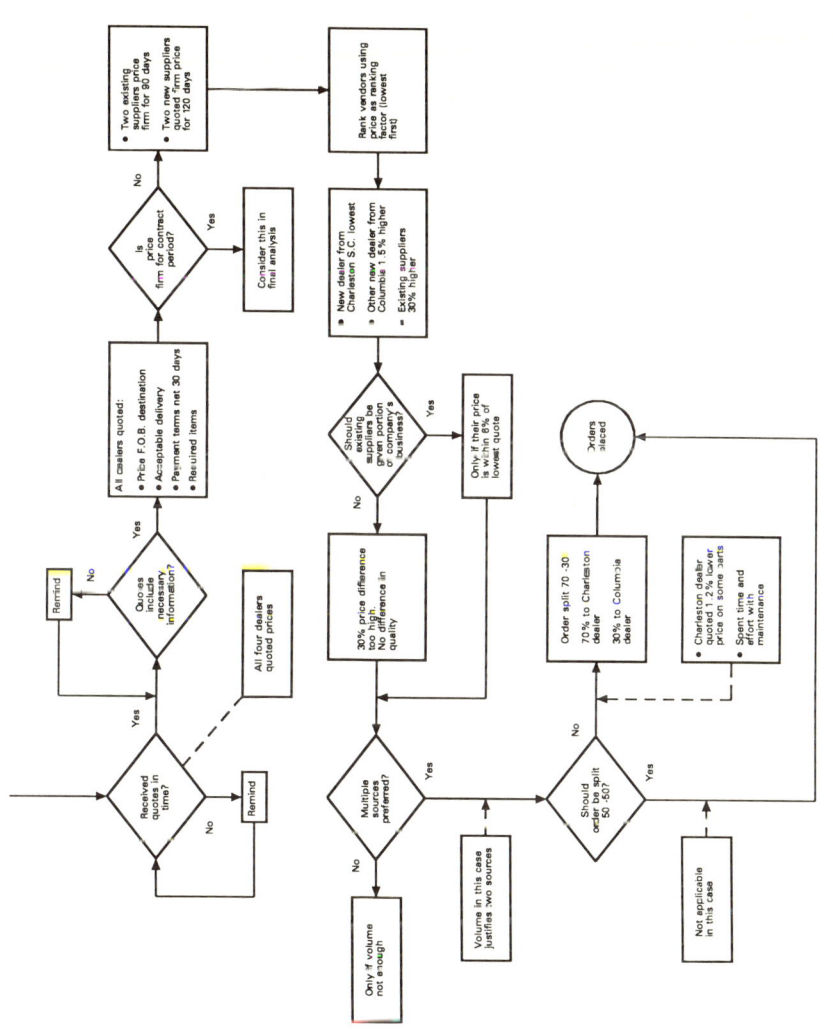

Figure 5–3. Purchase Decision Process: Parts for Lift Trucks

Because it is easier to unload oil from railroad tanks than from trucks, Mr. Carter prefers delivery by rail.

"Rosco's feedback is very valuable to us in evaluating the performances of the suppliers," Mr. Barnes explained.

Selecting Suppliers to Submit Bids

The company has been buying #6 fuel oil from Exxon for a long time. Exxon is the primary supplier at this point. The purchasing agent explained that many factors were involved in choosing Exxon as a primary source. First, because of the critical need for fuel oil, and the fact that the price is government controlled, the most important factor is capacity to meet the company's needs.

Exxon is one of the largest oil companies in the world, and has interests in the oil fields of the Middle East as well as the United States. It has its own refineries with ample capacity, and an excellent reputation as a quality oil supplier. Exxon has a large storage facility in Charleston, S.C., and has a contract with railroads in that area for transportation. Transportation is an important component of the delivered price of oil. A conveniently located storage facility saves a considerable amount of this transportation cost. Transportation by railroad is less expensive than truck transportation. Over the past several years, the company has developed an excellent relationship with Exxon; their service and shipping schedule have been extremely satisfactory.

To avoid a single-source situation, the company has developed a second source of supply. One criterion applied in developing this second source was ensuring that oil from this supplier was not from the same oil fields supplying oil to Exxon. If problems develop in the Middle East, such as the oil embargo in 1973, Exxon's oil supply will be affected drastically. Thus, a second source from different oil fields could compensate for this loss. A second criterion is that the refineries of the second source must preferably be located in different regions than Exxon refineries. Other factors considered are location of storage facilities, refining capabilities, quality of management, reputation for quality, and transportation facilities.

Amerada Hess was selected as the second supplier, based on the above criteria. It has a large storage facility in Charleston, S.C., an excellent management reputation, and its major sources of crude oil are Venezuela and Nigeria. Amerada Hess has a large fleet of delivery trucks to transport the oil. The company prefers to receive oil from the second source by truck. This ensures that the delivery of oil is not interrupted if a railroad strike or other railroad problems develop.

The senior purchasing engineer responsible for #6 fuel oil was advised in 1978 by his purchasing manager to analyze the purchasing practice for this item. He was then to suggest ways to improve the purchase procedure. The senior purchasing engineer recommended acquiring a third source for fuel oil.

He argued that both Exxon and Hess had storage facilities in Charleston, S.C. If a problem would develop in Charleston (such as flooding, earthquake, or a local labor strike), the supply of fuel oil would be cut off. He suggested including a supplier on the bid list who owned a storage facility nearby, in a place other than Charleston. Two primary reasons were given for the argument that the third suppliers' oil should come from oil fields other than the Middle East. First, Exxon's primary source is the Middle East; therefore in order to reduce dependence on Middle East oil, the third supplier should have oil sources elsewhere. Secondly, oil from the Middle East contains greater amounts of vanadium (a heavy metal), and this causes scaling in the boiler tubes. This scaling must be removed periodically by shutting off the boilers. This increases both boiler downtime and maintenance cost.

Late in 1978, the senior purchasing engineer received permission from the purchasing manager to search for a third supplier, with the above requirements in mind. He began to contact other renowned companies in the area. In early 1979, he recommended Colonial Oil Industries, Inc., in Savannah, Georgia, as a third possible supplier of #6 fuel oil.

Colonial Oil is one of the largest oil distributors in the southeast. They do not own any oil fields, nor do they operate any refineries. They are strictly fuel oil distributors, and have excellent contact with refineries. Their main sources are Chevron and Natomas, who own oil fields in South America and Indonesia. Colonial Oil has a large storage facility in Savannah, and can deliver oil by rail or truck. Colonial Oil is known for its dynamic management, which is capable of obtaining oil for their customers from anywhere in the world.

A sample of #6 fuel oil was supplied by Colonial Oil for analysis. The oil was found to be low in vanadium, and was acceptable. Based on the recommendation of the senior purchasing engineer, Colonial Oil was accepted as the third supplier for fuel oil by the purchasing manager, production service department, and the maintenance department.

When the purchase requisition for 1980 fuel oil requirements was received, the senior purchasing engineer had three suppliers on the bid list. The past performance of the existing suppliers were satisfactory; therefore, there was no need to drop any of them. Based on the earlier analysis, one new supplier was added to the bid list. At this time, the purchasing manager felt that it was not necessary to add additional suppliers. This was due to the extensive research, time commitment, and cost required.

The RFQ was sent to the new supplier for bid submission within two weeks. This situation was different from that of annual contracts. There was no need to send RFQs to the existing suppliers. The contract with Exxon was valid for five years, and did not expire until 1983. The contract with Hess was evergreen, and remained valid indefinitely until either party terminated it in writing, giving three months' advance notice.

The real purpose of the contract in this instance is to assess the company's long-range need for fuel oil and to periodically inform the suppliers of this. Exxon has the policy of reviewing contracts every five years, and thus will not accept evergreen contracts. Exxon and Hess simply receive planned purchase agreements concerning quantity of fuel oil to be delivered in 1980 according to the terms of the existing contract. Such intimation is usually sent in November of the preceding year. Thus, there is no need to send RFQs to Exxon or Hess.

Evaluating and Selecting Suppliers

The bid was received from Colonial Oil on time. It met the requirement for having a sulphur content of less than 2.5 percent. Colonial Oil also assured the company that the vanadium in their oil would not exceed 300 parts per billion (ppb).

The company decided to split the available volume of ten million gallons among the three suppliers. This volume was large enough to divide, without any one supplier losing interest in the company's business. The crucial decision concerned *how* to divide the available business among the three suppliers. Further analysis of the suppliers' offers was needed. Various considerations were salient. First, Exxon delivered oil by railroad. The price of the oil was the same, but the company must pay freight charges. In other words, the prices quoted by all three suppliers are FOB their storage locations. When the oil is delivered by railroad, it costs about one-half cent less per gallon in transportation compared to delivery by truck. However, because Exxon oil contains higher amounts of vanadium, it requires special treatment before use. The company hired a consulting engineering firm to solve the vanadium problem. They suggested a chemical treatment of Exxon oil that reduces the vanadium to 250 ppb. The company had two large storage tanks for fuel oil storage for up to two weeks. The operations department decided to use one tank to store Exxon oil for the necessary chemical treatment. The production service department estimated that the cost of treating Exxon oil was about one-half cent per gallon, which offset the savings in transportation cost.

There are additional advantages in railroad delivery. A large quantity of oil can be delivered by rail cars. They are extremely easy to unload compared to trucks. Further, rail cars can remain on company property for twenty-four hours without incurring demurrage charges. The company may unload the rail car at any convenient time within twenty-four hours. However, this is not the case for trucks. Trucks must be unloaded within two hours, as the truck driver must remain with the truck until it is unloaded. This sometimes causes a labor scheduling problem with the production service department. Truck delivery is scheduled ahead of time, but trucks may run late because of traffic problems or mechanical failure.

Colonial Oil can deliver by railroad. Their oil is low in vanadium, and does not require chemical treatment. Thus, its delivered price per gallon is about one-half cent less than the prices of Exxon and Hess. In addition it has the advantages of rail delivery. On the other hand, Colonial Oil is only a distributor, and is a new supplier for the company. Therefore, the purchasing agent did not give them a major share of the business.

In 1979, Exxon received 70 percent and Hess 30 percent of the company's business. In 1980, Exxon received 50 percent; Hess received 25 percent; and Colonial, 25 percent of the company's business.

"This will simplify scheduling by equally dividing the quantity delivered through road and rail. Because Exxon oil requires chemical treatment, the maintenance department wants no more than 50 percent of the oil from Exxon," Mr. Barnes explained.

This recommendation was made by the senior purchasing engineer to management. It was approved by the purchasing manager and the plant manager. Approval by the purchasing and plant managers was required, because of the size of the order, approximately $5 million.

According to the purchasing engineer, there was no adverse reaction from Exxon upon receiving a reduced share of the company's business. "We did not volunteer the information to Exxon about adding Colonial as a new supplier. They may find out about Colonial at some future date, but right now Exxon knows we are trying everything possible to reduce our oil usage by switching to other sources, such as gas and coal," Mr. Barnes stated.

The decision process is shown in figure 5–4.

Evaluation

Although the basic price of oil is regulated by the government and the oil-producing countries, this example reflects the use of nonprice criteria in selecting suppliers.

The purchasing engineer, through persuasive negotiations, was able to meet the conflicting requirements of the power and service department and the maintenance department. The service department wanted all of the oil to come from Exxon, for greater ease in unloading. The maintenance department wanted all of the oil to come from Hess and Colonial, because Exxon oil caused scaling problems in the boiler tubes.

The entire decision process was well-coordinated by the purchasing engineer.

96 • *Industrial Purchasing Strategies*

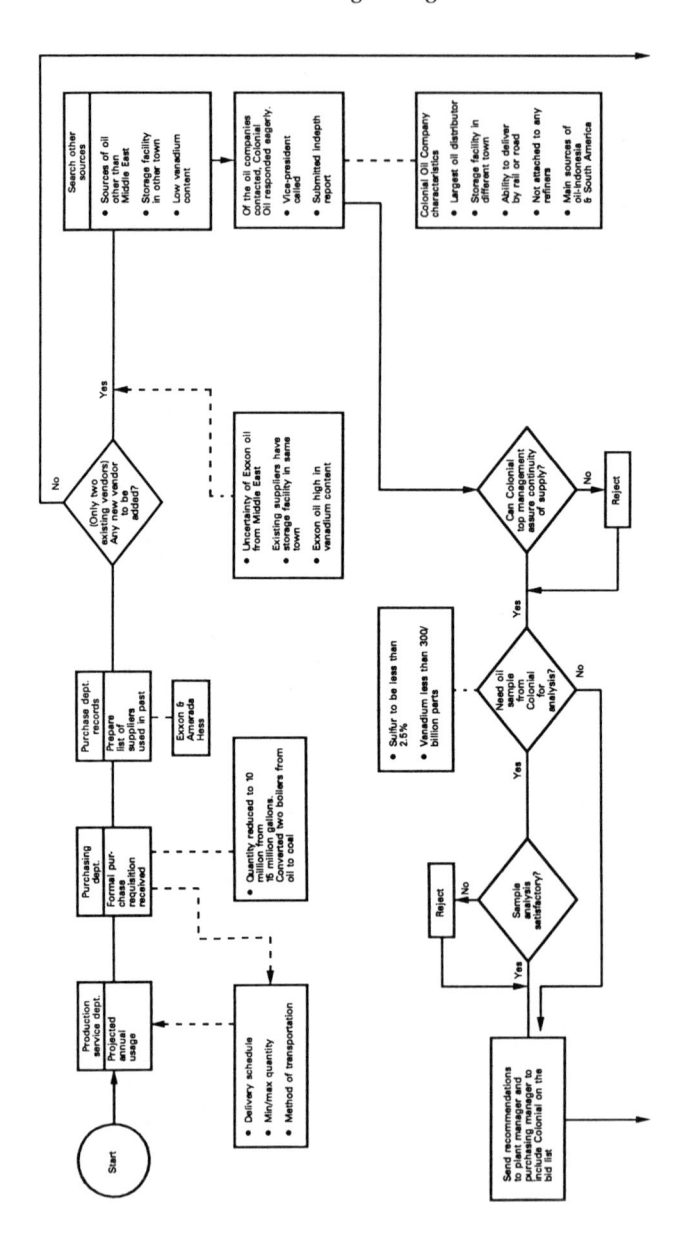

Evans Products • 97

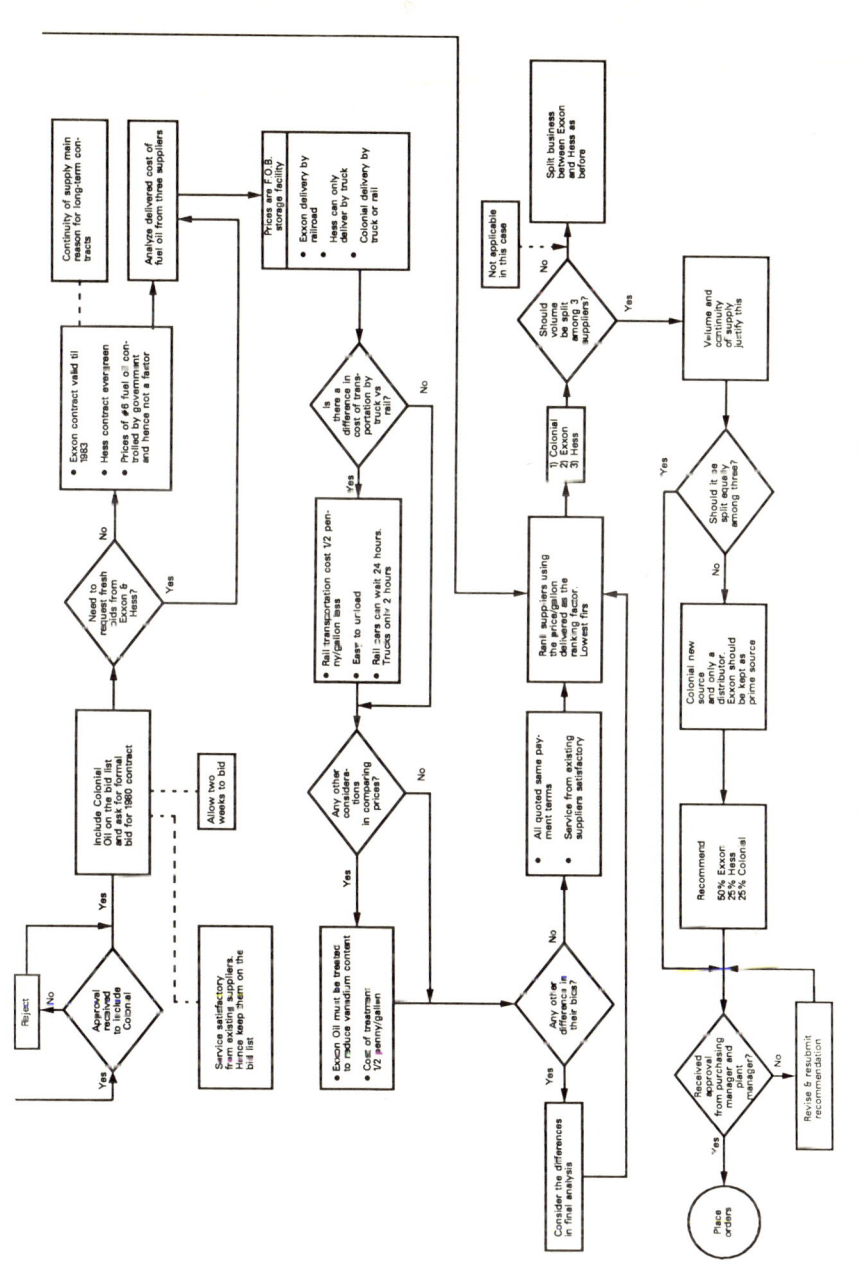

Figure 5-4. Purchase Decision Process: #6 Fuel Oil

6
Buying Acids, Pallets, and Gaskets at Diamond International Company

Diamond International is a diversified chemical company with its corporate headquarters in Dayton, Ohio. The company's worldwide sales in 1979 were $14 billion, up almost 20 percent from 1978 sales. The net income was close to $1 billion in 1979. Sales outside the United States in 1979 were almost $4 billion, approximately 30 percent of total sales.

The company employed more than 140,000 people worldwide in late 1979. Diamond operates more than 150 manufacturing plants and over a hundred research and development, sales service, and plant laboratories in the United States. Outside the United States, Diamond International has forty-seven subsidiaries, affiliated companies, and branches in thirty-four countries and territories. Altogether, the company manufactures about fourteen hundred products and product lines.

Background

Diamond International is an old company; it opened in 1800 as a producer of black powder. The founder of the firm, G. F. Diamond, was a chemist. He built a small powder mill in Dayton, Ohio, soon after arriving in this country from England. At that time, the quality of powder made in the United States was poor, and powder imported from abroad was expensive. Good powder was badly needed for mining, hunting, and self-protection; his product found a ready market.

During its first century of operation, the company remained primarily a manufacturer of black powder, with dynamite and eventually smokeless powder added to the product line in later years.

In the twentieth century, the company branched out into diversified chemical activities. Today, the company's interests include chemistry, biology, solid-state physics, electronics, pharmaceuticals, and the agricultural sciences.

Its product groups range from sulphuric acid to high-speed medical X-ray films; from fibers for the sheerest garments to materials that insulate people from the temperature extremes of the moon; from polyethylene industrial pipe to photopolymer printing plates; from paint to sophisticated analytical instruments. Diamond's product lines fall into four general categories: chemicals, plastics, specialty products, and fibers.

The chemical segment of the company consists of commodity chemicals, special-purpose chemicals, and pigments.

The plastics segment is comprised of thermoplastic resins, elastomers, films, and other plastic products. These products have a wide variety of applications in industrial and consumer goods.

The specialty products segment includes agricultural chemicals, explosives, paints and coatings, building products, medical products including pharmaceuticals, X-ray films and the automatic clinical analyzer, graphic arts products for printing, and a broad range of Remington sporting firearms and ammunition.

The fiber segment's products fall into four primary categories: apparel and home fabrics; carpet fibers and fiberfill; industrial fibers; and spunbonded products.

Nylon, Qiana, Dacron, Orlon, and Lyere synthetic fibers, sold in the apparel and home fabrics markets, reach the consumer in a variety of forms. Both nylon and Dacron are sold to the carpet industries, and Dacron fiberfill is used in such products as pillows and sleeping bags. The most important industrial fiber market is tire reinforcement. Spunbonded products are used in numerous applications, ranging from envelopes and packaging to operating room apparel and carpet backing.

Procurement Function

In 1975, the company created various staff departments reporting directly to the executive committee. The by-laws of the corporation provide that "during the interval between the meetings of the Board of Directors, the Executive Committee shall possess and may exercise all powers of the board, in the management and direction of all the business and affairs of the company."

One staff department created in 1975 was the energy and materials department, which is responsible for coordinating the company's overall efforts to obtain adequate energy suppliers and petrochemical feedstocks. This department is also responsible for purchasing and long-range procurement of raw materials, and all items required in the operation of the company's manufacturing and other activities. It also directs the company's efforts in exploration for reserves. It is involved in efforts to develop new sources of energy and basic hydrocarbon raw materials, and maintains liaison with government agencies and industry groups.

Top management has recognized that the organization's profitability is dependent on effective and efficient procurement policies, coordinated on a company-wide basis. The energy and materials department reports directly to top management. Prior to 1975, each manufacturing facility had its own purchasing department, which was responsible for all purchasing activities related to that plant. Thus, the purchasing function was decentralized; there were broad company procurement policies, but purchasing reported directly to respective plant managers. However, when the company was reorganized in 1975, the procurement function was elevated to management level, in line with engineering, research and development, and corporate planning functions.

Further, the purchasing departments at each plant location were consolidated into regional energy and materials departments. For example, one of the company's southeastern regional departments is located in Charleston, S.C.; it is responsible for all purchasing activities of the company's five manufacturing plants in the Carolinas. One regional department is in Atlanta, Georgia, and is responsible for the purchasing of six plants located in Georgia, Florida, and Tennessee. Figure 6–1 shows the related purchasing concept implemented by the company in 1975.

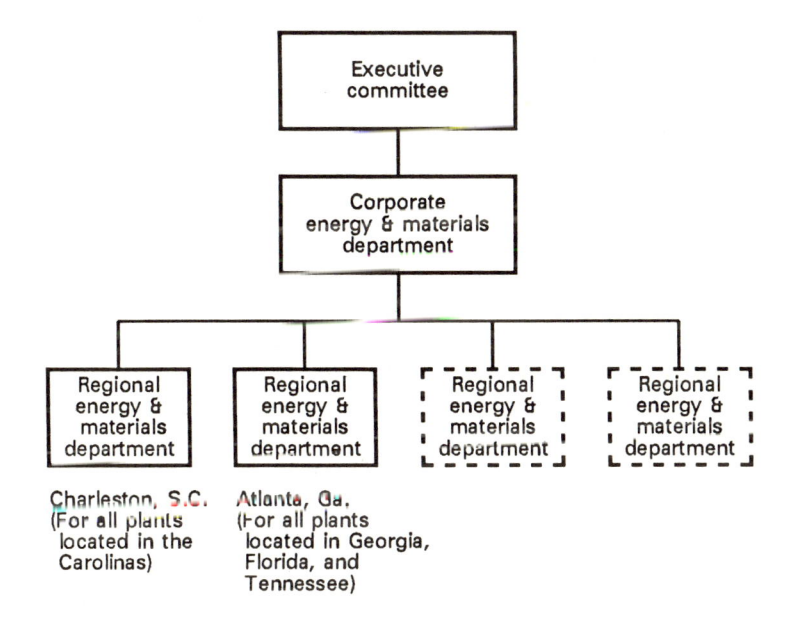

Figure 6–1. Diamond International's Regional Procurement Departments

Research for this study was conducted at the Charleston regional purchasing department. Mr. J. B. Cody is the manager of this department. A total of forty employees work at this location: twenty-one purchasing agents and supervisors, and nineteen clerical workers. Mr. Cody explained the regional purchasing concept as follows:

> Regional purchasing has many advantages—the most important one, of course, is in volume purchasing. It forces standardization of various items on plants. Previously, each plant had its own special need. Now at least we can analyze, without bias, if this need is really special or we can change it to fall in line with the needs of other plants. During the shortages of 1973, each of the regional plants of the company was competing for the same item with the same vendor without even knowing that this was happening. In the process we were responsible for pushing the price up. This may sound ridiculous, but it is true. The regional purchasing concept still keeps us close to the needs of each plant we serve. We have monthly meetings with plant personnel, we communicate daily over the phone, we have a central computer that receives a purchase requisition within minutes from any plant location. We have improved our purchasing efficiency, we are able now to plan ahead, our communications with vendors have been cut down but they are more effective, and our vendor relations have improved.

According to Mr. Cody, the company has saved more than $100 million over the past five years, after implementing the regional purchasing concept.

Three senior purchasing supervisors report to Mr. Cody. Each senior supervisor is responsible for a group of items to be purchased. For example, the first senior supervisor is responsible for the purchasing for the equipment group, the second for the supplies group, and the third for the contracts and essential materials group. Total purchases at this regional location amount to $300 million. The organizational chart for Carolina regional purchasing is shown in figure 6–2.

Finally, Mr. Cody pointed out that it is company policy that purchasing agents must have technical degrees in order to understand and use their expertise in buying the items they are responsible for, and must have worked at least five years in one of the Diamond plants before they can work in purchasing.

The following items purchased on long-term contracts were selected for the study: finishing ingredients (acids); wooden pallets; and sealing gaskets.

The regional purchasing manager suggested these items for the research for the following reasons: finishing ingredients, for the dollar volume involved ($16 million annually); wooden pallets, because of a minority vendor on the bid list; and sealing gaskets, for their variety (three thousand different varieties).

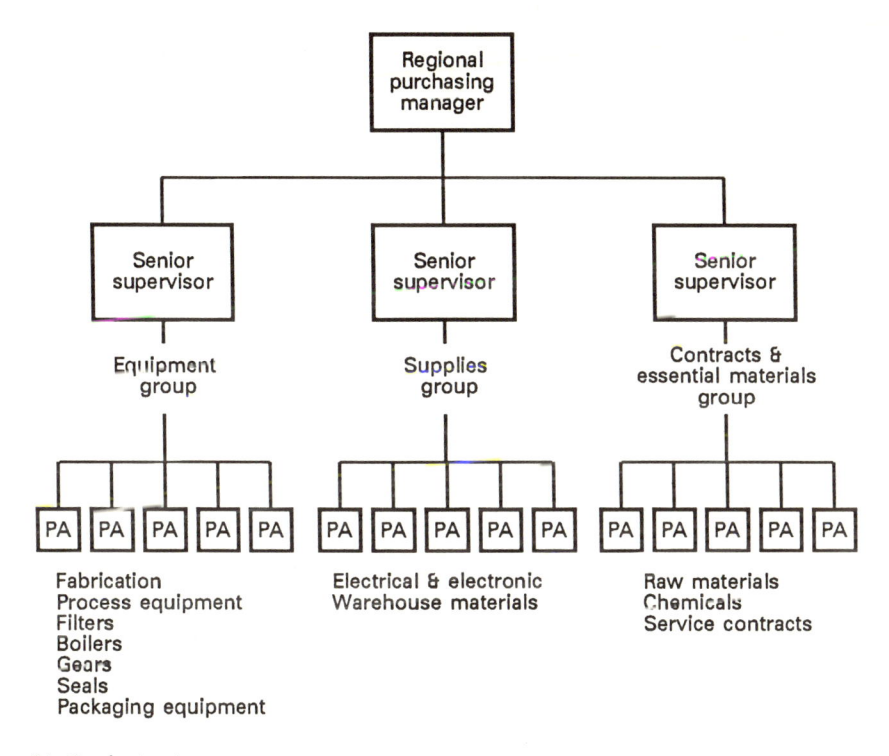

```
                    Regional
                    purchasing
                    manager
                        |
        ┌───────────────┼───────────────┐
     Senior          Senior          Senior
   supervisor      supervisor      supervisor
        |               |               |
    Equipment        Supplies       Contracts &
      group           group      essential materials
                                      group
```

Fabrication / Process equipment / Filters / Boilers / Gears / Seals / Packaging equipment

Electrical & electronic / Warehouse materials

Raw materials / Chemicals / Service contracts

PA: Purchasing Agent

Figure 6–2. Carolina Regional Purchasing

Purchase of Finishing Ingredients

Diamond International is one of the largest manufacturers of synthetic fibers in the United States. Synthetic fibers require a finishing process that gives them antistatic properties and lubrication. This is important for spinning and textile mills when producing an end product such as nylon cloth or carpets. The antistatic properties and lubrication of synthetic fibers facilitate weaving of the cloth.

Ingredients used for finishing synthetic fibers are fatty acids, oleic acids, surfactane, and mineral oils. One ingredient, oleic acid, was chosen for the study to learn the decision process involved in its purchase.

The Buying Center

The following people were interviewed: A. E. Davis, purchasing agent; J. B. Cody, regional purchasing manager, Carolinas region; A. W. Cave, senior supervisor.

Mr. Davis was in charge of purchasing finishing ingredients. He had a degree in chemical engineering, and had worked for six years in the Diamond central laboratory in Dayton, Ohio.

Mr. Cave was a senior supervisor in the regional purchasing department. Mr. Davis reported to him, and kept him informed about the number of vendors selected to submit bids, negotiations with vendors, and the final evaluation and selection of suppliers. Mr. Cave explained his vendor evaluation policy: "If everything is working fine, and the existing vendor is performing satisfactorily, it's very difficult to replace him. The new vendor has to more or less buy his way in by quoting a very competitive price—usually about 10 percent lower."

Mr. Cody was the regional purchasing manager. He authorized the decisions of Mr. Davis and Mr. Cave on purchasing finishing ingredients, because of the large amount of money involved ($16 million). Mr. Cody expressed his opinion about centralized versus decentralized purchasing: "Both systems have advantages and disadvantages. You can write a book on the subject. But the regional purchasing concept has combined the advantages of both centralized and decentralized systems: volume buying without sacrificing service to the individual manufacturing facility."

Oleic acids were used to manufacture the finished products. Delivery of this item was critical, and stock had to be maintained at each manufacturing location. Each plant in the Carolina region forecast its anticipated usage of oleic acids for one calendar year, based on its total synthetic fiber production requirements for a given year. The company's total purchase of oleic acids for the 1979 calendar year in the Carolina region amounted to about $15 million. According to the purchasing agent, Mr. Davis, the 1980 requirement would probably be around $16 million. Although the total volume purchased in 1980 would remain the same as that purchased in 1979, a price increase of about 7 percent was anticipated in 1980. This was based on price increases of raw materials used to produce oleic acids.

All Diamond manufacturing plants producing synthetic fibers used oleic acids as the finishing ingredient. Therefore, there were common corporate specifications for this product. These specifications were prepared by the corporate chemical engineering department in Dayton, in consultation with corporate research and development, along with production personnel at various manufacturing facilities. In drawing up specifications, many years of valuable experience of Diamond personnel were pooled together in the corporate staff of three engineers. These specifications were continuously monitored to include changes in technology, improvements recommended by manufacturers, and new processes developed by the company's research and development group.

Company policy was to purchase oleic acids on a yearly contract to maintain continuity of supply, and obtain a competitive price through volume buying. The company preferred not to have long-term contracts exceeding one year, because the demand for synthetic fibers fluctuates from year to year; thus, forecasting beyond that time period becomes difficult. The purchasing agent also noted that inviting fresh bids each year for annual contracts created competition among suppliers, who were likely to quote better prices.

To check the quality of oleic acids received from suppliers, the manufacturing facility at each company location had a laboratory. The test reports were submitted to the purchasing departments, with comments on whether or not the supplier complied with specifications. The specifications allow tolerances of the chemical composition of the acids, within certain limits. Consignments that fail to meet specifications are returned to the manufacturer along with detailed analysis reports.

According to Mr. Davis, "the quality of finishing ingredients has marketing implications. It adds color, shine, lubrication, and antistatic properties to the synthetic fabric, and these qualities are easily noticeable by the company's customers."

If finishing is not done properly, the fiber is likely to be rejected by the company's customer. Thus, the company's image is tarnished. Mr. Cave stressed that "for these reasons, the chemistry of oleic acids is extremely important for the company. Its quality is continuously monitored and its specifications are kept confidential to maintain the company superiority in producing quality synthetic fibers as compared to the competition."

Selecting Suppliers to Submit Bids

Over the years, the company has developed three dependable sources for the supply of oleic acids to Diamond plants located in the Carolinas. The purchasing agent was asked why the company did not have a truly centralized purchasing policy for this item, as finishing ingredients were required by all the company's plants (located all over the country and the world). He indicated that the high cost of transportation was the major factor against centralized purchasing. The acids were heavy, and required specialized care in handling. Transportation costs increased each year, and so it was not practical to purchase this item from one or two sources, and then transport it across the country to various plant locations. Each region has developed its own sources, especially because Diamond had decentralized purchasing before 1975, and each plant bought what it required independently. Mr. Davis quickly added: "The possibility of company-wide annual contract negotiations exists in the future when enough oleic acid manufacturers have manufacturing facilities available in the various regions of the country."

The second reason indicated by Mr. Davis for the regional purchase of this item was that it allowed a close relationship to develop between suppliers in one region and the nearby Diamond plants. These suppliers came to understand the process, needs, and idiosyncracies of those at each plant location. He explained:

> Chemistry has lots of grey areas. Although there are specifications for this item, each manufacturer's item has unique characteristics and any time you switch a supplier an extensive evaluation program has to be conducted. This consists of laboratory evaluation by the corporate research and development group, production department evaluation at plant locations, and evaluation by the customer. The customer evaluation consists of monitoring the manufacturing process in the end use of synthetic fibers and how it affects production efficiency. Such evaluation is a costly project involving anywhere from several months to as much as three years.

The performances of the three existing sources were satisfactory. No new supplier was evaluated for this item and therefore, the purchasing agent sent RFQs only to those three suppliers, allowing them two weeks to submit quotations. This also met the company requirement to preferably have three sources for bidding.

Diamond did not have a formal rating system for suppliers, but laboratory reports from plants, and feedback from production remained in the vendor's file. And this file was consulted in evaluating the vendors' performance.

Evaluating and Selecting Suppliers

The three suppliers, A, B, and C, submitted detailed quotations within three weeks. (One supplier had requested a week's extension in quoting his price. This extension was granted to all of the suppliers.)

The quotes were examined for the necessary information such as quantity, delivery schedule, point of delivery, freight charges, deviations from specifications (if any), terms of payment, and price escalation. The purchasing department requested information from each manufacturer on the date on which the labor contract would expire. All three suppliers were large and reputable manufacturers of oleic acids in the region.

The three quotes contained all of the necessary information required to evaluate the suppliers. Each supplier's offer met company specifications. Each supplier also met the required delivery schedules for various plants, and prices included delivery FOB destination. The terms of payment quoted by each supplier were net 30 days, which was standard industry practice. None of the suppliers quoted a firm price. The prices quoted were firm for thirty days, after which they were subject to changes in raw material prices. The next step was to tabulate the prices bid by each supplier.

Supplier	Total Price	Remarks
A	Lowest	Relatively new source Labor contract expires in 1980
B	2 percent higher than A	Established source Labor contract expires in 1982
C	3.7 percent higher than A	Established source Nonunion plant

Because of the critical nature of the item and the large quantity needed, the order was split among the three suppliers. The volume was large enough to split three ways, and still keep the suppliers interested. The purchase requisition made it clear to suppliers that Diamond reserved the right to order any quantity from a supplier, depending upon the evaluation of the quotation.

The next question was how to split the volume among the three suppliers. The purchasing agent invited preferences from individual plants. "This gives some muscle to the plant people," he said. The plant people were not given prices quoted by each supplier, but they were given the rest of the available information. The plants suggested the quantity to be ordered from each supplier. The final breakdown follows: Supplier A, 15 percent of the volume; Supplier B, 25 percent of the volume; and Supplier C, 60 percent of the volume.

The purchasing agent evaluated the split, approved it, and submitted it to his supervisor. They agreed to the breakdown.

According to Mr. Davis, "the quality, service, and overall performance of supplier C were the factors in giving him a larger share of the business. Supplier A, even with the lowest price, received the smallest share because his labor contract was expiring in 1980. Further, supplier A is relatively new for Diamond."

The purchase decision process is shown in figure 6–3.

Evaluation

This is an example where extreme importance was attached to established sources. Even among the established sources, those with the best quality and service record obtained the major share of the company's business. Each supplier's product had unique characteristics. The purchasing agent argued:

> Any time you switch to a new supplier, an extensive evaluation program has to be conducted; thousands of dollars are involved in laboratory evaluation, production evaluation, and evaluation by the customers. The time period ranges from a few months to a couple of years. Unless there are compelling

108 • *Industrial Purchasing Strategies*

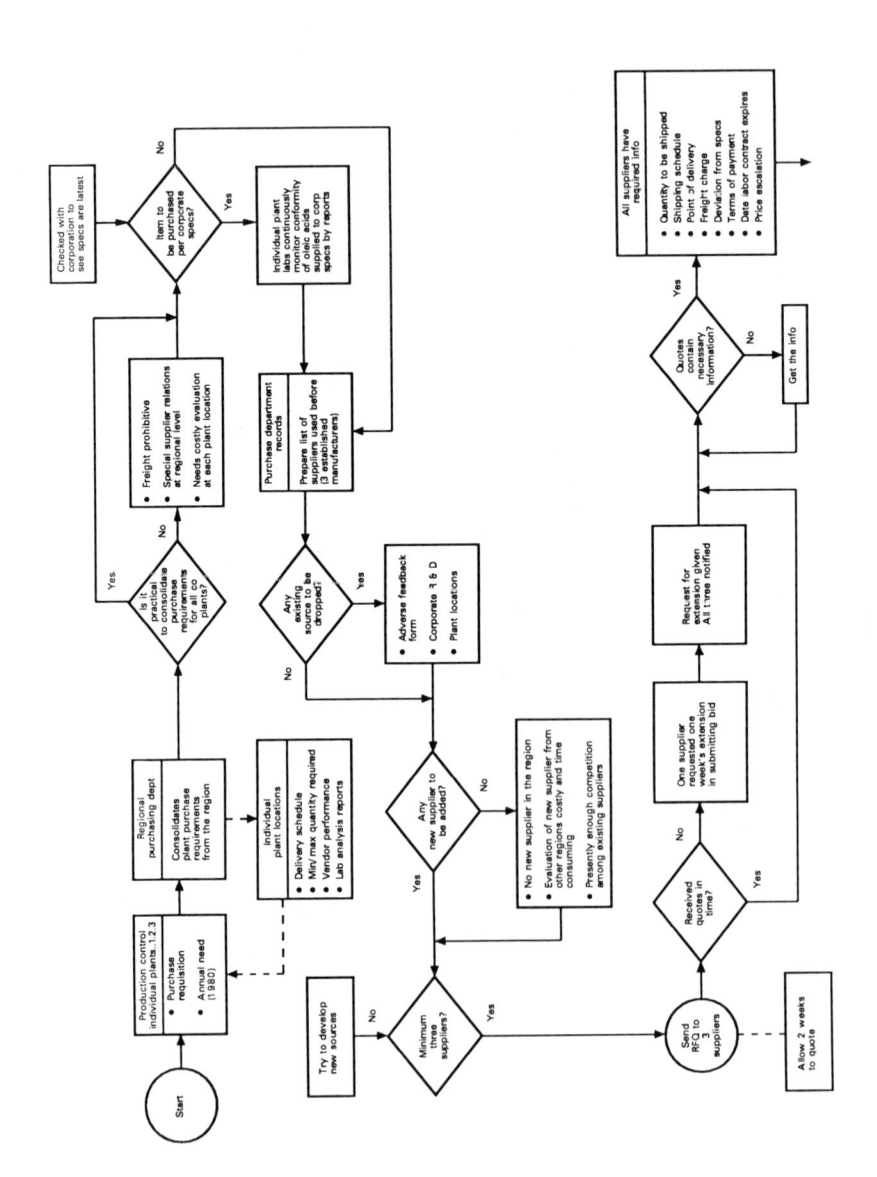

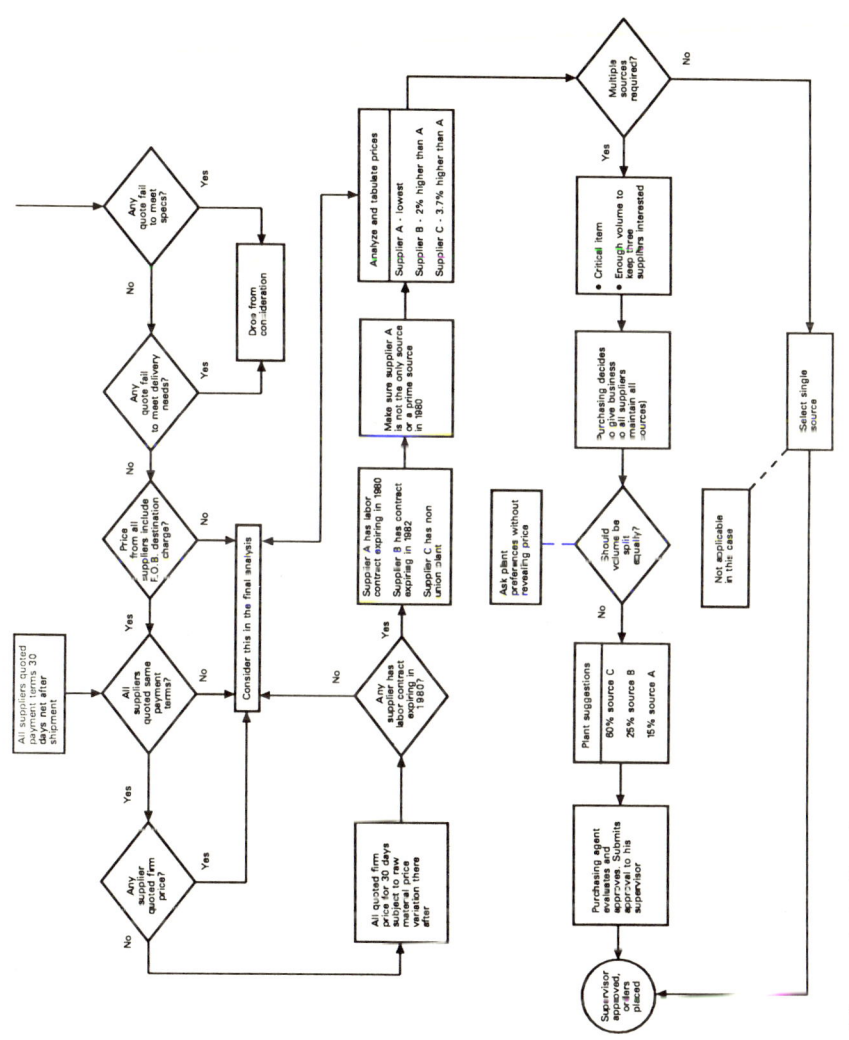

Figure 6-3. Purchase Decision Process: Finishing Ingredients (Oleic Acids)

reasons, such as if existing supplier's quality deteriorates or if delivery becomes unreliable or a new supplier quotes a very attractive price (10 percent lower), you don't add a new supplier.

No attempt was made to negotiate price with suppliers. This may be considered to be a weakness in the decision process. However, Mr. Cave explained: "Negotiating the price with the suppliers is a sort of bargaining with them, which is against company policy. You may save a few dollars now, but eventually the service and quality will suffer if you squeeze your suppliers. In the long range, it will cost you more."

Purchase of Wooden Pallets

Wooden pallets are used by Diamond manufacturing in the Carolinas for a variety of purposes. For example, the Diamond Sumter plant manufactures Mylar sheets, and uses wooden pallets to ship these sheets; the plant stacks the sheets on pallets, and ties them with plastic straps. Other plants use pallets for transporting different types of finished productions from the production area to stocking areas, and from stocking to the shipping area.

Wooden pallets may appear to be simple, but because they are used to transport finished products, two important factors must be considered. First, the safety of the individuals handling finished products on the pallets is important. If pallets are not designed properly, they can break, causing the heavy materials of the finished products to fall. Second, the product itself may be damaged if the pallet cracks, and the straps holding the Mylar sheets snaps. The design of the pallets should also be such that they are suitable for handling by fork lift trucks.

The size of pallets varies with individual plants. Therefore, a general meeting was held when the regional purchasing concept was implemented (1975) to discuss the variety of pallets used by Diamond plants in the Carolinas. The purchasing department, user departments, and packaging engineering departments from the various plant locations participated in this meeting. According to the purchasing agent, "the purpose of the meeting was to study the variety of sizes of pallets used at different locations, the reasons for using a specific size, and if the number of sizes could be reduced without sacrificing the flexibility in the end use." Several follow-up meetings were held, and the final outcome was that five different sizes of pallets were used by all plants in the Carolinas.

Why was this practice of standardization of pallets not extended to all Diamond plants in the United States? The purchasing agent had a good answer to this question:

As the number of plants increases, the variety of pallets we use also increases because each plant manufactures different items in various sizes and weights. Standardization then becomes a real problem. The fundamental reason for not using company-wide standardization is that pallets are bulky, and transportation costs are very high. At the same time, pallets are simple to produce, and therefore sources should be developed who are close to the plants using the pallets. Having a supplier who will take care of the needs of all the plants located in the Carolinas is much more practical because the distances are reasonable. Even if the same pallet sizes are required by a Diamond plant in Texas, the transportation cost from a supplier in the Carolinas would be prohibitive. The Texas plant will have to purchase these pallets locally, and they should not have any problems because there are many pallet manufacturers there. The whole idea of standardization is to take advantage of quantity buying. If you cannot achieve this, there is no point in standardization. The regional purchasing concept strikes a good balance in this respect between centralized and decentralized purchasing. The advantages of both systems are combined.

The specifications for pallets were written by the packaging engineering department at one plant—usually a plant using the maximum variety of pallets—and approved by their counterparts at other locations. If specifications had to be revised, the initiating plant first discussed this with the purchasing department. Purchasing then discussed these revisions with vendors, and transmitted the information to the packaging engineering department, which was responsible for specifications. They discussed the revised specifications with other plants, and finalized them after receiving their approval. If there was disagreement on final specifications, a joint meeting was held with the packaging departments and purchasing to resolve the differences. The purchasing agent stated that during his six-year career in purchasing, he was not aware of a single instance when differences were not resolved by mutual discussions. "The responsibilities are clearly defined, and each one tries to understand the problems of others," he stated.

The Buying Center

The following people were interviewed to study the decision process: J. W. Dodge, purchasing agent, Charleston, S.C.; Bud Kimble, store supervisor, Sumter, S.C.; and Wayne Turner, purchasing agent, Sumter, S.C.

Mr. Dodge was in charge of purchasing packaging material. Once the order is released, the store supervisors at individual plant locations contacted vendors directly to schedule delivery of the pallets. The packaging department at each plant submitted a report to Mr. Dodge about the pallets' quality. Mr. Kimble and Mr. Turner were interviewed by telephone from Charleston.

According to Mr. Dodge, the feedback from Mr. Kimble and Mr. Turner on delivery and quality of pallets was important in the purchasing process.

Selecting Suppliers to Submit Bids

The company has in the past used three suppliers to meet its need for pallets. The number of wooden pallets required for each plant for the calendar year 1980 was estimated by the plants' production control departments. They sent purchase requisitions to regional purchasing in Charleston, where the requirements from all of the Carolina plants were consolidated. The purchasing agent expected to purchase wooden pallets amounting to about $300,000 during 1980.

One manufacturer out of the three established sources had stopped manufacturing pallets in late 1979. This source was not an active supplier during 1979, but its decision to stop manufacturing pallets left the company with only two sources. The purchasing agent had been actively trying during the last few months to develop a new source and was able to interest a minority supplier in bidding for the company's 1980 pallet requirement. This supplier had supplied other wooden items to the company previously, and quality and workmanship were satisfactory. In the past year, this company had purchased new machinery; the purchasing agent found, after visiting the facility, that it had the capacity to meet Diamond's needs.

According to Mr. Dodge, "The company prefers to buy all wooden pallets on a yearly contract because of the savings obtained in quantity buying. It is difficult to forecast the pallet requirements beyond one year because of changing economic conditions. Therefore, contracts beyond one year are not realistic."

He further explained: "The two other existing suppliers are well known for their quality, and we are extremely satisfied with their performances. As a matter of fact, these are the two suppliers who have the contracts for 1979 to supply the pallets."

Thus, the purchasing agent sent RFQs to the two existing suppliers, and to one new minority supplier for the wooden pallets required for 1980, allowing them two weeks to submit quotes. This also met the company requirement to preferably have three sources place bids.

Evaluating and Selecting Suppliers

When the bids were received, all suppliers quoted per company specifications. All indicated delivery times as required by individual plants; all promised to keep a firm price for ninety days, after which it was subject to negotiations; and all quoted prices FOB destination.

The terms of payment quoted by all three suppliers were slightly different.

The minority supplier requested a 10 percent advance payment with the order, and the remaining amount within a week from the date of delivery. The two other suppliers quoted standard terms—1% 10, net 30 days. In analyzing prices, the minority vendor's price was 4 to 9 percent higher per item. Because of this, and the unfavorable terms of payment, the minority vendor was rejected. Mr. Dodge argued: "The company policy is to seek out the minority vendor for bidding. But they have to be competitive to get the business."

Further analysis of prices showed that one supplier quoted lower prices for three sizes of pallets, and the other quoted lower prices for the remaining two pallet sizes. The company split the order between the two suppliers, giving them orders for the items for which they quoted the best prices. Thus, the company had two sources of supply. Further, splitting the order in this particular way saved Diamond about 5 percent in total cost. The dollar volume split between the two suppliers was 62 percent to the first supplier, and 38 percent to the second.

The purchase decision is shown in figure 6-4.

Evaluation

It is clear from this case that minority vendors must be competitive to gain a share of this company's business, even though the company policy is to seek vendors out and encourage them to submit bids.

The major weakness in the decision process was that there were too few vendors submitting bids. Because pallets are relatively easy to manufacture, the purchasing agent should have attempted to develop additional sources of supply. Rather than simply satisfying the company requirement of having three suppliers on the bid list, efforts toward developing several more sources might have paid off, creating keen competition among suppliers, and thereby saving the company some money.

Purchase of Sealing Gaskets

Diamond manufacturing plants use more than three thousand varieties of rubber gaskets of various shapes, thicknesses, and types of material. The basic function of rubber gaskets is to seal the joints of pipelines handling chemical fluids.

The purchasing agent explained, "The rubber gaskets age because of heat cycling, the type of chemical they come in contact with, and the pressure inside the pipes. Periodic replacement of the gasket is common whenever a preventive maintenance is scheduled or in the worst case, when they fail. For this reason, the gaskets are kept in stock at each plant location. The operating experience gained over a period of years helps the plant operations people to forecast the

114 • *Industrial Purchasing Strategies*

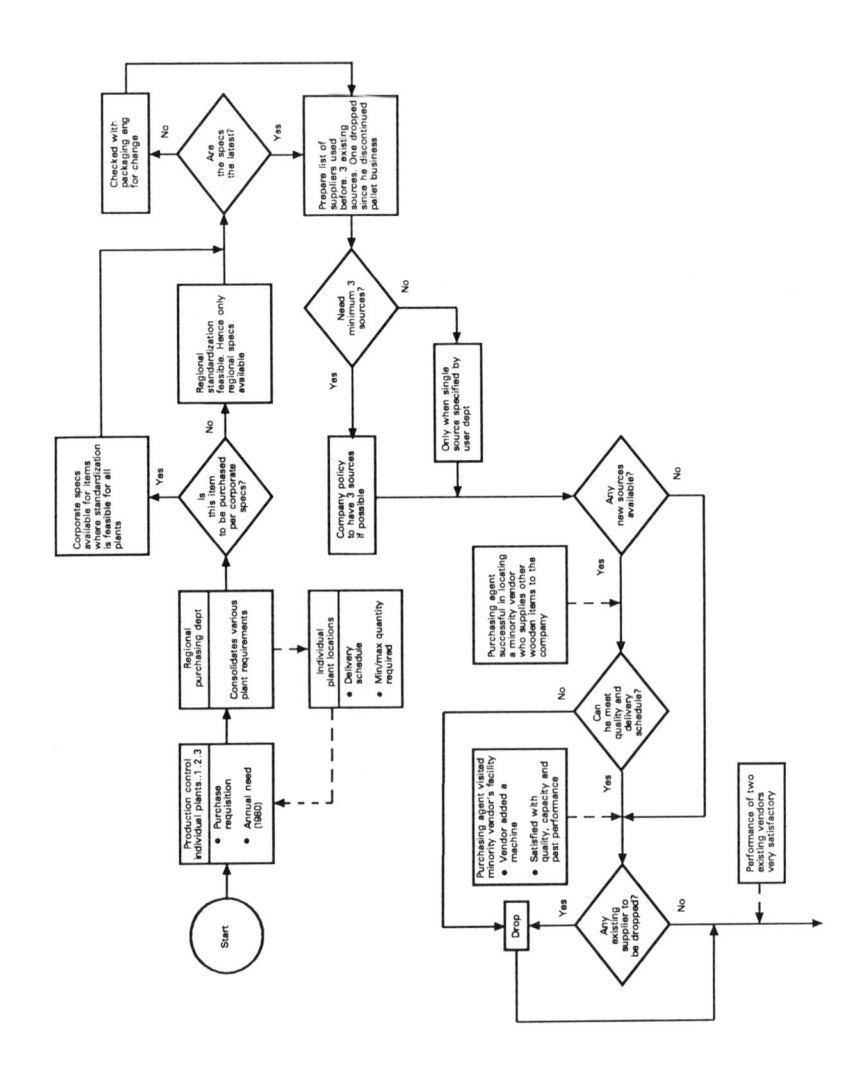

Diamond International Company • 115

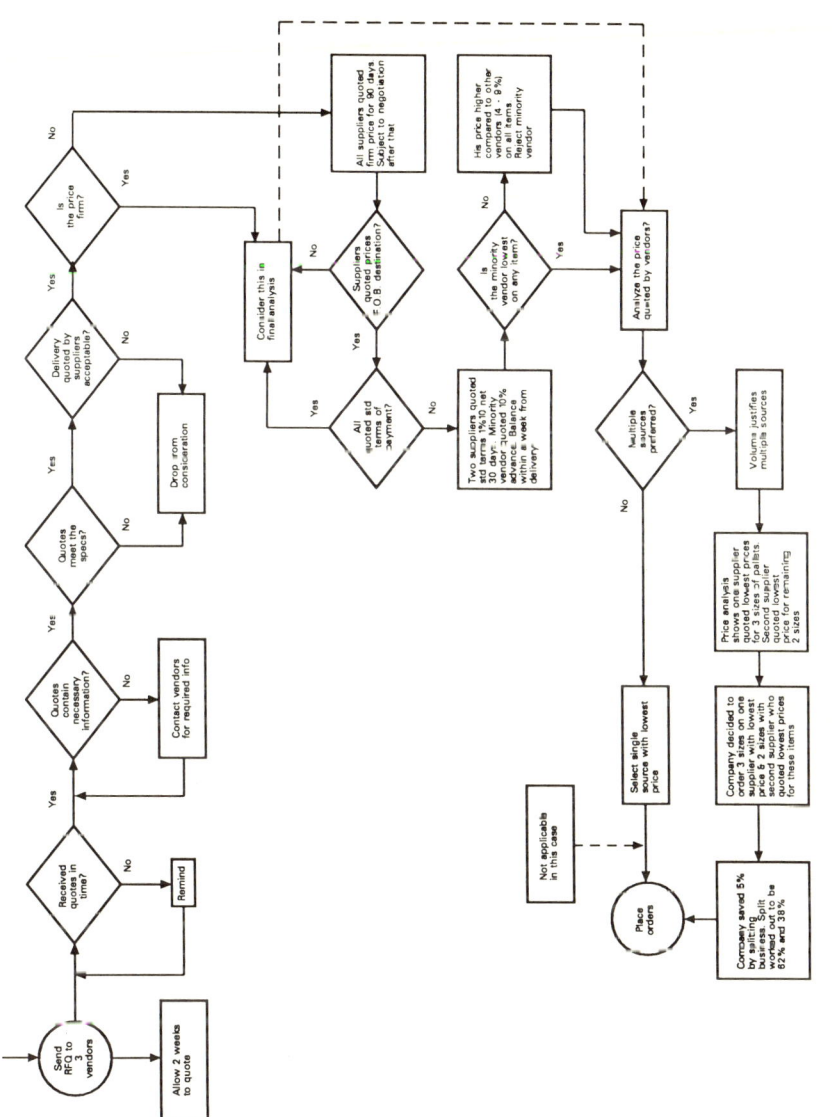

Figure 6-4. Purchase Decision Process: Wooden Pallets

annual usage of these items. The company policy is to purchase these items on annual contracts."

Decision to Select Manufacturers versus Dealers

Several manufacturers of rubber gaskets in the United States specialize in certain varieties. Their major sales are direct to original equipment manufacturers (OEMs), such as manufacturers of valves and pipe fittings. Replacement sales of gaskets are usually handled through distributors located all over the country. Because the gaskets are usually small and generally weigh little, they can be ordered from any manufacturer or distributor anywhere in the country without incurring high shipping costs. This is an example of an item for which requirements from all Diamond facilities in the United States can be combined and ordered from manufacturers directly, or through distributors. However, the purchasing agent explained why gaskets are purchased on a regional basis.

First, if gaskets were ordered directly from the manufacturers, a great number of manufacturers would be involved because of the thousands of varieties of gaskets required. No single manufacturer could supply all the different types of gaskets needed. Second, the volume required for each type of gasket, even when requirements from all Diamond plants are consolidated, is not large enough to earn special quantity discounts from the manufacturers. Therefore, the company decided to purchase gaskets through distributors.

The distributors, in quoting prices for gaskets, gave consideration not only to the quantity to be supplied, but also to the shipments they must make to individual plants. According to the purchasing agent, "There is not much savings whether the gaskets are ordered on a regional basis or on a national basis. However, the advantages in ordering the gaskets on a regional basis are the decrease in the response time and the improvement in the service given by the local distributor." These distributors agreed to stock all varieties of gaskets that Diamond uses; and if an individual plant runs out of a particular type of gasket, they will rush deliver the needed gasket, or the company can arrange to pick it up, when the distributor is located in the region. The policy, therefore, is to purchase these items on a regional basis through distributors. Most distributors are willing to stock all varieties of gaskets.

There are no common specifications for gaskets. Most are manufactured by one or two specialized manufacturers, and therefore, a gasket is identified by that manufacturer's part number.

A purchase requisition for gaskets consists of a computer printout, which lists all of the gaskets by description, the manufacturer's identifying part number, and the quantity needed. In short, no product specifications are available, and no coordination of specifications is needed among the plants buying gaskets.

The Buying Center

The following persons were interviewed to understand the purchasing process for gaskets: J. F. Hall, purchasing agent; H. J. Mack, purchasing agent; and A. W. Cave, senior supervisor.

Mr. Hall had taken over this product line from Mr. Mack within the past year, so both of them were interviewed. The total value of gaskets purchased in 1979 in the Carolina region was $150,000. Mr. Cave has the responsibility of approving decisions made by purchasing agents.

Selecting Suppliers to Submit Bids

Four suppliers have done business with the company. They are authorized distributors in the area for rubber gasket manufacturers. They have the financial ability and warehouse facilities to carry these items in stock and to supply them per delivery schedules. The company has been satisfied with the service and overall performances of these suppliers. There was no need to drop any from the bidders list.

The sales rep of a new supplier had called a few months earlier. This supplier had recently been appointed distributor for gasket manufacturers and indicated eagerness to do business with Diamond. The purchasing agent asked for details of the supplier's warehouse facilities, names of manufacturers represented, number of employees, and details about other items carried in stock. The financial check on the company and the details requested above were found to be satisfactory; therefore, this supplier was added to the bidders list.

The purchasing agent sent RFQs to five suppliers, satisfying the minimum requirement of three sources.

Evaluating and Selecting Suppliers

The suppliers were given four weeks to quote, because of the large number of items listed on the purchase requisition and the fact that they had to contact different manufacturers for price committments and quantity required in 1980.

After several reminders, all five suppliers submitted quotations within five weeks. Two suppliers did not quote on half of the items. In other respects, all quotations contained the necessary information.

All suppliers quoted prices FOB destination to various plants for the required schedules, and asked for payment terms of 2% 10, net 30 days. Suppliers quoted a firm price. The price would remain firm for thirty days but would change as manufacturers changed their prices. However, the suppliers would inform Diamond in writing thirty days in advance before price changes became effective. This was standard practice with all suppliers.

118 • *Industrial Purchasing Strategies*

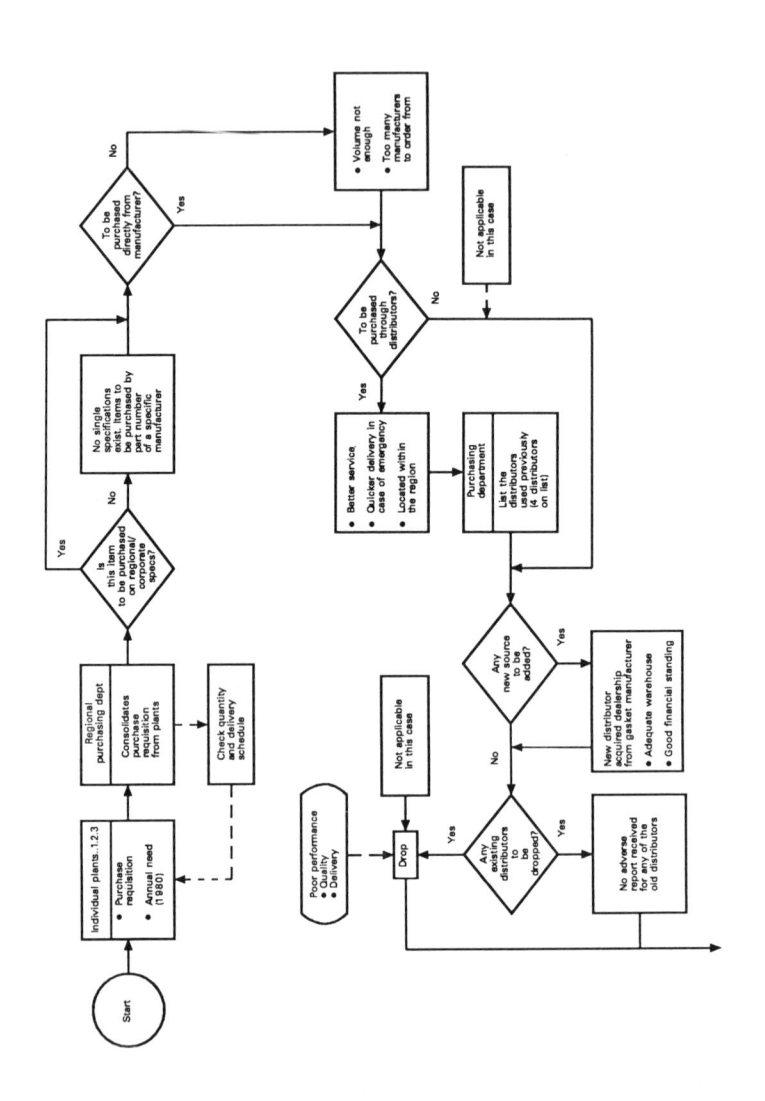

Diamond International Company • 119

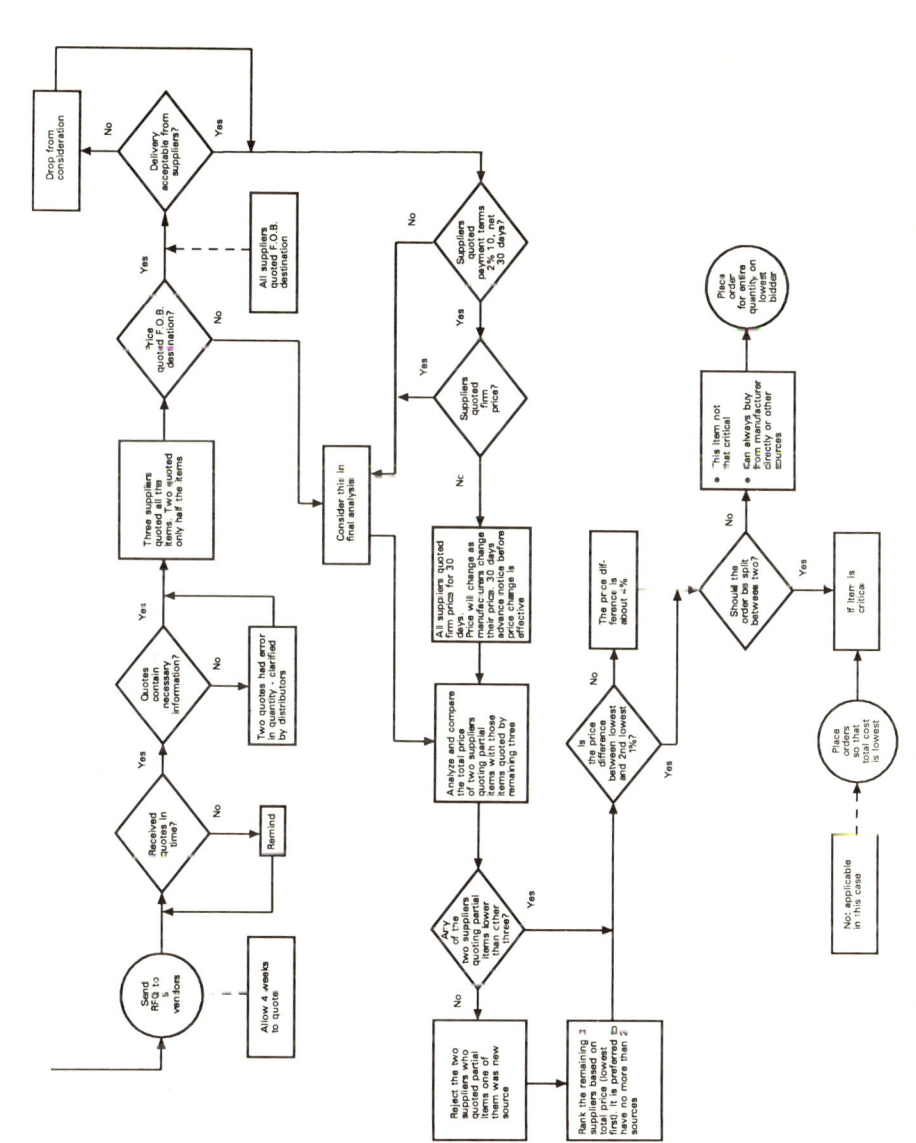

Figure 6–5. Purchase Decision Process: Sealing Gaskets

Finally, prices quoted by the five suppliers were compared. The two who quoted partially had higher prices than the other suppliers and were rejected. One of these was the new source. Of the remaining three, the two who quoted lower total prices were compared. The company had done business with both in the past. The price difference between the lowest and the second lowest bid was about 4 percent. The purchasing agent indicated that this difference was too high to justify splitting the business between the two. The supplier who quoted the lowest price was selected, saving the company money. The purchasing agent also remarked, "This simplifies order processing at each plant and avoids confusion."

The purchase decision process is depicted in figure 6–5.

Evaluation

This is an example of consolidating several thousand items that are identified by the original manufacturer's part numbers. When different distributors quote identical items and offer the same delivery and service, the purchase decision is based strictly on price. The quantity to be purchased was not split among distributors in order to save money and simplify the processing of orders at the individual plant locations. The purchasing agent could have explored the possibility of buying gaskets from independent manufacturers of rubber parts.

7
Buying Coal, Gases, and Cable at Southeast Electric Company

History

Southeast Electric Company and its predecessors have been in the electric, gas, and transportation business in North Carolina for many years. The history of one constituent company dates back to 1838.

The present Southeast Electric Company was incorporated in 1920 under the corporate name of Carolina Power Company. The name was changed to Southeast Electric Company in 1938.

Service Area

Southeast Electric Company's service area covers more than twelve thousand square miles in the central, southern, and southwestern sections of North Carolina. With a population of approximately 1.8 million, this area represents roughly a quarter of the state's land area, and a third of its population.

The company provides electric service to over 127 communities, and natural gas service to over seventy communities. The electric customer mix is well balanced, with residential, commercial, and industrial customers accounting for approximately 30 percent, 37 percent, and 33 percent, respectively, of total kilowatt-hour (kwh) sales during 1979. Primary industries include textile mill products; chemical and allied products; paper and related products; stone, clay, and glass products; and lumber and wood products. The company also provides urban bus service in two of the state's three largest cities.

During the past decade, approximately $8 billion has been invested in new and expanding industries in North Carolina, with over a third of that investment occurring within the company's service area. The rate of population growth within the service area has been excellent, outpacing both the state and national rates for the ten-year period through 1976.

As of December 1979, 380,000 electric customers were connected to the lines of this company's system. There were 190,000 natural gas customers at that time.

Electric Generating Facilities

The company operates nine steam stations with a generating capacity 900,000 kilowatts (kw) and twenty gas turbine generators which produce 300,000 kw.
Fossil fuel used in electric generation in 1979 cost $200 million.
At the time of our research, the company was constructing a 9-million-kw nuclear-powered generating facility, which was scheduled for completion in 1980.
The latest published forecast indicated a continuing program of construction and expansion, with a projected budget of approximately $900 million for the next five years, and $199 billion for the next ten years (1979–88).

Operating Revenues and Management

Total operating revenues for 1979 were in excess of $650 million. For the twelve-month period ending 31 December 1979, the company's payroll amounted to $5 million, at which date four thousand people were employed. This did not include employees of contractors engaged in construction work.
The company is governed by a seventeen-member board of directors, three of whom are executive officers. The nonemployee board member are outstanding business and financial executives, who live in and have interests in the company's service area.

Regulatory Bodies

The operation of the company is subject to regulation by a number of governmental bodies. The North Carolina Public Service Commission supervises accounting, and rates charged for services, and the quality and dependability of services. The Federal Energy Regulatory Commission rules on rates for the resale or exchange of power, issues or denies licenses for the construction of hydroelectric plants on navigable waters, and performs certain other regulatory acts that affect private companies at national levels. The Securities and Exchange Commission has jurisdiction over certain phases of financial operations of the company, involving certain stocks and/or bonds. Several other agencies, both state and federal, regulate Southeast Electric Company, including the Nuclear Regulatory Commission, HHS, and the Department of Labor.

The company has made large investments in preservation of the state's environment through the modernization of facilities to control air and water pollution. All coal-burning steam plants have electrostatic precipitators that remove over 99 percent of the fly ash from furnace gases. Cooling towers and spray ponds are used to control the temperature of cooling water and bring it to a temperature compatible with nature before returning it to the state's rivers.

Purchasing Department

The company has a central purchasing department located at corporate headquarters. The purchasing department orders about forty-eight thousand items from several thousand vendors located all over the United States. The 1979 estimated purchases were approximately $400 million, out of which $250 million was spent to buy fuels such as coal, oil, and gas.

The purchasing responsibility is divided among three supervisors: D. H. Parker, director of fuel purchasing, is responsible for the purchase of coal, oil and gas; Jim Boland is the supervisor for purchasing materials for new construction, production, and maintenance; and D. Miller is the supervisor for purchasing distribution- and transmission-line materials, transit department equipment and items required for the automotive department.

A total of fourteen purchasing agents work under these three supervisors. In addition, there is one value engineer in a staff position who assists the purchasing department in the technical evaluation of products. The value engineer reports directly to H. C. Palmer, the general manager of purchasing. The supervisors and purchasing managers have bachelor or associate degrees, and have been in purchasing from two to twenty-two years. The basic organizational chart for the purchasing department is shown in figure 7–1.

Long-term purchase contracts are used in the purchase of high-dollar-volume items required continuously for the operation of power plants, and for the transmission and distribution of electricity.

Except for fuel supply items, all items purchased on long-term contracts must be approved by two other departments: engineering and operations. The engineering department can reject the item based on their technical evaluation; operations can reject it based on the past experience of failure in the field during operation, or equipment not meeting the department's installation and operation standards. Thus, the purchase of items under long-term contracts requires continuous communications and cooperation among the purchasing, engineering, and operations departments. Each department has the power to veto a bidder and the item offered.

Communications among these three departments, as well as with vendors, are well documented, because the company is a public utility, is subject to outside audits, and operates under several regulatory bodies.

124 • *Industrial Purchasing Strategies*

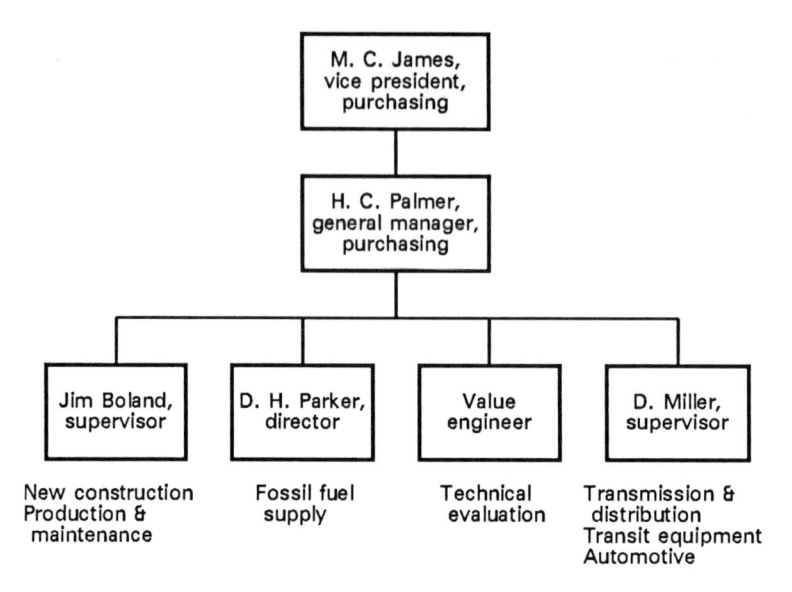

```
                    ┌─────────────────┐
                    │   M. C. James,  │
                    │  vice president,│
                    │    purchasing   │
                    └────────┬────────┘
                             │
                    ┌────────┴────────┐
                    │   H. C. Palmer, │
                    │ general manager,│
                    │    purchasing   │
                    └────────┬────────┘
         ┌───────────┬───────┴──────┬────────────┐
    ┌─────────┐ ┌──────────┐  ┌─────────┐  ┌──────────┐
    │Jim Boland│ │D. H. Parker│ │  Value  │  │D. Miller,│
    │supervisor│ │  director  │ │engineer │  │supervisor│
    └─────────┘ └──────────┘  └─────────┘  └──────────┘
New construction  Fossil fuel   Technical   Transmission &
Production &       supply       evaluation  distribution
maintenance                                 Transit equipment
                                            Automotive
```

Figure 7–1. Southeast Electric's Purchasing Department: Organizational Chart

The following three items purchased under long-term contracts were selected for the research: coal; purging gases; and 600-volt cables.

Coal and purging gases have multiple sources of supply; 600-volt cables are purchased from a single source. These items represent a broad variety of products with annual usage ranging from $200,000 to $25 million. The supplier choice processes for each item is described in the rest of this chapter.

Purchase of Coal

Fuel Supply Department

The fuel supply department of Southeast Electric Company is accountable for the system-wide purchase and delivery of all fossil fuels, including coal, #6 fuel oil, #2 fuel oil, propane, gasoline, and diesel fuel. The director of the fuel department follows the company's procurement practices and policies to obtain the greatest possible value for each dollar spent consistent with maximum reliability.

The fuel department is responsible for providing a constant supply of fossil fuel, such that it will be procured in quantities sufficient to meet the company's needs and to maintain stockpile levels consistent with current environmental and performance standards. According to Mr. Parker, director of the fuel supply department:

Fuel market conditions are continuously monitored in order to assess current market conditions, short-term trends, and long-terms trends as they affect the company's fuel purchasing strategies. Fuel is procured based on a mix of supply sources: long-term contracts, and spot market purchases, as specified by the company's guidelines. Fuel supplier performance is monitored and controlled relative to quantity, quality, price, and delivery schedules. The department analyzes transportation alternatives that will maximize fuel procurement costs.

Mr. Parker also stressed the need to be vigilant about market trends:

We remain familiar with fossil fuel market conditions through supplier contact and field visits to coal mines and other supplier facilities, paying particular attention to supply availability, price trends, and unusual circumstances developing in the market place. In addition, we monitor the fuel market through meetings, conferences, trade publications, and other industries in an effort to create a more efficient fuel supply department.

Spot Coal

The fuel supply department maintains an open bidders list, in that it does not evaluate and approve those vendors offering coal to Southeast Electric Company. The company requests a letter from each bidder, describing the company and its operations prior to adding the firm to the spot bidders list. Telephone bids are also accepted, but confirmation in writing is requested from the coal supplier. The department attempts to collect as many bids as possible for each month's purchases.

Each month a bid invitation containing quality specifications is mailed to those on the company's spot bidders list, requesting bids for coal to be delivered during the following month. Spot coal is purchased by the company in quantities sufficient to make up the difference between projected coal burned (furnished monthly by the production department), and quantities supplied under long-term contract. The amount purchased is also dependent upon the inventory levels of the company's stockpiles.

According to Mr. Parker, "each bid is evaluated on the basis of price, freight cost, quality (Btu/lb), quantity (tons), past experience with the supplier, if any, and car rating at the loading point (unit train or volume movements)."

Upon determining the amount of spot coal required, the fuel department normally attempts to negotiate the price and premium/penalty provisions of the purchase. Mr. Parker explained:

Depending upon the market conditions and the number of bids received, we will often counteroffer a bid at a price lower than the seller's bid price, in hopes of lowering the purchase price, and obtaining a price more in line with or less than the market price as we see it in the coal market.

Coal is a commodity, and as such, its price it very susceptible to changes in supply and demand. When the price is down and there is ample supply to meet demand, the buyer can use purchasing actions not available during a seller's market to lower cost. One example of such an action is the company's current practice on premium/penalty. It has a premium/penalty clause in its purchasing agreements, whereby the company pays a premium if the coal quality received exceeds the quality called for in the purchase agreement, and it deducts a penalty if the quality falls below the quality specified. This straight-line premium/penalty is based on total delivered cost, including the coal price and freight charges.

The purchasing department is successful at times (depending upon market conditions) in increasing the penalty provision from the straight-line method (approximately $.25/ton/100 Btu) to $.50/ton/100 Btu if the quality falls over 500 Btu/lb below that guaranteed by the seller. The increased penalty provision not only reduces the company's coal cost if it receives poor-quality coal, but also deters the producer from shipping poor-quality coal. This provision is negotiated with each purchase, and its inclusion is based strictly on market conditions at the time of sale.

Contract Coal

The fuel supply department strives to have under contract approximately 75 percent of the coal burn as specified by company guidelines. The amount under contract varies from year to year, depending on the burn forecast. The objectives of coal contracts are to have an assured supply at a reasonable price. To obtain these objectives, the department has negotiated and entered into contracts with shippers and/or producers for periods of one to five years, with options to review or extend contracts for as long as fifteen years.

Purchasing methods used to obtain these contracts are bids, negotiations, and a combination of these. Mr Parker said:

> We feel that a combination of bids and negotiations offers the best method of purchasing coal. By this method, we take the bids and attempt to further reduce the price through negotiation. A thorough study of the producer, his ability to mine and load, and the quality of his product is made before accepting the contract.

In all renewed and new contracts, Mr. Parker has been successful in negotiating pricing and adjustments, whereby price remains constant for a fixed time period, usually quarterly, semiannually, or annually. Price adjustments are based on independent indexes that reflect the changes in mining costs including labor, equipment, and supplies. Mr. Parker stated: "By using indexes based on cost, we avoid tying the price of contract coal to rapidly changing coal prices that occur in the market."

The fuel department directs the administration of all existing contracts to include contract performance regarding quality and quantity of coal supplied, price escalations, explanations for nondelivery of coal, and the resolution of major discrepancies regarding coal quality and quantity, payments, and premium/penalty adjustments.

Handling Coal: Railroads

Freight cost is about 30 percent of the total delivered cost of coal. Therefore, the fuel department attempts to control this cost closely. Most coal purchased on long-term contract is shipped from mines in four southeastern states.

The movement of coal from Kentucky, Tennessee, Virginia, and West Virginia to the company's electric generating stations occurs via Louisville and Nashville Railroad Company, Carolina, Clinchfield, and Ohio Railroad, Chesapeake and Ohio Railway Company, Norfolk and Western Railway Company, and Southern Railway Company.

Freight rates for rail transportation of bituminous coal to company plants are covered by tariffs. Unit Freight Tariff SFA 4174 requires a minimum of five thousand tons or seventy-two cars per train, with an annual volume requirement of two million tons. The single-car Freight Tariff SFA 4160 requires a minimum of 225,000 tons per year. Contract coal is moved via Freight Tariff SFA 4174, which results in substantial savings for the company. Most spot coal purchases are transported via Freight Tariff SFA 4160, due to the inability of a shipper to participate on a unit train basis.

The fuel supply department monitors the development of unusual events (including railroad car shortages and railroad strikes) as they may affect the supply of coal to the company's plants. The department negotiates and is a liaison with railroads on major claims, rate problems, receiving problems, and general movement of coal. It coordinates the scheduling of unit train and single-car deliveries between plants, suppliers and railroads. The fuel supply department maintains a close relationship with railroad representatives, and keeps in constant contact with railroads on shipments to meet delivery dates, rerouting when necessary and improving freight rates.

Most of Southeast Electric Company's fossil fuel generating plants use coal for firing boilers to produce steam, which in turn produces electricty. Therefore, coal is the lifeblood for continued operations of these generating plants. Advance planning for the purchase of coal is required. The systems planning department prepares forecasts for the usage of coal, considering the future expansion of existing generating stations, and the conversion of oil-fired stations into coal-fired stations. The three time periods covered by this forecast are:

1. *Long-range forecasts* cover the twenty-year period from 1980 to 2000.
2. *Intermediate forecasts* cover the five-year period from 1980 to 1985.
3. *Short-range forecasts* cover the year 1980.

The company plans to buy 4 million tons of coal during 1980. This constitutes about 80 percent of the company's operating costs. Out of this, about 2.9 million tons will be purchased on long-term contracts; the remaining 1.1 million tons will be purchased from the spot market.

Coal Specifications

Stressing the need for good-quality coal, Mr. Parker said, "To maintain the quality of the coal purchased, it is very important to specify the type of coal required by the company. The boilers are designed to operate using a specific type of coal only, and to maintain their efficiency the quality of the coal is monitored continuously."

The coal specifications also assure management that the company need not purchase higher-quality coal and produce better boiler efficiency. For example, the coal's sulphur content is specified between 1.5 and 2 percent. The existing boilers are designed to operate with this sulphur content. However, if a sulphur content of less than 1 percent is specified, the coal price increases 15 to 20 percent, without higher operational efficiency. According to R. M. Wells, the director of environmental compliance at Southeast Electric Company:

> The Environmental Protection Agency has set the limit of less than 2.5 percent sulphur content in the coal to be used for the company's existing boilers. But the agency insists that any new boiler installed by the company just burn coal having sulphur content less than 1 percent. We have finalized plans to convert Williams Station, which uses oil, to operate on coal by 1982. The coal required for this station must have sulphur content less than 1 percent to meet the standards set by the EPA.

The other items included in specifications are Btu/lb, percentage of ash content, ash fusion temperature, fluid temperature, size, moisture content, volatile percentage, and grindability.

The company specifies Btu/lb of no less than 12,000 Btu/lb. However, the higher the Btu/lb of coal, the greater the efficiency. At the same time, if the Btu/lb falls below 2,000, boiler efficiency decreases. Therefore, in this instance it is worthwhile to buy better-quality coal, when evaluated only in terms of Btu/lb. As mentioned earlier, the company has a premium/penalty clause in the purchase agreement, which assures the quality of coal received. If the Btu/lb falls below the value guaranteed by the seller, a penalty is assessed; but if it exceeds the value guaranteed, a premium is assessed, based on a formula agreed upon earlier in the contract.

Each shipment of coal received is sampled and analyzed by the company's quality department; then, based on the actual Btu/lb determined by tests, the premium or penalty is calculated.

The Buying Center

In-depth interviews were conducted with the following people. D. H. Parker, director of the fuel supply department; J. W. White, purchasing agent; B. A. Dailey, director of quality control; and R. M. Wells, director of environment compliance.

Mr. White is responsible for preparing the bidders list for compliance coal, inviting bids, and analyzing them in consultation with Mr. Parker.

Mr. Dailey performs the analysis of coal received from the vendor, and supplies this information to purchasing. Individuals from this department assist purchasing in reviewing the wording of long-term contracts and coal specifications, visit suppliers and their test facilities, give technical assistance, and keep abreast of the latest technology.

Mr. Wells is in constant contact with operating personnel at each generating plant and monitors boiler efficiency and sulphur content released into the atmosphere. Certain boilers operate better with coal from specific mines. Mr. Wells instructs the purchasing department to ship certain types of coal to specific plants. He also assists in setting up specifications, and keeps records of the sulphur content of coal from various suppliers.

Operating personnel at each plant level are informed of the scheduled shipments of coal from the mines. Each generating plant in turn supplies figures of its weekly coal usage and quantity of coal received. From this information, the purchasing department prepares the schedule, indicating the quantity of coal on hand, and how many days this quantity is expected to last.

Coal suppliers are important in keeping the company's power lines energized. Continuous contact with these suppliers is maintained by the purchasing department and is essential. Purchasing ensures that the analysis of coal by quality control is fair and consistent with the contract, that suppliers receive payments on time, and that all other departments work in close cooperation with them. If this is achieved, suppliers are willing to work with the company and offer better terms. As Mr. Parker stated, "Better relations with suppliers are essential; my second employer is the fuel supplier."

Selecting Suppliers to Submit Bids

The *Keystone Coal Industry Manual* lists the names of coal suppliers, coal mines, their locations, and types of coal they mine. In addition, it gives information on the size of companies, railroads they use for shipments, shipping points, and other general information. This manual, however, is rarely referred to when seeking out a new supplier. Mr. Parker, the director of fuel supply, said: "The company has been purchasing coal for over fifty years. When we purchase coal in such a quantity, we don't have to go and seek out suppliers. They seek us out."

The list of potential suppliers is continuously updated, as salesmen from coal suppliers visit the purchasing department and request that their company's name be added to the bidders list.

The company has about 125 suppliers on the bidders list for spot coal purchases. The locations of mines and shipping points are very important factors, because freight accounts for about 30 percent of the total delivered cost of the coal. Therefore, most suppliers on the bid list are located in Kentucky, Virginia, West Virginia, Tennessee, and Pennsylvania. When a new supplier is added to the bidders list, its location is used initially to screen it.

Of these 125 suppliers, only eighteen could deliver the compliance coal in the required quantity on long-term contracts. Company policy dictated sending requests for bids for long-term contracts only to those suppliers who have supplied coal to the company in the past, either in the spot market or on long-term contracts. The rationale behind this policy was explained by Mr. Parker: "We have past experience in dealing with these suppliers and have some idea of the quality and quantity they can supply. We usually also get to know the management of these suppliers."

Of these eighteen suppliers, two were dropped because of consistent problems with their coal's quality. The remaining sixteen suppliers were asked to submit bids. However, only nine suppliers actually quoted; seven suppliers indicated "no bid."

Evaluating and Selecting Suppliers

Once bids from various suppliers were received, the purchasing department prepares a bid evaluation table. This includes the name of the producer, if it is different from the supplier. The name of the producer is important in gathering information on the consistency and quality of coal produced, capacity and capability, financial strength, and labor relations, including the time period for which the labor contract is valid. Other information includes shipping point, annual tonnage promised, time period of the contract, Btu/lb of the coal, sulphur, ash and moisture content, volatile percentage, ash fusion temperature, grindability, size, railroad car rating, railroad district, price (FOB mine), freight rate, and dates indicating the shipping schedule. From this information, the purchasing department calculated the cost in dollars per 1 million Btu (MMBtu).

Mr. White, the purchasing agent, explained his supplier selection process:

A bid evaluation table simplifies the supplier selection process. Those suppliers who fail to meet specifications (on one or more evaluation criteria) are eliminated first. Further, because coal is a critical item for the operating of the generating plants, a single-source situation is avoided. In a case like this, the company policy is to have at least two suppliers or preferably three from different areas. The reason behind this is that if there is a railroad service disruption in one area or a natural disaster in certain mines, then the supply of coal will not be completely cut off.

The next step was to select four suppliers based on lowest dollar cost per MMBtu from those suppliers who met specifications completely. These suppliers were screened again, according to their capacity, consistency of quality and past performance. If two suppliers were from the same vicinity, the one with the lower cost/MMBtu was selected. Using this elimination process, three suppliers were selected for final negotiations.

Conditions in the spot market are a good indication of the supply and demand situation. The purchasing department used this information shrewdly to negotiate long-term contracts. The following items were negotiated:

1. Most suppliers quote a firm price for a period of three months. The purchasing department tries to get a firm price for one year, or at least six months.
2. The purchasing department tries to attain the best premium/penalty terms.
3. The price adjustment quoted is based on increases in labor, fuel royalties, and equipment costs. The purchasing department strives to get the best terms with certain maximum limits stipulated in the contract.

Quantity ordered from each supplier is used as a negotiating tool; the supplier who offers the best terms qualifies for the larger share of the company's business.

Negotiations were under way when this research was being conducted. Later, Mr. Parker indicated that the three suppliers had offered very similar terms, and he split the available business equally among them. "This way the order execution will be simple and easy," he explained. The decision was approved by the general manager of purchasing.

Figure 7–2 shows the flowchart of the purchase decision for this item.

Evaluation

The decision process was well coordinated by the purchasing department. This case provides an example where members of purchasing continuously monitor the fuel market, and attempt to negotiate the purchase when the situation is favorable.

132 • *Industrial Purchasing Strategies*

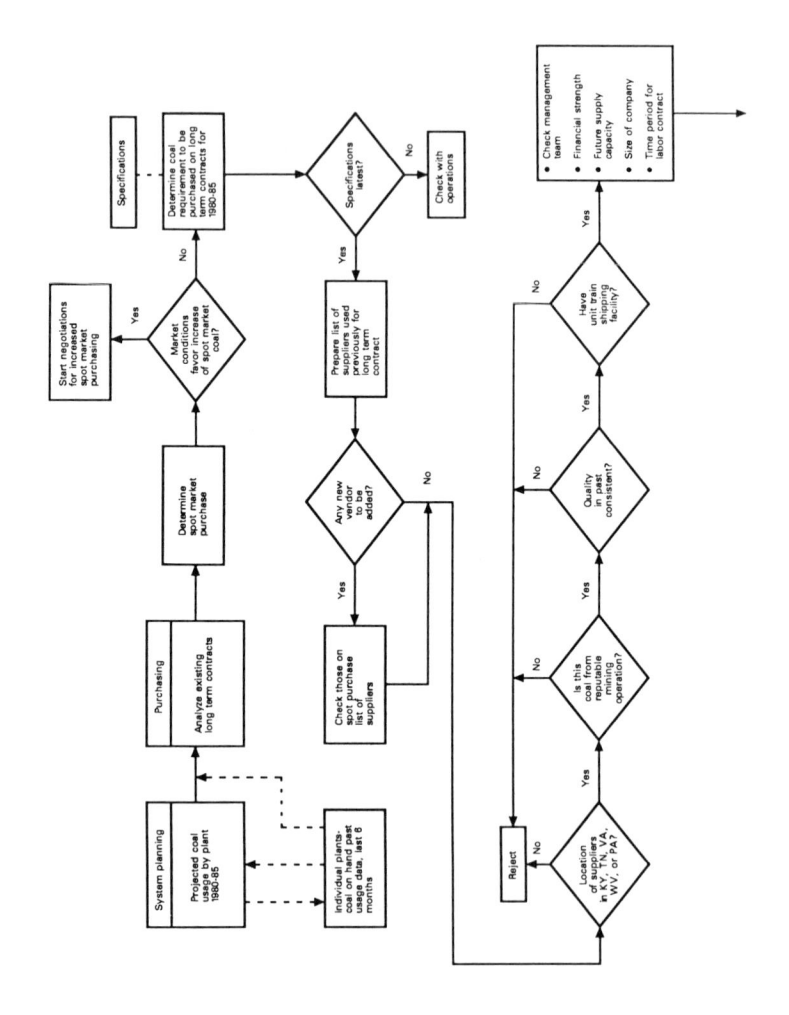

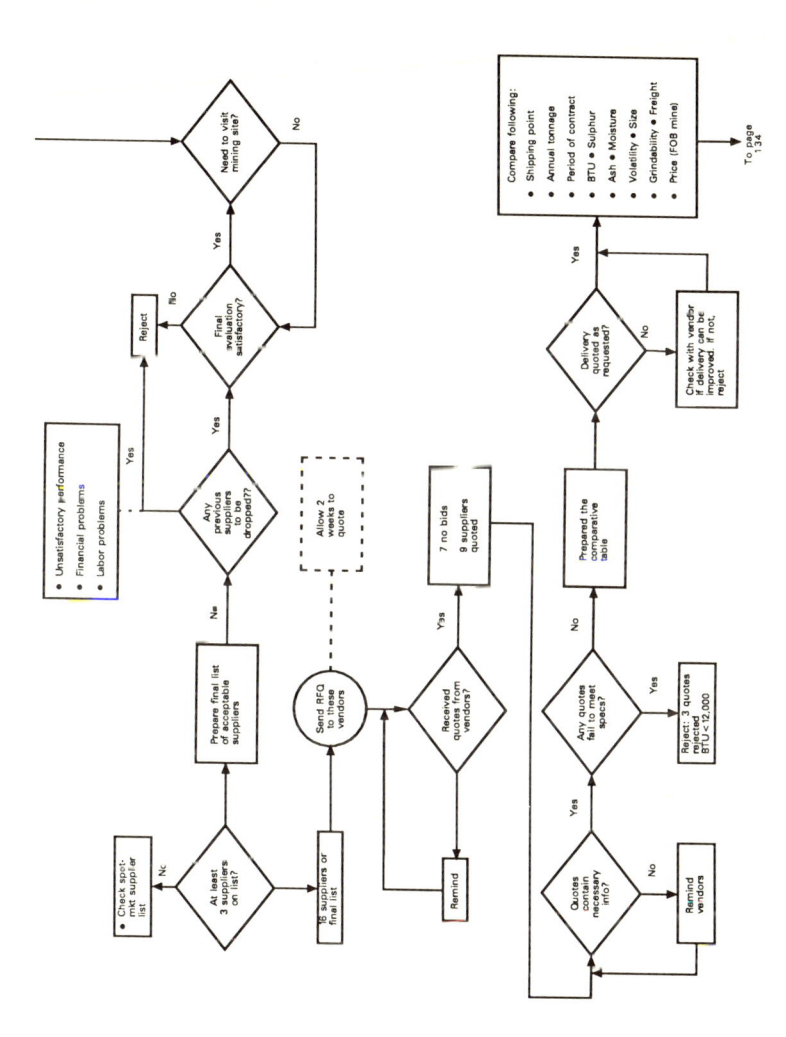

Figure 7–2. Purchase Decision Process: Coal

134 • *Industrial Purchasing Strategies*

Figure 7–2. Purchase Decision Process: Coal (continued)

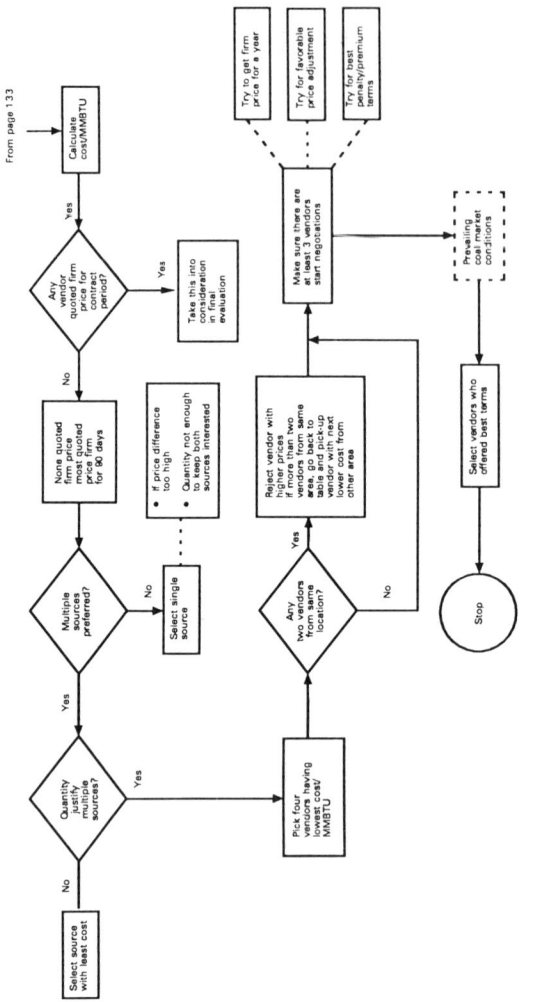

NOTE: In this instance three vendors remained for final negotiations. They all offered practically same terms. All three vendors were selected and awarded equal business since price difference was not much.

The company's policy to purchase coal on long-term contracts as well as from the spot market is very effective in lowering the purchasing cost, according to Mr. Parker. He substantiated this statement by showing a study made by an independent energy consulting firm in Washington, D.C. The study indicated that Southeast Electric Company had the lowest fuel cost in 1979, when compared to all other electric utilities in the southeastern region of the United States.

The series of negotiations with vendors in the final stage of the decision process to attain better contract terms seems to be the major strength of the purchasing process. The lack of a formal vendor rating system is a weakness of the process.

The Purchase of Cooling and Purging Gases

Cooling and purging gases are required for everyday operation of the generating stations. The company purchases these gases in various sizes of gas cylinders directly from the manufacturer, or from authorized dealers. The plant operations department at each generating station determines the annual usage of different gases for purchasing. A large number of gas cylinders is required for continuous operation of generating stations; therefore, company policy is to buy these gases via annual contracts. Because of changing market conditions, suppliers are unwilling to contract for a period longer than one year.

Hydrogen, acetylene, oxygen, nitrogen, carbon dioxide, and argon are used by the company's generating stations.

In addition to the quantity required annually, generating plants prepare delivery schedules monthly for each of these gases, so that a minimum level of inventory is maintained at each plant. The company expected to purchase cooling and purging gases worth $180,000 in 1980.

These gases are compressed and shipped in metal cylinders. Some electric utilities, including Southeast Electric Company, own cylinders. These cylinders undergo a hydrostatic test each year per safety regulations, which adds to the cost of owning cylinders. Further costs of insurance, cleaning, and maintenance must also be added. Based on the results of a detailed analysis by its industrial engineering group, the company decided two years ago not to purchase any more gas cylinders. Instead, it would be less expensive to lease or rent cylinders from gas suppliers.

The company's generating stations are located all over the southern half of North Carolina. Therefore, it is standard practice for the company to invite bids for each generating station separately, although suppliers can submit bids to meet the requirements of all the various stations. The reason for this approach, as explained by Larry Cape (the purchasing agent) is to obtain the best price from each supplier, which reduces the overall cost of gases to the company. For example, gas cylinders are heavy, and must be handled with care. Certain suppliers are located close to certain generating stations, and can quote better prices for delivery to one plant than to others.

Because the company owns some gas cylinders, purchasing requested separate bids for gases to be supplied only in company-owned cylinders and gases supplied in cylinders rented by the company.

The Buying Center

In order to understand the purchase decision process, the following people were interviewed: Larry Cape, purchasing agent; Jim Boland, purchasing supervisor; and Jack Schwartz, operation supervisor, Cedar Station.

Mr. Cape is the purchasing agent responsible for buying cooling and purging gases. Mr. Boland is his supervisor, and approves Mr. Cape's decisions. Mr. Schwartz is the operations supervisor at the Cedar generating station; he was interviewed by telephone. Mr. Schwartz gives feedback to Mr. Cape on suppliers' delivery and service.

Selecting Suppliers to Submit Bids

According to Mr. Cape, "Unless it is an unfamiliar item to be purchased for the first time, one does not look in the Thomas Register or Yellow Pages to find out who are the suppliers for the required item."

In this case, the company had been buying gases for a number of years. The company had done business with certain established suppliers in the area. Their sales reps visited the company regularly, kept it informed about market trends, as well as new dealerships carrying the item, and supply–demand situations. Five known suppliers in the area carry these gases. The company was familiar with their sizes, stocking, types of insurance carried for this type of business, and quality of employees. In the past two years, no new dealer was appointed for these items in the area, and the company felt that there was adequate competition among suppliers.

Name of Supplier	Location
National Welders	Columbia/Charlotte
Liquid Air	Columbia/Augusta
Piedmont Welders	Charlotte
Arco Welders	Hanahan
Air Products	Charlotte

These suppliers were asked to submit bids. Their past performances were satisfactory, so there was no reason to drop any of them from the bidders list. When asked if there was a formal rating system to measure suppliers' performance, Mr. Cape replied: "There is nothing permanent in the marketplace; the employees of suppliers can change, technology may change, supplier management can change, and you may spend your entire time evaluating vendors. If something drastically goes wrong, there is a record on file."

Evaluating and Selecting Suppliers

There are no special specifications for gases. All manufacturers produce these gases per common national standards. Therefore, each supplier's product is identical. Thus, once bids were received, they were evaluated on the following criteria:

> Delivery: Does it meet the requirement of the plant? If not, can the supplier improve delivery?
>
> Price: Is price firm for the contract period? If not, for how long is it firm? Is there a price adjustment?
>
> Cylinder rental
>
> Cost of cylinder testing
>
> Past service and cooperation from the supplier

When bids were received from suppliers, they were tabulated for comparison. One supplier did not bid. One submitted a partial bid. The remaining three suppliers submitted complete bids. National Welder quoted the lowest prices for all items, including the price of renting cylinders. Because the volume was not large enough to split, the entire order for Cedar Station was placed with National Welder.

The purchasing agent noted that National Welder had also been the supplier for the previous year: "They know the persons at individual locations, they understand company requirements very well, they are eager to do business with the company, and therefore end up quoting very attractive prices."

The purchasing agent pointed out an interesting technique he had been using to attain better prices from even the lowest bidder. He called that supplier on the telephone, and told him he had a good chance of getting the order if he could better his price. According to him, this technique worked 80 percent of the time. In this case, National Welder reduced its price by 5 cents per cylinder for two of the six items. When using this technique, the purchasing agent did not refer directly to the bids received from other vendors. If asked by the supplier, he responded that it was his company's policy not to discuss with vendors the bids received.

Figure 7–3 shows the purchase decision process in detail.

Evaluation

In this case, the most important factor in the purchasing decision was whether to buy, lease, or rent air cylinders. If the company owned or leased cylinders, insurance and upkeep costs had to be added to the cost of the gas. Based on past experience and cost analyses, the company rented cylinders.

Some researchers (Pettigrew 1975; Mogee and Bean 1976) have observed that purchasing agents jealously guard their position as "gate keeper" to the firm, and do not like sales reps to talk to the technical people in purchasing. Mr. Cape expressed his opinion on this issue: "We encourage sales reps to go and visit our generating stations and talk to the operations people. If sales reps are willing to go there, get dirty, and collect first-hand details about our needs, they make our job simple."

The purchasing agent was willing to negotiate even with the vendor quoting the lowest price. These negotiations resulted in savings to the company, because the supplier reduces its prices. Thus, the policy to negotiate price and other terms with the supplier is effective in saving money for the company.

Purchase of 600-Volt Cables

The company buys about one million feet of 600-volt cable every year for distributing electricity to its commercial and industrial customers. To assure continuity of supply and attain better prices based on volume, the company purchases these cables from suppliers on long-term contracts. The contract period is usually one year. Because of uncertainty in the metal and insulating materials market, suppliers are unwilling to quote and negotiate contracts for longer than a year. The company's budget for the purchase of cables of this type for a one-year period is $750,000. The cables are intended to provide secondary service on underground distribution systems and are suitable for direct burial or installation in ducts, in wet or dry locations.

The engineering department writes detailed specifications to ensure that cables of the proper quality are purchased for trouble-free service. The operations department is responsible for actually installing the cables underground. The department keeps detailed records of problems or cable failures encountered in the field. Based on experience, they suggest necessary revisions in specifications to engineering, after investigating the cause of failures operations has experienced. The purchasing department works in close cooperation with operations and engineering. Because cables are complex technical items, the purchasing department relies on the engineering and operations departments to conduct technical discussions with suppliers. According to company policy, suppliers are free to contact and discuss technical and installation problems directly with engineering and operations, and keep purchasing posted on such discussions. However, suppliers are not allowed to discuss price or other commercial terms with the engineering and operations departments.

The cable specification is a very important document; therefore, it is written with great care to clarify the company's requirements to suppliers.

The Buying Center

The following persons, who constitute the buying center for this item, were interviewed: D. Miller, purchasing supervisor; Bob Sidney, purchasing agent; Charlie Watson, senior engineer, engineering department; Jim Corey, administrative manager, operations department; and Ed Shull, administrative assistant, operations department.

Mr. Sidney is the purchasing agent in charge of purchasing cables. He reports to Mr. Miller, and submits his final recommendations to him for approval. Mr. Miller has been in purchasing for over twenty-two years. He summed up his experience in purchasing as follows: "It's hard to apply black-and-white rules in purchasing. Purchasing changes continuously, and we will never be able to keep the human element out of it. It's a constant learning process."

He added, "A good purchasing agent must keep an open mind and should be willing to change."

According to Mr. Sidney, "Supplier sales reps are your best sources of information. If you keep your eyes and ears open, you learn a lot from them. There are no dumb sales reps; only smart ones survive!"

Mr. Sidney favors nonunion suppliers located in nearby states. He argued: "They have less operating constraints, their deliveries are reliable, and in general it's easy to deal with them."

It is company policy to revise the bidders list continuously. Mr. Miller explained: "We take a hard look at it at least once a year. We always add one or two and remove one or two from the bidders list to make sure that existing suppliers remain competitive and don't take us for granted."

Commenting on the effect of personal friendships with the sales reps in the supplier evaluation process, Mr. Miller argued, "It's a two-way street. If the sales rep has helped you when you are in a bid, you may like to help him."

Mr. Watson of engineering is responsible for writing specifications for cables. He stressed: "We do a better job at writing cable specs, as compared to 90 percent of other utilities. We have the lowest rate of cable failures in the southeast."

Mr. Watson said that he received valuable input from operations in writing specifications for cables. Mr. Corey simplified his supplier evaluation by

140 • *Industrial Purchasing Strategies*

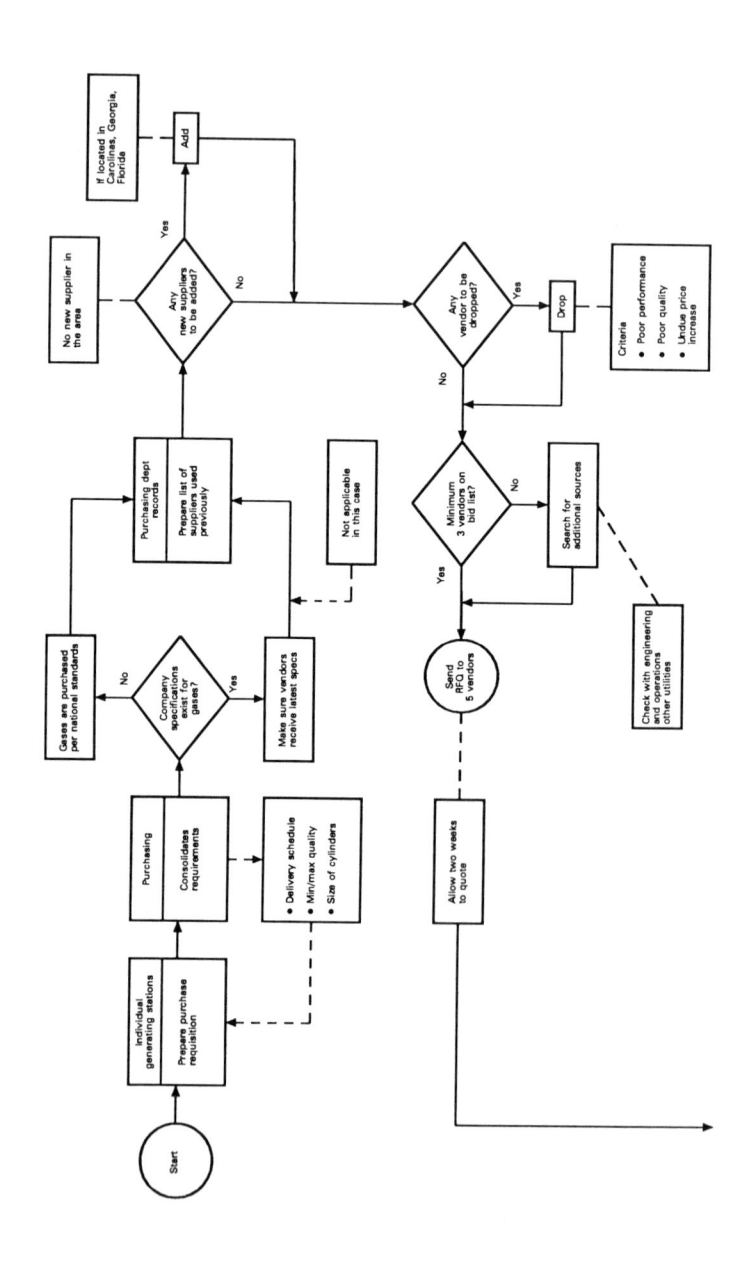

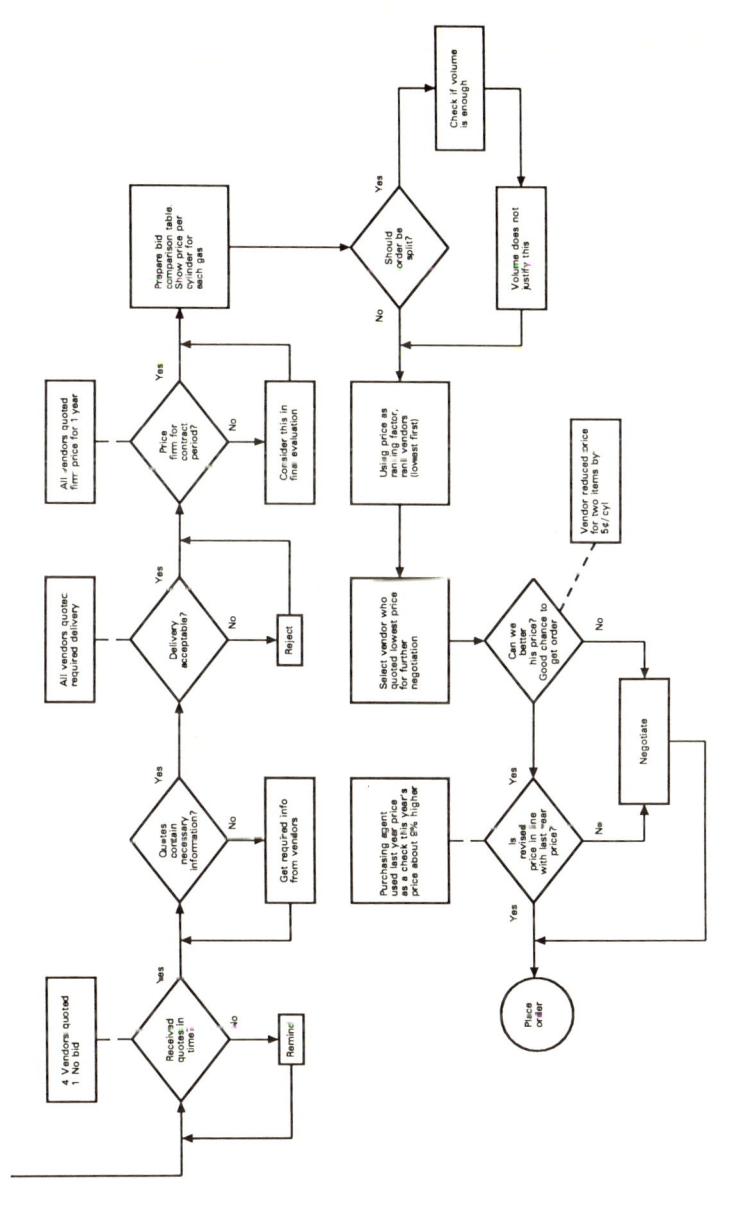

Figure 7-3. Purchase Decision Process: Gases

contacting other utilities. He explained, "The proof of the pudding is in the eating. Ask other utilities who have used the products of the supplier."

Selecting Suppliers to Submit Bids

Over the years, the company had purchased 600-volt cables from various suppliers. These suppliers were aware of the company's needs, the potential volume of business available, and the company's specifications for cables. Their sales reps visited the company every two months to keep in touch with the company's changing needs, not only for 600-volt cables, but for other types of cables, and a variety of other items manufactured as well.

Because the cables are installed underground, the type of soil, moisture, and other environmental factors affect the operation and life of the cables. The company relies heavily on the past experience of other manufacturers with cables in choosing suppliers. If their experience was good, there is great reluctance to change. Experience has shown that though it is tempting to place orders with a new source and save money initially, if the cables fail, the company incurs heavy costs in replacing them, loses revenues from customers due to service interruptions, and disrupts work schedules, because failures must be attended to quickly. Other work might therefore be left unfinished and laborers forced to work around the clock to finish that work. For these reasons, the company is extremely careful in selecting vendors to submit bids. Based on past experience, suppliers who are approved for the bidders list are continuously evaluated. This list is prepared by purchasing and must be approved by engineering and operations.

The engineering department, before approving a supplier for the bidders list, examines the supplier's manufacturing facility, including the following:

1. What type of machinery do they have? Is it modern? What is its production capacity?
2. Who are their suppliers? Do they supply raw materials of good quality?
3. What type of incoming material inspection procedures does the supplier have? Do they have a quality assurance program that checks the quality of cables at each stage in manufacturing?
4. Do they have good research and development facilities? Who manages them? What experience do they have? How long have they been with the company?
5. What kind of test facilities do they have?
6. Do they have stable labor relations?
7. Do they have good, experienced engineering and management staffs?

The engineering department checks these items and visits the supplier's facilities. When they are convinced that the supplier has the technical ability to produce and service the required item, the supplier is approved.

The operations department scrutinizes suppliers differently. This department's primary concern is with ease of installing cables. What type of service are suppliers capable of providing in an emergency? How reliable is their delivery schedule? What type of stocking program do they have? How good is their packaging? Can it take the rough handling in the field? Who are other customers of this supplier? What is their experience? Once operations is satisfied with the answers to these questions, they approve the supplier for the bidders list.

Jim Corey of the operations department pointed out that one of the suppliers, Essex Group Inc., "was excluded from this list because of delivery problems we have experienced with them over the past six to eight months for 28kv cables."

The purchasing department wrote Essex a letter, stating that unless they did something to correct these problems, they would be removed from the bidders list for all items the company buys from them.

The production manager and the quality control manager of Essex had arranged a meeting with the purchasing, engineering, and operations departments of Southeast Electric Company. The researcher was working with purchasing at that time and was permitted to attend the meeting.

Both the production and quality control managers had joined Essex within the past six months. They admitted that there had been scheduling problems in the past, but went into great detail explaining that the situation was now under control. Shipment of 28kv cables would begin within the next two to three weeks.

Essex had been taken over by a larger company; as a result, some management personnel had left the company. Some changes were introduced in the production machine layout, causing a delay in scheduling. Also, communications from Essex to Southeast Electric were admitted to be poor, and Essex representatives agreed that they should have kept Southeast informed of these developments. Finally, representatives stressed that Essex valued the business of Southeast, and major problems were now behind them. The meeting lasted for about an hour and a half.

After the Essex representatives left, the meeting continued. Mr. Miller of purchasing explained that they had tried to purchase 28kv cables from other sources, but were unsuccessful for two reasons. First, specifications were very restricted; no other utility company used them. Second, the quantity needed by the company was small for 28kv cables, and other manufacturers were reluctant to quote. Two manufacturers who quoted after a few weeks of constant follow-up quoted almost double the price of Essex, and their delivery schedules were unacceptable.

Mr. Watson of engineering explained that Essex had machines that produce this cable at a much lower cost than the others, and their quality was extremely good. Essex was therefore given a second chance as a supplier, because they were at that time the only source for 28kv cables. However, Mr. Miller was instructed to monitor the performance of Essex closely, and to continue to search for a second source for 28kv cables. In the end, Essex was retained on the bidders list for 600-volt cables.

Requests for quotations were sent to all ten suppliers on the bid list; the suppliers were given two weeks to submit the bids.

When the bids were received, seven suppliers had quoted, and the remaining three returned the RFQs with no bid.

Evaluating and Selecting Suppliers

After receiving quotations, the purchasing department made two copies; the quoted prices were removed from these. These copies were for the evaluations of engineering and operations. Prices were kept secret from these two departments, so that their technical and operational evaluations were not influenced. Mr. Watson in engineering, and Mr. Corey and Mr. Shull in operations stated that they disliked this procedure. They felt that they were capable of judging how much more a specific supplier should be paid for a better score on certain attributes than others. However, company policy required following this procedure, and they could do nothing about it. Their past attempts to change this procedure had been unsuccessful.

Engineering and operations returned their evaluations of the quotations to purchasing. They approved all quotations as submitted by vendors. Two suppliers did not indicate reel sizes, and Mr. Watson pointed out that this had to be clarified to satisfy specifications. The purchasing department prepared a bid evaluation table to finalize selection of suppliers.

One supplier quoted forty-two to forty-three weeks delivery, and its price was the second highest. This was unacceptable, and this supplier was dropped. Delivery from the rest of the suppliers was acceptable. All suppliers quoted a price adjustment subject to variations in the price of aluminum, from the base price of $.63 per pound. In addition, one supplier quoted an adjustment based on changes in the Bureau of Labor Statistics index. This supplier had quoted the highest price, and was rejected.

All of the remaining suppliers except for one quoted a price adjustment effective immediately upon shipment; one quoted a firm price until 30 June 1980. Thus, for this supplier price adjustment would occur only during the later half of the year. This supplier also quoted the lowest price. The price difference between this supplier and the one quoting the second lowest price was 6 percent. Further, the supplier quoting the lowest price had nonunion labor.

The next issue, according to Mr. Sidney, was that of possibly splitting the order between two or more suppliers. The purchasing agent indicated that because the price was so attractive, and service and delivery so reliable, the order for the entire quantity would be placed with South Wire Company, the lowest bidder.

The purchase decision process is depicted in figure 7–4.

Evaluation

This case shows how technically complex items are purchased by means of a joint decision among the purchasing, engineering, and operations departments. This raises the issue of differences that arise during joint decision-making processes. All respondents indicated that this was not a problem. Whenever differences did arise, they were resolved through mutual discussions. In dealings with the Essex company, this held true.

Before a supplier qualifies to receive the bid, it must be approved jointly by engineering, operations, and purchasing. Each department applies different criteria for its approval of a supplier. After bids are received, the engineering and operations departments again evaluate the bids independently, and each has the authority to reject the bids. They are not aware of the price. "Their evaluation is strictly technical and is not influenced by the price quoted," according to Mr. Miller. Once the joint evaluation process is complete, successful bidders are evaluated strictly by the purchasing department.

No attempt was made by purchasing to negotiate price or other terms of the contract. In this respect, the purchase decision process was weak. The absence of a formal vendor rating system is another weakness in evaluating suppliers. Those involved in the decision process seem to rely heavily on their memories in evaluating vendors.

Unlike most other industries, utilities operate in a captive market. They do not view other utilities as major competitors and therefore, it appears that they are willing to share operating experiences. This includes product performance, and services rendered by various suppliers. This is an excellent method for evaluating suppliers and their products.

146 • *Industrial Purchasing Strategies*

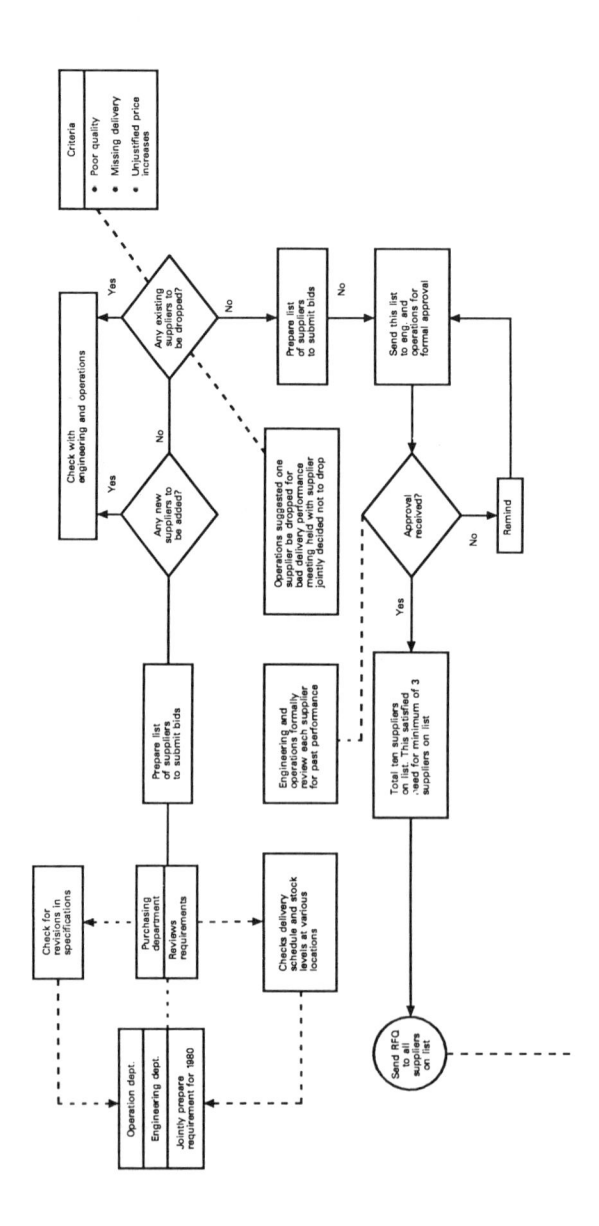

Southeast Electric Company • 147

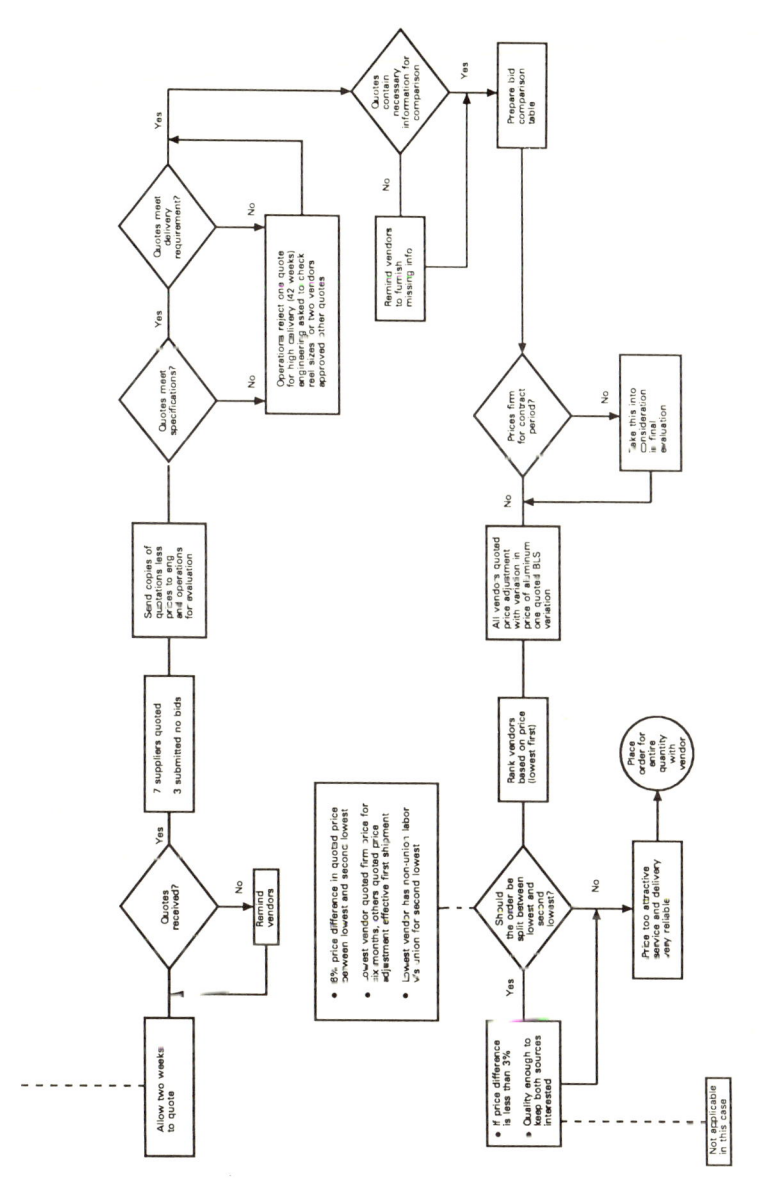

Figure 7-4. Purchase Decision Process: 600-Volt Cables

8
Purchase Decision Processes Involving Annual and Long-Term Contracts

The intent of this chapter is to unify the results of the research study and to develop a general overview helpful in constructing a descriptive model of purchase decision processes involving long-term contracts. The complete descriptive model is presented in the final chapter. This chapter presents an elaboration of the five basic phases of industrial buying behavior for long-term contracts that were described briefly in chapter 1. The present chapter focuses on how decision-makers divide and simplify large-scale industrial purchasing problems into more manageable subproblems. Very specific decision rules are applied to each subproblem; the decision rules can be viewed as a series of rules-of-thumb that are affected by situational constraints found during the process of solving the problem. For example, buyers do not search actively for new sources in the decision processes for all plant purchasing agreements. Search depended on the characteristics of the specific purchasing problem, for example, the number of approved vendors or the current bid list on the level of satisfaction with current suppliers.

Purpose of Long-Term Contracts in Industrial Buying

What are the basic reasons for purchasing some items via long-term contracts? Purchasing agents were asked this question when they were interviewed. Their responses are summarized below.

1. Long-term purchase contracts assure continuity of supply for critical items, especially during shortages. All purchasing agents interviewed considered this the most important reason for entering into long-term contracts with suppliers. The word "contract" has certain legal connotations, and purchasing agents believe that suppliers are likely to give priority to fulfilling these contracts during shortages. Even when the price of the item to be purchased was

controlled by the government (as in the case of fuel oil), the company entered into long-term contracts with suppliers; this was to ensure continuity of supply.

2. Long-term contracts imply quantity buying over a specified period of time. This results in better prices from suppliers. Suppliers are able to plan ahead, purchase raw materials in volume, schedule production efficiently, reduce inventory cost, and exercise better quality control.

3. Long-term contracts reduce the number of individual orders that otherwise would have to be issued; this reduces paperwork, follow-up, and control required from the purchasing department. Thus, the efficiency of the purchasing department is increased. Secondly, the company's inventory cost is reduced, as suppliers are informed as to what quantity is needed in each time period. The company is also forced to plan ahead and forecast the quantity needed for the contract period. This results in the preparation and implementation of better delivery schedules, the avoidance of rush deliveries, and the reduction of freights charges, as suppliers are allowed to use the least expensive means of transportation.

Out of eighteen items studied in six companies, fifteen items were purchased on an annual contract. At the end of the contract period, fresh quotations were invited from suppliers. If the performance of an existing supplier was unacceptable, it was dropped from the bidders list. Similarly, a new supplier was added to the bidders list if it exhibited keen interest in the company's business and met company requirements as an acceptable source.

Annual contracts are preferred by both suppliers and purchasers. Because of fluctuations in the price of raw materials, suppliers are not willing to enter into contracts for longer than one year. Even for annual contracts, no suppliers of the fifteen items studied quoted a firm price for the entire contract period. The prices quoted were firm for only ninety days, with the exception of one supplier, who quoted a price firm for six months. Prices were subject to negotiation thereafter, or some sort of price adjustment was quoted based on the variation of prices of raw materials. Therefore, it was of little value to have a contract period longer than one year, because suppliers changed prices every few months.

The purchasers believed that inviting fresh bids each year introduced an element of competition, keeping suppliers honest. It also gave them a chance to evaluate the performance of existing suppliers, and to add new potential suppliers to generate healthy competition.

Evergreen contracts were observed in only three situations. The first situation was when the company was locked into a single-source situation, as in the case of the purchase of heavy axle assemblies for large tamper machines. The time period of this type of contract is indefinite. Secondly, when the price of the item is controlled, as in the case of fuel oil, the time period of the contract can be indefinite. The main purpose of the contract is to assure continuity of supply. The third situation is when price adjustments quoted by suppliers are precise, and based on the cost of labor and equipment used, as in the case of the purchase of coal. In addition, the company was, in this case, also buying coal from the spot market. Thus, if there was a glut in the market, the company could increase its spot market purchase to reduce cost. But if there was a shortage, the company would continue to receive contract coal without paying higher prices, and would also maintain assured sources of supply.

Stages in the Purchase Decision Process

Initiating the Purchasing Process: Preparing the Purchase Requisition

For all of the items studied, a purchase requisition was required to initiate action from the purchasing department. Items purchased on long-term contracts are usually required for regular production; hence, the purchase requisition is issued by production control or production planning. In general, the user department recognizes the need for the item to be purchased; that department in turn requests that the purchasing department purchase the item by issuing a formal purchase requisition.

Information Required in the Purchase Requisition

The purchase requisition contains information on the quantity needed, a brief description of the item including the company part number when available, reference to company specifications, and drawings to which the purchased items must comply. When the item is manufactured as per national or international standards, a reference is made to these standards, as in the case of the purchase of #6 fuel oil and steel rods (bar stock). Sometimes, the purchase requisition indicates the preferred mode of transportation, days of the week and times of the day when deliveries should be made, location of the warehouse or receiving section to which the item should be delivered, and special markings on the packages (if desired). The purchase requisition sometimes suggests the names of potential suppliers, for the benefit of the purchasing department.

All purchasing agents interviewed checked the purchase requisition thoroughly to ensure that it contained the necessary information. Taking a few minutes to check the purchase requisition was helpful in avoiding future problems.

Product Specifications

The engineering department is usually in charge of preparing and revising specifications. Three purchasing agents mentioned that old specifications were pulled out and attached to the purchase requisition by the user departments. In one case, the purchasing department did not check to see if specifications were the most recent, and the supplier manufactured the items per old specifications. These items were rejected by the company's quality control department. The vendor refused to take the delivered items back because they had been manufactured according to the specifications received. The company spent several thousand dollars on making the items usable. Experienced purchasing agents ensure that the latest specifications are sent to vendors to avoid such problems.

Search for Potential Suppliers

The next step is to prepare the list of potential suppliers who are able to supply the required item. Out of eighteen items investigated, only one item was being purchased for the first time. For these "repeat purchase" items, purchasing agents perused the existing list of suppliers in the company files. Interestingly, all six companies have the policy of preferring that a minimum of three suppliers should be requested to submit bids for the required items. If the purchasing agent is unable to locate three acceptable potential vendors, this must be recorded and filed for company auditors. Each company has a printed form entitled "Request for Quotation." When these forms were compared, all of them had three spaces for vendor addresses, indicating that the RFQ should preferably be sent to three vendors.

No restrictions were set for the maximum number of suppliers requested to submit bids. However, this was dependent upon the item, and the amount of time and effort the purchasing agent was willing to devote. Usually three to six suppliers were sent RFQs, (although sometimes as many as twelve to sixteen received RFQs). This was the consensus of all purchasing agents interviewed. According to the experienced agents, the optimum figure is between six and eight, beyond which the benefits gained do not justify the extra time and effort expended.

If there were less than three suppliers on the bid list, the purchasing agent actively sought new sources. The response to a sales call from the representative of a new potential supplier was very enthusiastic; and the agent provided as much information as possible to the new source, and was very willing to develop new sources.

In order to find new suppliers in such a situation, the purchasing agent first contacted others in the company close to the item required, such as manufacturing engineers, design engineers, electrical engineers, industrial engineers, or packaging engineers. This included persons in the company's other divisions or plants. The other sources of information mentioned were sales representatives manufacturing similar products. *The Thomas Register* and trade magazines were also consulted.

However, when there were twelve to sixteen suppliers on the bid list, the purchasing agent's priorities changed. No new sources of supply were actively sought. It was very difficult for a new supplier to get on the bid list, unless it had something special to offer. The purchasing agent's evaluative criteria were tough in this situation, and was likely to reject new sources. This was especially true when approval from other departments was required before the new supplier could be included on the bid list, or when extensive testing of product samples from the new source was required. Such approval and sample testing is time-consuming and expensive for the company.

These arguments also apply when there are about six suppliers on the bid list, and the performance of the existing suppliers is acceptable.

Evaluating and Selecting Suppliers for Bidding on the Required Item

Purchasing agents indicated that they usually preferred to drop one or two suppliers from the old bidders list and add one or two new suppliers each year. For example, if a supplier consistently quoted the highest price, it was dropped. This indicates to suppliers that their price must be competitive. Those suppliers who did not respond to the company's request for bids were also likely to be dropped. According to purchasing agents, if the supplier does not even bother to respond, it is inferred that it is not interested in the company's business.

Existing suppliers may be dropped from the bid list for various reasons. According to 78 percent of the purchasing agents, unsatisfactory past performance was the primary reason for dropping a supplier. Unsatisfactory performance included poor quality of the item delivered, constant delays in delivery, unwillingness to resolve problems pertaining to quality and delivery, or other errors in shipping and invoicing. If a supplier continues to ask for a price increase after initially submitting a low bid to get the order, purchasing agents may drop the supplier from the bid list.

The overall attitude of sales representatives was a factor influencing the decision to drop a supplier. Purchasing agents did not like sales reps who used high-pressure techniques, who had poor product knowledge, who did not keep their promises, and did not plan their sales calls.

Except for severe quality or delivery problems, purchasing agents usually dropped a supplier for a combination of reasons, rather than for one single reason.

In this situation, a new supplier is added to the bid list when initiative is taken by a new source—usually through a visit from the sales rep. If the purchasing agent was unhappy with any sources on the bid list, he cooperated well with new sources, helping them to gain approval from other departments as required, and ultimately being included on the bid list.

154 • *Industrial Purchasing Strategies*

The factors influencing the decision to add or drop a supplier from the bid list are summarized below.

1. Purchasing agents actively seek new sources when there are only one or two suppliers on the bid list. The purchasing departments follow the company policy of preferably having three suppliers on the bid list when competitive bidding is required, as in the case of long-term contracts. The rationale behind having three suppliers on the bid list is that it is easier for two suppliers to enter into colllusion rather than three.

2. When the number of suppliers on the bid list is greater than three, and the performance of suppliers on the bid list remains acceptable, the purchasing agent generally does not take initiative to seek out new sources of supply. The bid list consists of suppliers used previously, and is compiled from purchasing department records. A new supplier may be added to the bid list if it takes the initiative, and has something better to offer. The bid list consists essentially of suppliers whose sales reps are in contact with the company's purchasing department. However, when the new vendor is a minority vendor, it always gets a chance to quote, according to all purchasing agents interviewed, provided that the item is of acceptable quality. Purchasing agents actively seek out minority vendors in order to fulfill government requirements, especially if the company has some government contracts.

3. It is very difficult for a new supplier to get on the bid list if there are already twelve to sixteen suppliers on the list, and their performance is acceptable, and if approval from other departments is required before a new vendor is added to the bid list.

4. Dropping a supplier from the bid list is a purchasing department decision, although this decision may be based on feedback received from other departments. Adding a supplier to the bid list may require approval from other departments, but the purchasing department plays a pivotal role in obtaining this approval.

5. If a supplier is on the company's bid list for one item, it is easy for it to be added to the bid list for other items, if the product meets company requirements. This occurred in the case of hydraulic valve castings and wooden pallets. In both cases, new suppliers who were already supplying similar items to the company were added to the bid list.

Type of Information Collected on Suppliers

When a new supplier is to be added to the bid list, purchasing gathers information to determine if the supplier is indeed qualified to satisfy the company's needs. Generally, the information collected on potential suppliers includes product brochures describing the items manufactured and their features; the size of the manufacturing facility; number of employees; financial report; the company's annual report; and the names of existing customers.

The type of information gathered depends upon the item and the quantity needed. For example, if the item is bulky and heavy, location is important. The cost of transportation increases continuously; therefore, purchasing agents prefer suppliers with mining, manufacturing, or storage facilities nearby. This was evident in the case of the purchase of coal, fuel oil, wooden pallets, corrugated boxes, and bale caps. This preference for local suppliers was evident when the purchasing function was decentralized. Purchasing departments developed a good rapport with local suppliers. Such suppliers were easily accessible, sales reps visited regularly, and they developed good contacts with inside personnel. Purchasing agents believed that it was a good policy to do business with local suppliers, which also fostered community development.

If the item is technically complex and critical in nature, it is necessary to gain the approval of other departments, as in the case of 600-volt cables, and processing ingredients such as oelic acids. This might require a visit to the supplier's facility, analysis of the type of equipment they have, and evaluation of their engineering capability, research and development facility, quality control procedures, reputation in the industry, and capacity to produce quality items consistently. When samples are required, they are tested and evaluated extensively before the vendor is included on the bid list.

Purchasing agents indicated that the quantity of the item to be purchased is an important consideration in including a new supplier on the bid list. The capacity and capability of the supplier become conclusive factors when the quantity is large. One purchasing agent summed this up as follows: "There are only a few players who are qualified to play in the major leagues—same thing applies to the suppliers. When a large quantity of a critical item is required, there are only a few who can play the ballgame right."

Policy on Seeing New Suppliers' Sales Representatives

If a sales rep from a new supplier visits a company without an appointment, the rep is always permitted to talk with someone in the purchasing department. This was a policy of all the companies in the study. Although visits without appointments were not encouraged, reps' sales presentations were at least listened to. As one purchasing manager stated, "This is a good company policy because you may stumble into someone you were looking for for years."

This was not true, however, for reps of suppliers on the bid list, or those known to the company. Purchasing agents might or might not see them, depending upon the purpose of the visit, and how busy the agents were at the time.

All of the companies visited have a common policy regarding vendor sales reps visiting other departments of the company. They were not to visit other departments without informing purchasing of this intention. Further, during such visits, the equipment price and other commercial terms and conditions were not to be discussed.

A copy of any written communications between the supplier and departments other than purchasing had to be sent to the purchasing department. Research findings indicate that this guideline is followed by vendors. The purpose of this policy, as expressed by the purchasing agents, was to ensure that other departments did not commit the company to suppliers regarding any purchasing decisions, which were to be made only by the purchasing department.

Inviting Bids

Once the bidders list was finalized, an RFQ was sent to each supplier on that list, requesting them to submit quotes within a specified time, usually within two to four weeks.

The RFQ contained the company's standard terms and conditions on a printed form. In addition, it briefly described the item needed, quantity, delivery schedule, exact delivery location, preferred mode of transportation, marking requirements, and any other special requirements indicated on the purchase requisition. The RFQ might also require suppliers to quote separate prices for the basic item and the associated cost of tooling.

When suppliers receive an RFQ, most respond within the time specified. Some suppliers ask for an extension on the due date for bids if they are busy and there is not enough time to prepare the quote. Such requests are invariably granted by purchasing agents.

Purchasing agents, in some cases, must remind suppliers to submit bids; but, after a couple of reminders either by phone or in writing, most bids are received within three to four weeks. Those suppliers who do not bother to respond make a bad impression on purchasing agents, and are likely to be removed from the bid list.

Some suppliers may respond, stating "no bid." This may occur for a variety of reasons. The supplier may have all production capacity filled, and may not be able to meet the required delivery schedule. The item may be too complicated to produce. This occurs when a supplier is added to the bid list without being fully investigated as to capacity. The sales rep, out of overzealousness to increase business, may indicate to the purchasing agent that the company is capable of supplying the needed item. But when the time comes to actually bid, the company's manufacturing and engineering departments may realize that the company is unable to supply the item. Another reason for a "no bid" is that the supplier has stopped production of the needed item because it has the opportunity to produce another item that yields a higher profit. Depending upon the supplier's stated reason, the purchasing agent decides whether or not to drop it from the bid list.

Analyzing Bids

The next step is to analyze quotations from suppliers who have submitted bids. The purchasing agents examine all quotes to determine whether they contain all of the necessary information as requested in the RFQ. If any of the required information is missing, or any aspects of the suppliers' bids are unclear, vendors are requested to immediately provide the missing information.

Bid Comparison and Evaluation

Once all of the bids with complete information are received, a bid comparison table is prepared. Bids are evaluated in two steps: a technical evaluation, and a commercial evaluation.

Does the supplier's offer meet the required specifications? Did it make any exceptions to the technical features specified? These are the basic questions raised during a technical evaluation. If the supplier's offer has failed to meet certain specifications that cannot be relaxed, the offer is rejected. For example, if local regulations require that the sulphur content in the coal to be burned must not exceed 2.5 percent and the supplier cannot guarantee such coal, the offer is rejected. However, if the supplier's offer has failed to meet a portion of the specifications that can be relaxed, but results in additional costs to the company, these costs are added to the quoted price during the final comparison. For example, during the purchase of #6 fuel oil, the oil from Exxon contained a higher amount of vanadium than that desired, but this could be reduced by a chemical treatment. Therefore, the cost of chemical treatment was added to the quoted price of Exxon oil during the final comparison.

Technical Evaluation

For some technically complex items, vendors' bids are sent to the engineering and/or production departments for technical evaluation. When this is done, quoted prices are deleted from the bids, so that evaluation is strictly technical, and is not influenced by the quoted price. Technical evaluation usually results in accepting or rejecting the supplier's offer. In some cases, the offer is acceptable on the condition of certain features being included by the supplier. In this case, the purchasing department engages in additional communications with the vendor.

Commercial Evaluation

The bids that survive technical evaluation are reviewed next for commercial evaluation. The quoted prices from all suppliers are converted to a common base, so that they are directly comparable. First, if the majority of suppliers quoted prices FOB destination and one or two suppliers' prices are FOB shipping point, these suppliers are asked to quote prices FOB destination. Similarly, if payment terms quoted by all suppliers are not the same, suppliers are asked to agree to the same payment terms. For example, if one supplier's payment terms are net 30 days and the others' are 1% 10, net 30 days, the first supplier is asked to accept 1% 10, net 30 days. If it agrees, the price is then directly comparable with that of the other suppliers. If the supplier does not agree, the price is increased by 1 percent to make it comparable. If any other costs need to be added to a supplier's quoted price to make it comparable with the result of the suppliers' prices, this is done during commercial evaluation. Total price, with a common base quoted by each supplier, is now tabulated.

How long will the quoted price remain firm? When price is subject to escalation after a specified time period, what is the basis for escalation? These are the next items to be analyzed. Again, the purchasing department attempts to determine what the majority of suppliers have done, and asks the others to comply to make prices directly comparable.

Final Evaluation

The crucial stage of supplier elimination now begins. Those suppliers who have failed to meet the required delivery schedule are checked first. Those who quoted higher prices and failed to meet the delivery schedule are dropped. A supplier quoting a lowest or second lowest price and failing to meet the delivery requirement may receive a second chance. The purchasing agent checks to see if the delivery schedule can be improved. If the supplier agrees to improve the delivery schedule, the supplier remains on the active list.

The supplier quoting the lowest total price receives first attention. If it was the primary supplier last year and its performance was satisfactory, both technically and commercially, it automatically gets the order. If its labor contract is due to expire during the contract period of the purchase order, the purchasing agent may decide to split the order with another supplier to ensure continuity of supply.

If the supplier quoting the lowest price is a relatively new source, it may not get the order for the entire quantity. Similarly, if the established source quoted the lowest price, but past performance was not satisfactory, it may get the order for only a portion of the total requirement. Purchasing agents argue that poor performance is an added cost in doing business with a vendor, and this must be taken into consideration.

Here, the term "poor performance" is used differently than the term "unsatisfactory performance" used during the supplier selection process for inclusion on the bid list. There, unsatisfactory performance referred to those factors that disqualified the supplier from being included on the bid list. The term "poor performance" during bid evaluation includes those factors that the company can accept, but add to the time and efforts of various employees. These include errors in invoicing, minor delays in delivery, minor delays in responding to a problem, or infrequent rejection of the items delivered.

Absence of a Formal Vendor Rating System

There was no formal vendor rating system in any of the six companies studied. Although the purchasing department files contained records of problems encountered with vendors, all of the purchasing agents evaluated the various vendors from memory during the vendor selection process.

All purchasing agents interviewed opposed a formal vendor rating system. They argued that such a system was cumbersome, time-consuming, and difficult to implement, as there was no common agreement on how vendors should be rated. Rating systems would have to vary with the type of purchase, and could be used as a political tool.

Splitting the Volume among Suppliers

All of the purchasing agents interviewed preferred to purchase from more than one source if possible, as this was one way to ensure continuity of supply. However, out of eighteen items investigated, orders were placed with more than one supplier for only eight items. The main reason for not having more than one supplier was related to the amount of available business. The decision was made not to split the business if the quantity needed was too small to keep more than one supplier interested. In the case of castings and molded parts, the tooling cost prohibited splitting the volume of available business.

When the order was split, the volume of business available determined the number of suppliers who shared the total requirement. To facilitate order execution, the number of suppliers was usually two, and seldom more than four. Price was the main factor used in determining the amount of business each supplier would get, if competition was between established known sources. But, if the price differences between an established source and a relatively new source was within 2 to 3 percent, the established source would still get the major share of business, even if its price was higher. Or, the established source might get an amount of business equal to that of the new supplier quoting the lower price.

When the business was not divided equally between two suppliers, the split might be 60–40, 70–30, or in some cases, 80–20. The purchasing agent may consult other departments on how business should be divided between sources, but the final decision remained with purchasing. There was no evidence of specific guidelines from management on how the volume might be split among suppliers. Such decisions were left to the individual purchasing agent, and the agent used past experience and personal judgment in making the final choice.

Average Time Period for the Decision Process

From the date the purchase requisition is received in purchasing, it takes about a week to send the RFQ to suppliers. Suppliers were usually given two weeks to respond, but it often took as long as four weeks for most suppliers to send in their written quotations. Once all quotes were received, they were analyzed within two to three weeks. The purchasing agent prepared a list of recommendations, which were approved within a week by the purchasing supervisor, purchasing manager, and the materials manager, or a higher-ranking official of the company, depending upon the dollar volume involved in the purchase. Thus, the average time from the date a purchase requisition was received to the time final orders were placed was about nine weeks. Depending upon the item, the purchase decision process may take anywhere from six to twelve weeks.

Input from Other Departments during the Purchase Decision Process

The purchasing department needed and received input from various other departments of the company, depending upon the item to be purchased. Purchasing performed a service function for the user department, usually production or operations, for the items investigated in this study. The engineering department prepared specifications of the item to be purchased, and quality control ensured that the item received from the vendor met company requirements. Each of these departments interacted with vendors and purchasing to improve the purchase decision.

Vendor performance was continuously evaluated by these departments, and the purchasing department was informed of the results of this evaluation.

During long-term contract negotiations, all correspondence to vendors was channelled through purchasing. Other departments were consulted, but actual negotiations with suppliers were conducted exclusively by purchasing for all of the items studied.

The responsibilities of various departments in the purchasing process were well defined by the companies. Clearance from purchasing was required before a supplier's representative could visit persons from other departments of the company. It was also necessary that the purchasing department remain informed about these discussions. Further, company policy dictated that discussions be confined to technical details or application problems. Pricing information and commercial terms were to be discussed only with the purchasing department. This policy gave a great deal of authority and power to purchasing.

Understanding Priorities of Other Departments

In this study sixty-two people in various departments, including purchasing, were interviewed. All of them stated that usually all the departments worked together, and extended their full cooperation in improving the purchase decision. Differences did arise occasionally, but these were mainly the result of poor communications within the company. These differences were resolved immediately through a meeting arranged on a one-to-one basis, without involving superiors.

Differences arose due to the differing priorities of various departments. One purchasing agent indicated that his company could save about $25,000 per year by switching to another supplier for filters. The filters used at that time were of a specific type available from only one source. The filters were an extremely critical item, and production was happy with the existing supplier's quality. A change in supplier would require changing specifications of the item, changing the mounting arrangement, and conducting extensive production tests before the new filters could be accepted. This was an expensive process, but it would be only a one-time expense. From then on, the company would save $25,000 each year. The purchasing manager explained:

> Every time I have made the suggestion, production turned it down. I really feel frustrated. Finally I went to my boss. He told me to write a memo to the production department showing my analysis of cost savings with a copy to the plant manager who has the ultimate authority in the decision. The production manager replied with a list of project priorities he has from the plant manager. According to his backlog, he will not be able to consider the change in filter design until sometime in 1982, unless the plant manager changes his priorities. The plant manager suggested that this project be considered after 1982. You see, I do not know the priorities of the other departments. The production manager is under the gun all the time. I realize this now. I feel that I have done my job. The plant manager and my boss, the purchasing manager, are aware that there is a potential to save $25,000 per year. It is their decision when they want to start saving.

Importance of Communications

All purchasing agents interviewed mentioned that the primary function of the purchasing department was to communicate efficiently with other company departments to ensure that vendors received fair treatment for the services they performed. One purchasing agent indicated:

> Just as it is the responsibility of the company's marketing department to make sure that the customer is treated fairly for the long-range survival of the organization, it is the responsibility of the purchasing department to ensure that the vendor gets fair treatment to build up a long-term relationship with the suppliers.

Personal Factors Influencing the Purchase Decision

"Do you think friendship with suppliers' representatives influences your choice of suppliers?" was one question asked of purchasing personnel. Out of the thirty interviewed, sixteen responded that it did not occur in their case, but hastily added that individual likes and dislikes were extremely difficult to separate from the rational decision process. When the choice was clear, such factors hardly influenced the decision.

Six purchasing agents indicated that when other things were equal, these factors did influence the decision unknowingly. Responses from seven individuals indicated that they gave friendly suppliers the chance to bid. "Beyond that, you have to be a pro," stated one purchasing manager. The company's auditors have access to all files, and they audit them each year. One purchasing manager indicated that he got tough in analyzing offers from vendors who were his personal friends. "Most of the time they do not get the order and I feel I have been unfair to them. The best way is to keep only a working relationship with the vendors. Otherwise, it is likely to cloud the evaluation process one way or the other."

Personal factors were observed to influence the decision process when the prices quoted by two suppliers were very close, or the volume of available business was to be split among suppliers.

One purchasing agent said: "We all know that personal factors should not influence the purchase decision, but in reality whether they do or not depends upon the mental discipline of the purchasing agent, his upbringing, and his personal ethics."

All six companies included in this study had guidelines for purchasing agents regarding acceptance of gifts from suppliers. Going out for lunch with a vendor's representative, or accepting a ballgame ticket or a bottle of liquor once in a while was not considered accepting a gift. One purchasing agent indicated that although it was not a company policy, whenever he went out with a vendor's rep for lunch, he always paid for it.

Someone from vendor management having a personal friendship with persons in the management of the purchasing company could influence the purchase decision. This was mentioned only once by an individual from engineering, who was instructed to design equipment using only a specific component made by one certain company. He knew the reason for this. "In an instance like this, if you want your job, you just do it and don't argue," he said.

Interaction with Suppliers

The frequency of visits by sales reps increased during the purchase decision process. This was because representatives were eager to supply addition information if needed, and were interested in knowing if the purchase decision was in their favor. If they did not get the order, they wanted to know why they had lost it. For example, they wanted to know if their delivery was unacceptable, or if prices were too high. The purchasing agents mentioned that they would try to give them this information without revealing who had received the order and at what price. The sales reps gave this information to their management to keep them aware of the competitive situation.

Once purchase orders were placed, sales reps of the successful suppliers visited regularly. For example, once a month they checked to see if everything was going smoothly, or they visited as needed to take care of a specific problem. Sales reps from unsuccessful suppliers visited two or three times per year to keep in touch with purchasing agents and brief them on the market situation; this included such items as new products from their company, and changes in their company management.

Some general comments were made during the various interviews about sales reps' visits. One experienced purchasing agent remarked that 50 percent of the sales reps' visits were a waste of time. They did not plan the visits; they had nothing new to say; and they seemed to visit just to satisfy their management requirement for a certain minimum number of sales calls. One visit by a supplier's representative observed during the research was a case in point. A sales rep walked into a purchasing agent's office and shouted, "Hello everybody. I'm Jim Roberts." He made a few remarks about the weather, asked the purchasing agent how he was and about business, asked the agent to contact him if something came up, and left. The purchasing agent immediately pointed out that he knew the salesman by face, but did not remember which company he represented or the product he sold. The sales rep did not bother to leave his calling card.

Some sales reps worked diligently to build rapport with the purchasing agents. They took an interest in the agent's personal hobbies, and built credibility and trust.

Price Negotiations after Awarding Contracts

No suppliers quoted a firm price for the contract period for any of the items studied. The price was firm only for a portion of the contract period, and subject to negotiation thereafter. The suppliers then asked for a price increase, and tried to justify it by citing increases in the price of raw materials and/or labor cost. If the purchasing agent was convinced that the requested price increase was fair and justified, it was granted after tactful negotiations. One purchasing manager remarked: "If we blindly keep on granting each and every request for a price increase from a supplier, we are guilty of accelerating the rate of inflation. We have a tremendous responsibility to fight against this tendency in the national interest, and a good purchasing agent does this constantly."

Negotiations concerning a price increase are strictly between the supplier and purchasing, who has the authority to make the final decision. Purchasing agents dislike the tactics of suppliers who quote the lowest price to get the order, and then repeatedly ask for a price increase. These suppliers are likely to be dropped during the contract period if they become too greedy, or may be dropped from the bidder list for the following year.

Centralized versus Decentralized Purchasing Functions

A centralized purchasing department performs all purchasing functions for the entire organization at one central point. In the case of decentralized purchasing, a separate purchasing department is set up for each operating division or plant location with a considerable degree of autonomy in buying.

Southeast Electric operated about twenty generating stations within about 150 miles. The company operated a centralized purchasing department. The requirements of the generating stations were easy to consolidate because they used many common items. For similar reasons, Diamond International operated a centralized regional purchasing department for the company's plants located in the Carolinas. According to the purchasing agents of these two companies, a centralized purchasing department improved purchasing efficiency and took advantage of volume buying, especially if the plants used common items and were located within a hundred-mile radius. The close locations of plants was important for better communications, understanding special needs, and developing local sources to cut down on shipping costs for heavy items.

The remaining four companies in this study used decentralized purchasing, although each company had a centralized purchasing office headed by a corporate purchasing manager responsible for establishing basic policies and procedures.

The purchasing agents of these companies preferred decentralized purchasing. They argued that company plants were scattered all over the country, they produced diverse products, and as a result, the advantage of volume buying did not exist. They emphasized the advantages of better communications with the user department, understanding user needs, and developing efficient local sources through a decentralized purchasing department.

Corporate purchase agreements (CPAs) existed for common products used by all plants, such as computer cards and office furniture. But according to the purchasing agents interviewed, these items could be purchased from other sources if these sources quoted better prices than those negotiated in the CPA. Purchasing agents indicated that in most cases, other sources were able to quote lower prices.

Observations of centralized and decentralized purchasing operations suggest that both systems have advantages, depending upon the location of company plants and homogeneity of manufactured products. The major steps observed in the purchase decision process are summarized in a flow chart shown in figure 3–1.

9
Summary and Conclusions

In this final chapter, we will (1) review the research objectives and methodology; (2) discuss results and conclusions; (3) offer analyses of models for requesting quotations and awarding contracts; (4) discuss weaknesses observed in purchasing decisions; (5) explore theoretical implications; (6) compare and contrast our findings with those of existing research and highlight unique aspects of our research; (7) touch on managerial implications; and (8) propose areas of further research.

Research Objectives

The following objectives were established in conducting research on long-term contract negotiations concerning supplier choices, in naturalistic settings:

1. *To identify the process of selecting suppliers to bid on required items.* This phase included research focused on such questions as: How are potential suppliers identified? What information sources are used? What criteria are used in adding a new supplier or deleting an existing supplier from the bidders list? What is the minimum/maximum number of suppliers preferred on the bidders list? Are special preferences given to minority vendors?
2. *To understand the process of analyzing bids received from suppliers and evaluating vendors.* This phase of the research included questions such as: Is a formal vendor rating system used to evaluate suppliers? If so, what are the details? If not, why? If differences arise in choosing suppliers or selecting evaluative criteria, how are these differences resolved? Do trade relations (reciprocity) or attitudes toward sales representatives affect the vendor evaluation process?
3. *To investigate the process of selecting suppliers to award contracts*, such questions were asked: What are the choice criteria used in selecting or

168 • *Industrial Purchasing Strategies*

rejecting suppliers? Is there a preference for a single source, or multiple sources? What factors influence splitting the volume of business between suppliers, or increasing or decreasing their share of available business, in the case of multiple sources?

4. *To identify persons (departments) involved in the supplier choice process* and determine if there is centralization in negotiating long-term contracts in the case of companies with multiple manufacturing plants or divisions.

Methodology

A combination of data collections methods, termed "triangulation," was used to investigate the supplier choice decision process. The following methods of data collection were combined:

1. *Protocol analysis combined with Decision System Analysis (DSA)*: Protocol analysis involves instructing subjects to verbalize their thoughts while in the process of making a decision. DSA is the process of developing detailed descriptions of information-processing and decision-making systems existing in the firms.
2. *Structured and unstructured interviews*: A special questionnaire was designed for structured interviews. During unstructured interviews, no specific questions were asked, but respondents talked freely about the purchase decision process they used.
3. *Experience survey*: A survey of fixed alternative questions was developed to investigate the reasons buyers switch suppliers.
4. *Direct observations*: The researcher, with the permission of the purchasing department, sat in on several meetings between the suppliers' sales representatives and purchasing agents. This was useful in studying the experiences of those involved in the purchase decision process as intimately as possible.
5. *Unobtrusive techniques*: The unobtrusive method removes the investigator from direct participation in the events at hand. Purchasing records were well kept in company files, and were a very convenient data collection tool in this study.

Research was conducted in six industrial organizations located in the southeastern United States. An in-depth study of the purchase decision process concerning choice of suppliers was carried out for three items within each company. Thus, eighteen items were investigated thoroughly. Sixty-two persons involved in the purchase decision process from various departments of the companies were interviewed. An additional forty-three purchasing agents participated in the experience survey, which consisted of a structured questionnaire focusing on factors contributing to adding a new supplier, dropping an existing supplier, or increasing or decreasing the supplier's share of business for a new contract period.

The majority of past investigations of industrial buyers have used static methodologies, examining what buyers say they do, or what they say they have done (for example, Webster 1968, 1969, 1970; Ozanne and Churchill 1968, 1971). The triangulation technique used in this study combines segmented protocol analysis, direct observation, and unobtrusive method; this allows for examination of what buyers actually do in the real-world buying situation. This is the greatest strength of the research findings presented here.

Discussions of Results and Conclusions

The purchasing agents, in making supplier choice decisions, used a rather formalized procedure for reducing the number of alternatives to be considered. This procedure, similar to "heuristic programming," consists of successive applications of appropriate rules, so that the number of alternatives is reduced to a manageable amount. Supplier choice decisions seem to become a case of heuristic programming in a broad sense. This is evident from the analysis of two flow chart models developed from the findings of this study. Figure 9–1 is the supplier selection model for requesting quotations; figure 9–2 is the final supplier choice model for awarding contracts.

Analysis of Supplier Selection Model for Requesting Quotations

When the purchasing agent or buyer received a purchase requisition to buy an item, the buyer first asked what that item was (figure 9–1). Was it a new item being purchased for the first time, or a repeat purchase? If it was a repeat purchase, the buyer checked company records for previous suppliers. This was true for all of the repeat purchase items studied. If the item was new, the specifying engineer or user departments usually suggested sources. In the case of two new items investigated, the engineering department named two or three sources with whom they had contacts. All six companies investigated preferred to have a minimum of three suppliers on the bid list for items purchased before; however, for an item being purchased for the first time, most purchasing agents preferred to have six suppliers on the bid list. This was because all suppliers receiving RFQs might not quote. To ensure that these suppliers did quote, company records were examined for vendors supplying items similar to the one

170 • *Industrial Purchasing Strategies*

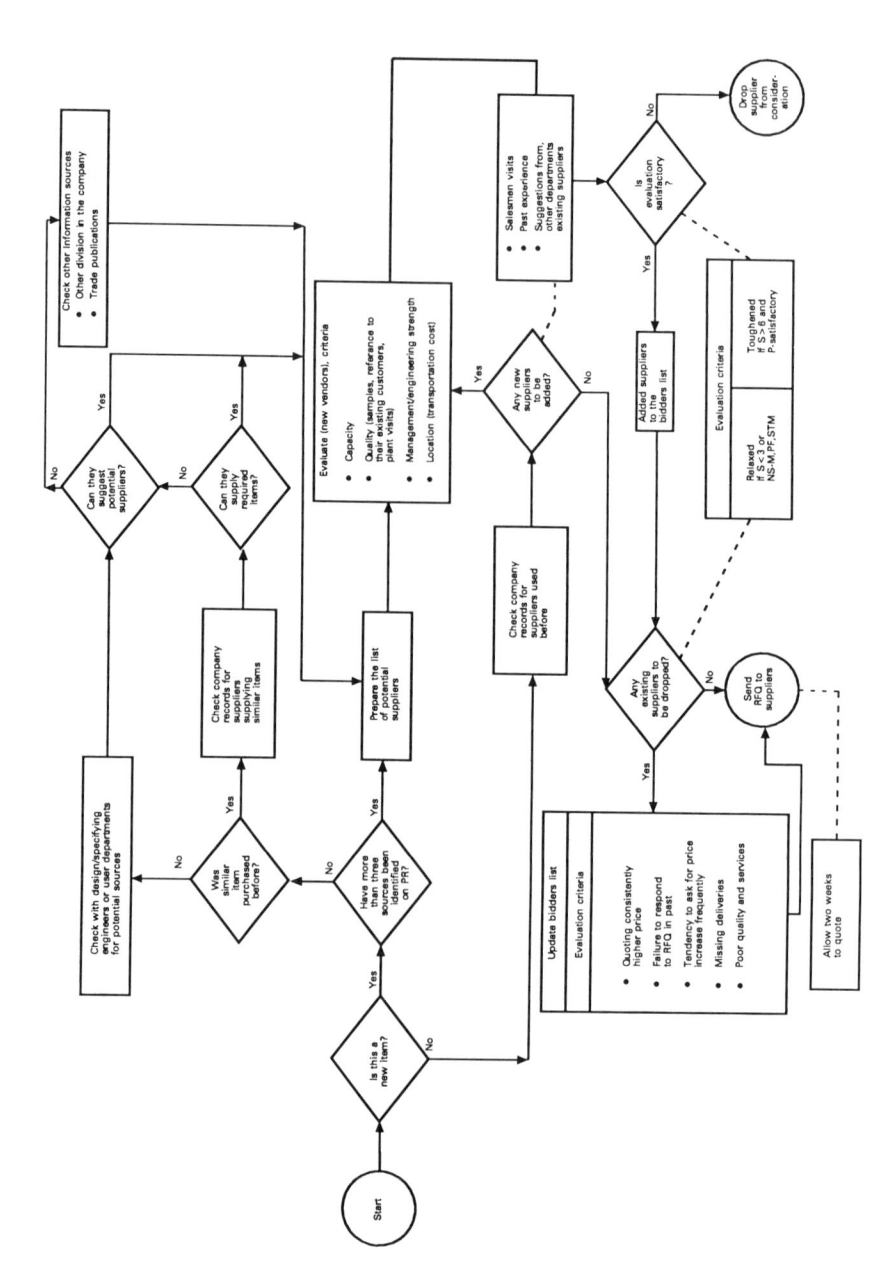

Figure 9–1. Supplier Selection Model for Requesting Quotations

being purchased. These vendors were then asked if they were interested in supplying the new item; if they were not, they were asked to suggest other potential suppliers. The purchasing agent might return to the specifying engineers and user department, who read technical magazines, receive technical literature directly from manufacturers, and attend trade shows, to obtain names of additional sources. This search for new sources continued until the desired number of sources was found, or the information sources as shown in the model were exhausted.

These observations concur with findings by Wind (1968), and are in line with the behavioral theory of the firm developed by Cyert and March (1963). Wind observed that

> search follows the simplest route.... The buyers, whenever engaged in search activities, start in their immediate neighborhood and initiate a search that is perceived to be the least expensive.... Only if this search does not produce the desired outcome do they engage in a more "distant" and expensive search process.

The search was carried out to the final stage of a buyer referring to trade publications for only one of the two new items studied. In the other case, the search was not even attempted, as three potential suppliers had been suggested on the purchase requisition, and the buyer found that all of them had keen interest in submitting quotes.

Of the sixteen repeat purchase items investigated, the search terminated with checking company records for previous suppliers whenever the number of suppliers found was three or greater. For only two items were there less than three potential suppliers. For one item (the front axle assembly) with a single-source situation, the purchasing agent located five additional potential suppliers from his previous experience with the other company. For the second item (#6 fuel oil), the search for potential suppliers was motivated by company management, because the two existing suppliers had storage facilities in the same town; the purchasing agent was asked to locate a third supplier in another area. His information was gathered from existing suppliers, asking them which of their competitors had storage facilities located elsewhere.

When the initiative was taken by a new potential supplier wishing to receive an RFQ, the purchasing agent evaluated this supplier using a noncompensatory, conjunctive evaluation model. For example, the purchasing agent established a minimum level of each attribute included in the evaluative criteria, and any potential supplier meeting those minimum levels was considered acceptable. The evaluative criteria included capacity to meet fluctuations in demand; quality of product offered (judged from sample performance, plant visits, or reference to existing customers of the potential vendor); location (which affects transportation costs); and management/engineering strength.

172 • *Industrial Purchasing Strategies*

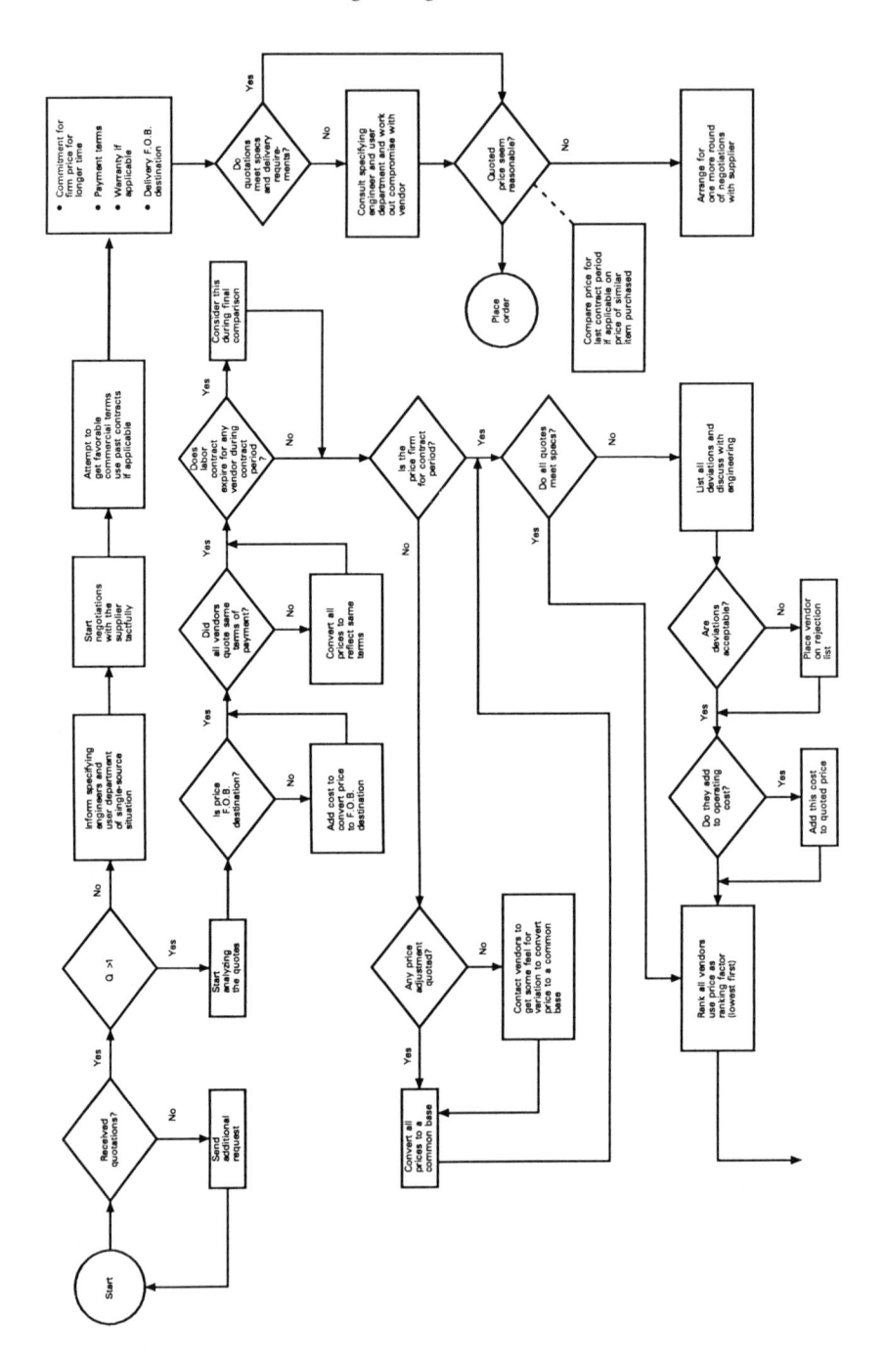

Summary and Conclusions • 173

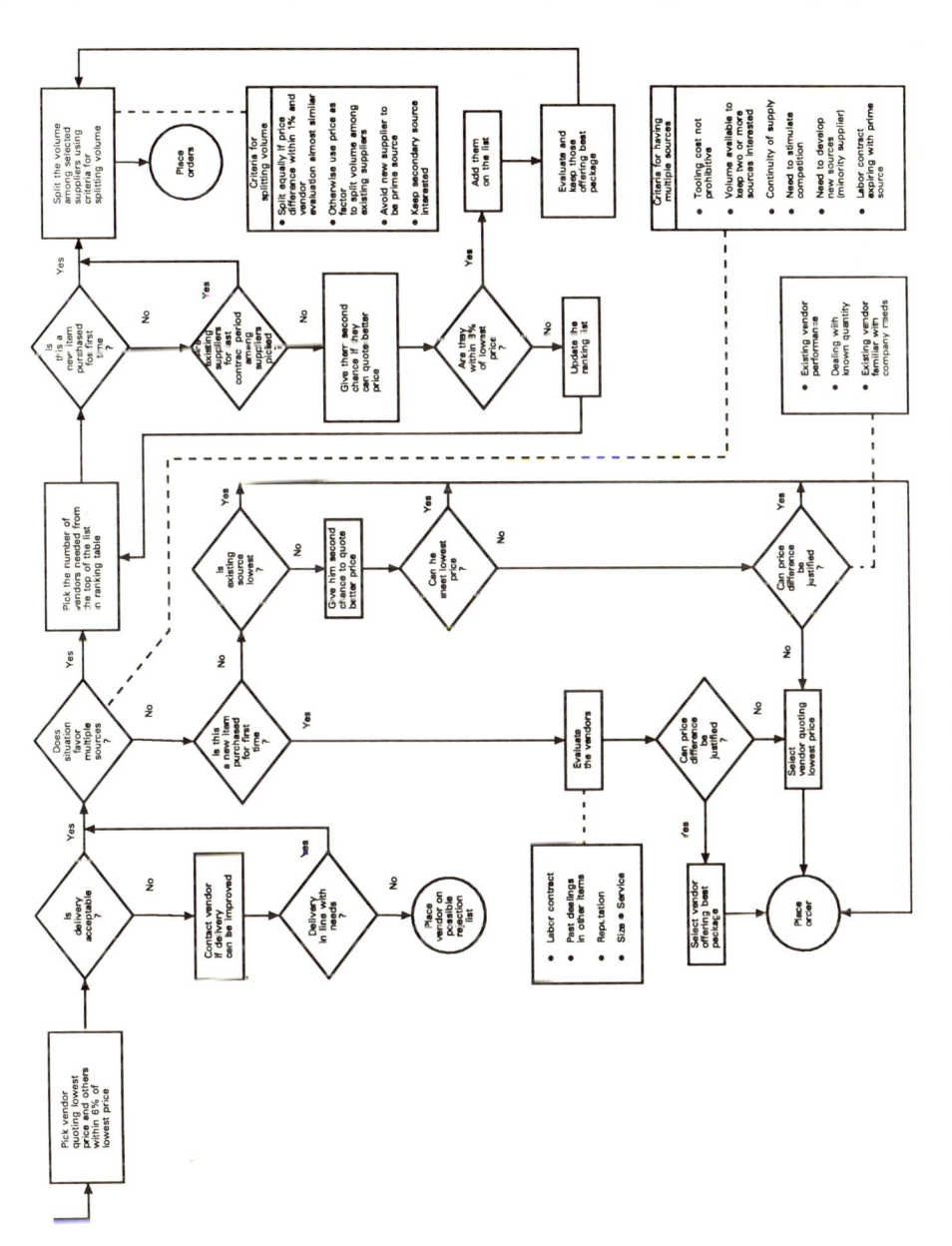

Figure 9–2. Supplier Selection Model for Awarding Contracts

Evaluative criteria are dynamic in nature. The importance of particular evaluative criteria varies from item to item. Also, the minimum acceptable level established for each criterion is also influenced by situational factors. For example, if there are less than three suppliers on the bid list, the acceptance level is lowered. This also occurs when a new supplier if recommended by someone in top management (for example, with the case of hydraulic motors), there is a need to develop a minority source (for example, for wooden pallets), or the supplier's representative is a personal friend.

However, if the performance of existing suppliers is satisfactory, and the number of suppliers on the bid list is greater than six, minimum acceptance levels are raised. Even with this tougher evaluation, if new potential suppliers qualify to be included on the bid list, the purchasing agent then turns to another decision rule. The agent evaluates the performance of existing suppliers, and drops one or two of them who have maintained a poor quality and service record, missed deliveries consistently, ask for price increases frequently, have consistently quoted a higher price, or have failed to respond to RFQs in the past. Suppliers are dropped using a screening procedure based on a lexicographic model in the order of attributes named above.

The simple decision rules used by purchasing agents when requesting quotations from potential suppliers are summarized below:

1. Seek new potential sources actively when the number of suppliers on the bid list is less than three. Identify potential sources using procedures that are least expensive in terms of time and cost.
2. Maintain the status quo when the performance of existing suppliers is satisfactory and the number of suppliers is greater than three.
3. Toughen the standards of acceptance for potential suppliers when the number of acceptable vendors on the bid list is greater than six. Relax the criteria when the new vendor is suggested by top management, is a minority, or is a personal friend.
4. Drop one or more existing vendors with poor performance records, especially when new vendors are included on the bid list.

Rules (1) and (2) can be explained in terms of the reward–balance model suggested by Wind (1971). This model suggests that "the buyer's behavior is directed toward satisfying the objectives which he perceives as being critical in the evaluation of his performance and hence in his reward."

Because the organizational requirement of having three suppliers on the bid list is not met under (1), the purchasing agent actively seeks new sources to avoid adverse comments from superiors and company auditors. Because there is no reward for change under (2), maintaining a balanced state requires inaction, and turning attention to another activity in the buyflow.

Rules (3) and (4) are in line with observations made by Cyert, Simon, and Trow (1956). They found that "in place of searching for the best alternative, the decision maker is usually concerned with finding a satisfactory alternative—one that will attain a specified goal and at the same time satisfy a number of auxiliary conditions."

The auxiliary conditions in the supplier selection process are: keeping the workload of the purchasing agent at a manageable level; weighing the cost of new vendor evaluation in time and effort, versus advantages gained from having the supplier on the bid list; and meeting other organizational needs of the purchasing agent.

Analysis of Final Supplier Choice Model for Awarding Contracts

Bid Evaluation Process: Single Supplier Submitting Acceptable Bid

Once the bidders list is finalized, the RFQ is sent to potential suppliers, allowing them two weeks to submit bids. If bids are not received in that time, a second request is sent (see figure 11–2). If only one acceptable bid is received, the purchasing agent begins tactful negotiations with the supplier and, at the same time, informs the specifying engineers and user department of the single-source situation. For example, in the case of front axle assembly (Chapman Machines), only one supplier submitted a quotation. Thus, the purchasing agent's negotiating power was severely curtailed. Because the purchasing agent was unsuccessful in developing new sources, his only choice was to begin tactful negotiations with the single supplier submitting an acceptable bid.

During tactful negotiations, an attempt was made to attain favorable commercial terms, using the previous contract or a similar item as a reference. The buyer tries to get a commitment for a price firm for a longer time period, better terms of payment and warranty period, and delivery terms FOB jobsite. The next question was: Does the quote meet specifications and the delivery requirement? If it did, the last item checked was price, to determine if it seemed reasonable. The price paid during the previous contract period served as a guide. If the price seemed to be out of line, another round of negotiations was conducted with the supplier, and the order was then placed. If the quotation did not meet specifications and/or delivery requirements, a compromise was worked out. Negotiations were extremely important in concluding the contract in a situation such as this. Usually the supplier is not aware of the fact that its quotation was the only one received by the purchaser. The purchasing agent, after awarding the contract, actively continued to search for additional sources. Out of eighteen items investigated, a single supplier submitted a quotation for only two items.

Bid Evaluation Process: Multiple Bids

When more than one quotation was received, the purchasing agent began the analysis by making all of the quotes as comparable as possible. For example, if one supplier quoted price FOB shipping point and another quoted FOB destination, the buyer asked the first supplier to revise the quote to make it FOB destination. If the supplier does not agree to this change, an estimated cost of transportation and insurance from shipping point to jobsite is added to the quoted price. This same process occurs regarding terms and payment and price escalation. If a supplier's labor contract expires during the contract period, this is also taken into consideration during the final comparison between vendors.

During the initial phase of analysis, prices quoted by all vendors are converted to a common base to make them comparable. This analysis is carried out strictly by the purchasing agent; other departments are not involved in the actual decision process.

Technical Evaluation

Technical evaluation is the next step in the decision process. The purchasing agent checks quotations from vendors to determine whether they meet the required specifications. Some vendors might have deviated slightly from specifications. These deviations are discussed with engineering and/or user departments to see if they are acceptable. If the deviations are acceptable, their additional cost, if any, is added to the quoted price. If the deviations are not acceptable, the vendor is placed on the possible rejection list. Vendors are rarely rejected during technical screening, as their technical capability is investigated thoroughly before they are included on the bid list. Crucial negotiations center around deviations from specifications. Some vendors may have quoted their standard process or component that deviates slightly from required specifications; however, the item may still perform the necessary function. In such a case, purchasing performs an important function as it attempts to convince the engineering/user department to accept deviations. The company may save money by accepting a standard component from the supplier.

Final Evaluation

Next, vendors are ranked according to price. The vendor quoting the lowest price is first on the list.

Summary and Conclusions • 177

The procedure to this point has established a ranking of suppliers. However, the actual purpose of the decision process is to determine a dollar value (premium) that can be paid to vendors offering higher levels of performance on important criteria.

Most purchasing agents feel that it is important to reward suppliers for good performances in delivery, reliability, research and development, as well as service to engineering, purchasing, and maintenance. However, it is difficult to place a monetary value on these criteria. None of the companies interviewed attempted to quantify these criteria. Instead, informal evaluation of these criteria was encouraged and carried out by the buyers. The data for such evaluations were gathered from engineering, maintenance, quality control, purchasing records, and suppliers themselves.

The crucial question at this stage of the decision process is: How much more is the company willing to pay for better levels of performance compared to lowest priced acceptable quote? This is a difficult question, and the answer is dependent upon how critical the item is, the dollar value of the contract, and the user company's competitive position in the market. However, most buyers studied indicated that they were willing to pay a 3- to 6-percent premium to the supplier offering significantly higher performance compared to the lowest priced acceptable quote. The remaining buyers indicated a willingness to pay a premium of 4 to 10 percent.

Buyers were observed to establish a price cut-off level, once suppliers' offers met the company's minimum requirements. This cut-off level was about 6 percent. Therefore, in the final evaluation, only those vendors quoting prices within 6 percent of the lowest price were considered.

One last screening was performed regarding delivery before the final evaluation was begun. If the delivery quoted did not meet the requirement, vendors quoting a competitive price were usually given a chance to improve their delivery. Contacting vendors by telephone for delivery improvement indicated to these potential suppliers that they were under serious consideration; further it motivated them to improve delivery. If delivery could not be improved, such vendors were put on the likely rejection list.

Vendors, up to this point, were selected using a noncompensatory, conjunctive evaluation model; that is, the selected vendor had to meet certain minimum acceptance levels on commercial terms, specifications, price, and delivery requirements. The remaining vendors were dropped if a minimum number of suppliers (usually two) survived this initial screening process. If only one supplier passed this screening, it received the order. If no suppliers passed, additional negotiations were necessary.

Criteria to Split Volume among Multiple Sources

The next step was to determine whether the situation warranted multiple sources. The deciding factors usually were: the availability of enough volume to keep more than one source interested in the business and, in the case of items requiring tooling, ensuring that the cost of tooling was not prohibitive. Other factors considered were: continuity of supply (labor contract with prime source expiring during contract period); need to stimulate competition, in service from suppliers, as well as in price; and need to develop a new source, for example, a minority supplier, to meet government regulations.

If the item was being purchased for the first time, the vendors required as multiple sources were chosen from the top of the vendor ranking list, and the volume was split according to these rules:

1. Split volume equally if the price difference is within 1 percent. This makes it easier to monitor the execution of the contract.
2. If the price difference is greater than 1 percent, split the volume using price as the deciding factor, and considering that the secondary source should receive enough volume to keep it interested in the company's business. In applying this rule to existing suppliers, it is assumed that there is no appreciable difference in the vendors' past performance. If there is a difference in past performance, this is weighed against the price difference, and the order is split accordingly.
3. When the volume is to be split between an existing supplier and a new supplier with whom the company has not previously done business, do not permit the new supplier to be the primary source.

If the item to be purchased was not new, and the existing suppliers were not among those chosen from the ranking table, most purchasing agents preferred to give them a chance to improve their quoted prices. If they quoted within 3 percent of the lowest price, their past performance was evaluated against that of other suppliers to arrive at the final decision of how to split the volume.

When the situation did not warrant multiple sources and the item to be purchased was new, the vendor quoting the lowest price was given preference, provided that its labor contract did not expire during the purchase contract period. If other vendors have quoted within 2 percent of the lowest price, they are evaluated on such additional factors as past performance with other items supplied to the company, reputation, size, and service organization. The vendor offering the best overall package received the order if the price difference (in actual dollars) could be justified. The price difference in actual dollars was dependent on the size of the order. For example, if the dollar value of the total order was $700,000, the 2 percent price difference amounted to $14,000. Was it worthwhile to pay $14,000 more to a vendor offering a better overall package? The answer to this question dictated the final vendor choice. At this point, for the first time in the decision process, purchasing agents appeared to use the compensatory evaluation (expectancy-value) model.

When the item to be purchased was not new, and the situation required a single source, the existing vendor was favored if its performance was satisfactory. If the price was not the lowest, the vendor might have had the chance to lower the price. The price difference was then calculated and weighed against other factors, such as familiarity of the existing vendor with company procedures, and its understanding of company needs, versus time and effort required to groom a new vendor. Most buyers interviewed felt that this price difference could be a maximum of about 3 percent. This was the most purchasing agents were willing to pay to avoid uncertainty.

Weaknesses Observed in Purchase Decisions

Investigating the supplier choice process using DSA provided an accurate picture, and an improved understanding of the entire decision process. Using this analysis, problems, biases, and oversights were identified. Specific weaknesses observed in the buyflow included the following:

lack of initiative in locating new sources;

lack of value analysis technique to reduce the cost of purchased items;

few serious attempts made to negotiate price or contract terms with vendors;

absence of a formal vendor rating system;

no clear policy on selecting single versus multiple sources;

absence of written guidelines on splitting volume among suppliers when multiple sources are selected; and

lack of formal training programs for buyers.

Lack of Initiative in Locating New Sources

New suppliers were added to the bid list for only four out of eighteen items investigated (chapter 7, fuel oil and list truck parts; chapter 8, rubber gaskets and wooden pallets). Initiative was taken to locate a new supplier for only one of these items. For the remaining three items, a new source was added due to the initiative (sales call) of a sales representative.

Most purchasing agents argued, "We operate in a marketing-oriented society, and usually the suppliers seek us out." This may be true, but countless small manufacturing firms are in existence today that lack nationwide, or even region-wide, marketing organization. These firms have low overhead, and produce high-quality products. Purchasing agents could reduce costs by making special efforts to locate such firms. These efforts should include locating foreign suppliers. Healthy competition from foreign suppliers is likely to encourage local suppliers to be more efficient.

Lack of Value Analysis

Value analysis is defined as the organized and systematic study of the function of a material, part, or component to identify areas of unnecessary cost that can be eliminated without impairing the capacity of the item to satisfy its objective.

The purchasing departments did not perform a formal value analysis for any of the items studied. They felt that this was the responsibility of those specifying the item. However, purchasing agents are frequently exposed to new literature and sales calls from companies introducing new items or alternative materials, and their input to value analysis could be beneficial. Purchasing managers should encourage purchasing agents to take an active role in value analysis to improve purchasing efficiency.

Lack of Negotiations with Vendors

Only one out of the six companies studied negotiated price and terms of contract with vendors (Southeast Electric Company, chapter 9). Purchasing agents of the remaining companies indicated that price negotiations were against company policy. One or more of the following reasons were given against negotiations:

> If the vendors know that price will be negotiated, they will quote a higher price to begin with. Vendors quote their best price when price revisions are not permitted after bids have been submitted.

> If suppliers are squeezed too much their product quality and service will decline.

> During shortages, suppliers will drop customers whose prices and terms are least attractive.

> The market competition is intense and suppliers quote attractive prices, leaving little room for negotiations.

In spite of these arguments against negotiations, buyers who engaged in price negotiations did obtain lower prices than those who did not (for example, chapter 9—purging gases and coal). Negotiating with vendors is a powerful way to reduce cost and improve purchasing efficiency. Although product price looms large in any procurement price negotiations, it is only one of many price elements discussed between parties. Other elements include freight charges, payment terms, warranty, penalty for late delivery, price escalation terms, and service charges.

Buyers need to develop a training program on the strategy and tactics of negotiations. Strategy is planning and directing negotiations to achieve goals and objectives. Tactics include maneuvers employed to implement strategy. This training might include role playing, counseling, and observing a master negotiator in action. Joint participation by corporate and local purchasing agents in the training program should be encouraged (see Woodside and Samuel 1981).

Absence of a Formal Vendor Rating System

No companies studied employed a formal vendor rating system. Without such a system, the purchase decision process is likely to be influenced by subjective factors, such as friendship or dislike for a supplier's sales representative. A simple but formal rating system is recommended; this would allow for quantification of various criteria used in the final vendor choice. The system should serve to complement personal memory as a guide for future decisions.

Absence of Written Guidelines in Selecting Single versus Multiple Sources or Splitting Volume among Suppliers

Buyers of the companies researched used their own personal judgment in selecting single versus multiple sources, or splitting the volume of business among suppliers. Although buyers received general guidelines from their immediate superiors, the absence of a clear-cut policy on the subject was confirmed by all respondents. Because such decisions are important for inducing competition and ensuring delivery of critical items, a formal written policy on the subject should be developed by purchasing management.

Lack of a Formal Training Program

There were no formal training programs in any of the firms studied. Purchasing decisions have a direct impact on the profitability of the company; thus, a good training program for purchasing agents would be a wise investment. Purchasing management should develop and implement such a program, incorporating these suggestions, to remove observed weaknesses in the purchase decisions.

Theoretical Implications

Some efforts have been made to predict supplier choices in industrial buying, using linear attitude models (Scott and Bennett 1971; Wildt and Bruno 1974). However, analysis of the flow chart models developed from this research indicates that purchasing agents do not use one simple evaluation model, but rather a combination of evaluation models at various stages in the decision process.

Although the overall choice process may appear to be complex, the decision rules used at various stages in the choice process are relatively simple. This simplicity is not always evident to the decision maker (Morgenroth 1964); such findings are consistent with the propositions of organizational theorists (March and Simon 1958).

Another interesting observation about the decision rules concerns the influence of precedence. When purchasing agents were asked how they arrived at the decision rules, they answered, "This is the way it was decided before under similar situations." The rationale was that if the decision is questioned, the purchasing agent could explain that past precedent was a guiding factor. Lindblom (1959, 1965) noted similar behavior among decision makers in government and elsewhere. Hulbert (1979), in reviewing descriptive models of marketing decisions, also observed that for some repetitive advertising and stocking decisions, the effect of past precedent was quite evident.

It is also evident that important purchasing decisions are best viewed as part of an organizational decision system. This is not surprising, as the concept of a "buying center" is well accepted in industrial purchasing. The purchasing decision is a culmination of other organizational decisions made at earlier times, and is heavily influenced by the inputs of various departments.

The existence of similarities in the supplier choice decisions within and between industrial organizations supports the notion of "bounded rationality" (Archer 1964). The supplier choice decision process is also characterized by feedback processes, and is therefore better viewed as adaptive processes relating with both organizational interdependencies and environmental contingencies (March and Simon 1958).

Despite structural similarities, the choice processes exhibited both differentiation and integration (Lawrence and Lorsch 1967). For example, with respect to tactics for negotiating with suppliers, the single-source situation required a good deal more tactful negotiations than other situations. Some purchasing agents were more aggressive negotiators than others; also, depending upon the technical complexity of the item, negotiations sometimes required input from other departments. Thus, each supplier choice decision has special characteristics related to the requirements posed by the situation (differential).

On the other hand, interdependencies in the final decision process created the need for subsequent integration, as in the case of combining and evaluating choice criteria, considering the needs of different departments.

Comparison of Research Findings with Those of Other Studies

Similar Findings

This Study	Other Studies
Preference for a minimum of suppliers on the bid list.	Thain, Johnston, and Leighton (1959); Robinson, Faris, and Wind (1967); Cardozo and Cagley (1971); Stiles (1973); Cunningham and White (1973); and Crow (1974).
Buyers tend to limit their consideration to potential suppliers with whom they were already familiar, or about whom they could most easily obtain information.	Buckner (1967); Wind (1970); Brand (1972); Monoky (1973); and Luffman (1974).
Engineering department is responsible for specifying equipment, and approving changes in specifications.	Strauss (1964); Robinson, Faris, and Wind (1967); Buckner (1967); Parket (1971); Brand (1972); and Pingry (1972).
For purchaser-specified products, it is difficult for a new supplier to be accepted as a prime source.	Thain, Johnston, and Leighton (1959); Robinson, Faris, and Wind (1967); Buckner (1967); Bubb and Van Rest (1973); Abernathy and Utterback (1975); and Hill and Hillier (1977).
Dissatisfaction with the performance of the current supplier is a major reason for dropping the supplier (missed deliveries, poor quality, not responsive to complaints).	Brand (1972); Luffman (1974); and Woodside and Lichtenstein (1980).

184 • *Industrial Purchasing Strategies*

Conflicting Findings

This Study	Other Studies
None of the six companies used a formal vendor rating system. None of the purchasing agents favored vendor rating systems.	Numerous studies have found that purchasing agents favor a formal rating system: Dowst and Somerby (1967); Purchasing Survey (1968); Berman (1969); Nolan (1970); Ellis (1971).
No evidence of reciprocity	Evidence of reciprocity: Thain, Johnston, and Leighton (1959); Robinson, Faris, and Wind (1967); Dauner (1967); Wind (1970); and Deutsch (1973).
Differences among persons in the buying center are always resolved amicably through mutual discussions.	Differences in the buying center are not always resolved amicably. Strauss (1962, 1964); Weigand (1966); and Pettigrew (1975).

Comments on Conflicting Findings

These research observations, which contradict the findings of other studies, warrant some additional comments.

Vendor Rating System. The use of quantitative information in supplier analysis (which incorporates the criteria used in both the initial selection and final evaluation of suppliers) has been the subject of prolonged debate (Hill and Hillier 1977). The essence of such controversy has usually centered around the fact that quantified information has been developed from subjective rating scales. Thus, quantitative information, by its statistical nature, may imply a scientific accuracy that does not in fact exist because of the subjectivity involved. It should not, therefore, be regarded by itself as a panacea to all source management problems.

Reciprocity. All of the studies that found evidence of reciprocity were conducted in the 1960s and early 1970s. According to Hill and Hillier (1977), recent evidence for the existence of reciprocity is scant. This could be due to the fact that planned reciprocity is in many cases illegal.

Resolution of Conflict. The focus of this study was on items purchased via long-term contracts. Most of these items fall into buying situations of straight or modified rebuy, in which the buying center deals with established sources and well-accepted choice criteria evolved from past experience. Members of the buying centers interviewed indicated that they tried to avoid "tunnel vision," and work with open minds to understand the problems and priorities of other departments. This observation is more in line with the findings of Robinson, Faris, and Wind (1967). They found that the conflicting goals within organizations are resolved through "local rationality," that is, delegation and specialization of decisions and goals.

Research Findings Unique to This Study

In reviewing the research on the vendor selection process, this study was found, surprisingly, to be the first to investigate these important issues:

the criteria used by purchasing agents in selecting multiple sources of supply;

the criteria used in splitting the volume of available business between selected sources; and

special preferences given to minority vendors to include them on the bidders list.

These observations have important managerial implications. For example, a minority supplier usually receives preference in submitting bids; but in order to receive an order, prices must be competitive. The findings of this study indicate that a minority or new vendor stands a better chance of gaining business when multiple sources are preferred. Therefore, minority or new vendors should concentrate their efforts on items purchased through multiple sources.

Having multiple sources serves as inexpensive insurance against delivery interruptions. When the situation permits, purchasing management should use multiple sources.

Importance of Decision System Analysis

Investigating the supplier choice process using decision system analysis provides a rich picture and better understanding of the entire decision process. The research findings of this study clarify the important distinction between criteria used in qualifying a potential supplier for the bidders list, and, when quotations are received, criteria used in selecting suppliers to award the contract.

The purchase of items through long-term contracts is an ongoing process;

therefore, purchasing organizations have a clear idea of what is needed (product specifications), who acceptable sources are, and the strengths and weaknesses of these sources. Once the supplier's product meets specifications and the required delivery, price becomes a deciding factor in narrowing down the choice. At this point, additional factors are evaluated along with price to arrive at the final choice.

Once this process is understood, interorganization and intraorganization comparisons can be made among the decision processes observed to arrive at some valid generalizations. Arriving at such valid generalizations is the essence of DSA. This can only be appreciated when seemingly contradictory findings are reported by various researchers concerning the importance of choice criteria in vendor selection decisions (see Parket 1971; Cardozo and Cagley 1971; Kiser, Rao, and Rao 1974; and Gronhaug 1977). Most of these studies involved submitting a list of attributes to purchasing agents and asking them to rate them according to importance in vendor selection. None of these studies used DSA. These rankings obviously vary, depending upon whether the item is supplier-specified or specified by the buying organization; the item is new or purchased before; a single-source situation exists, or multiple sources are available; and even for the same item, criteria change depending upon situational factors. The dynamic nature of criteria used in actual practice can only be observed through DSA.

Managerial Implications

Purchasing Management

In order for participants in buyflows to make better decisions, they need to know how buying decisions are made. The buyflows of this study illustrate how current decisions are made. Purchasing management can use these findings to improve its decisions. This type of analysis yields considerable insight into operational problems and inconsistencies.

This study demonstrates the feasibility of constructing buyflows that describe the structure of purchase behavior. Such flow charts are recommended as a means of auditing purchasing activity. They can be used as powerful diagnostic tools for purchasing managers, and provide direct and immediate payoffs to the firm. For example, this study was a learning experience for many participants. They considered, sometimes for the first time, data inputs sought and criteria employed in making a decision. The process is fairly straightforward to apply, and the benefits flow as much from DSA as from system descriptions. DSA can identify problems, biases, and oversights. Such auditing can increase the efficiency of purchasing, because the majority of problems identified are amenable to managerial solutions.

Another implication for purchasing management is in the area of the training, rewarding, and controlling of industrial buyers. The results of this study indicate that to resolve interdepartmental differences in a beneficial and healthy way, purchasing agents should avoid tunnel vision, and attempt to understand the problems and priorities of the other departments. In two of the companies studied, the purchasing agent was required to work at least five years with one or two other company departments before becoming a purchasing agent. This allowed the agent to develop a better understanding of the functioning of other departments, and prepared the agent to work with them. The criteria identified in this study (used to evaluate suppliers at various stages in the decision process) can also be used as training tools for new buyers.

The concept of centralized regional purchasing (for multiple plants located in the same vicinity) used by one of the companies should be explored by other organizations. There is potential for substantial savings, without losing the flexibility maintaining local contacts with vendors.

None of the companies studied used a formal vendor rating system. A simple but formal system would allow for quantification of various criteria used in the final choice, to serve as a guide for future decisions, and reduce the reliance on personal memory. The formal rating system would be an excellent guide in sitting down with a supplier's representative and discussing strengths and weaknesses. Experience of other companies (Arizona Public Service Company 1979) has revealed that channels of communication, concessions on the part of suppliers, and suppliers' overall responsiveness to buyers have increased as a result of such formal systems.

The choice processes used by various purchasing agents showed that those who engaged in price negotiations with vendors usually obtained a better price than those who did not. Negotiations with vendors to obtain better terms and lower prices should be used frequently to improve purchasing efficiency.

Marketing

Several implications for sales and marketing management are apparent from the findings of this study. Purchasing agents use different decision rules during the vendor qualifying process (to receive RFQs), and final vendor selection to award contracts. Knowledge of these decision rules could be very useful in improving the effectiveness of marketing decisions.

If a company is purchasing a new product for the first time, it is advantageous to know this before product specifications are finalized. Having access to and communicating with those responsible for finalizing specifications is extremely important for a new supplier. The supplier will thus be able to understand clearly the needs of the buying organization, and influence the drafting of product specifications in favor of his or her company. A company's existing suppliers have an edge in this situation over other suppliers if they use their sales calls effectively. For example, sales representatives should remain familiar with plans for new developments that the buying company is about to undertake. They should continually explore their company's ability to offer any of the new items that will be required in the future.

If the company is already purchasing an item from existing suppliers, the new supplier, before spending too much time and effort for this business, should find out how many suppliers are already on the bidders list. The supplier should also find out if the performance of existing suppliers is satisfactory. The research findings indicate that the purchasing agent's qualifying criteria vary according to these factors.

For vendors already on the bidders list, it is important for them to respond and quote on time; to give as much information as possible with the bids; and to submit a competitive price to remain qualified to receive future RFQs. Meeting product specifications and delivery requirements are necessary for being a successful supplier. In addition, quoting a competitive price increases the supplier's chance of getting an order.

For existing suppliers, it is important to ensure that quality of the item is consistent, delivery is timely, and service is satisfactory. The supplier should respond to any particular problem quickly, and convince those in the buying organization that the supplier has the full support of management. The marketing manager must cooperate to resolve problems. It was observed that effective communications were of great help. Negotiations with buyers on price increases should be conducted tactfully. For example, all price increase requests should be justified convincingly, and should preferably be documented. This strategy assures that the existing supplier will remain a favorable source, and might even increase its share of available business from the buying organization. The only way a new supplier can obtain a small share of business from an established supplier is to quote a very attractive price when multiple sourcing is likely.

The foregoing discussion indicates that the sales manager should formulate strategies according to the manager's situation in relation to buying organizations. The sales manager must train the sales staff to collect the necessary information continuously, as essential input to decisions.

Limitations of the Study

The exploratory and descriptive nature of this study, as well as the use of a convenience sample, restrict generalization of the results to items purchased on long-term contracts only. Moreover, this study does not suggest that the findings are applicable to other product groups, such as MRO (maintenance, repairs, and operating) items, capital equipment, and other items purchased on a one-time basis. Further the research was conducted in medium and large industrial plants of firms with total sales from $400 million to $15 billion. The supplier choice process might be different in small organizations. Lastly, organizational buyers in situations other than industrial purchasing were not evaluated in this research. Thus, the findings may not be applicable to other organizations such as hospitals, universities, and other government agencies.

Areas for Further Research

Research should be extended to include small industrial organizations (total sales less than $200 million), as well as other organizations such as hospitals, universities, and government agencies. Such research should investigate how items are purchased on long-term contracts. What are the buyflows for those items purchased on long-term contracts in such organizations? The answer is needed for building a generalized inductive model of organizational buying behavior.

Other types of long-term contracts are negotiated, for example, maintenance contracts and lease-hold contracts (for computers or copying machines). The vendor choice process for these contracts should be an additional area of investigation.

A combination of data collection methods, termed "triangulation," was used to develop a detailed picture of the supplier choice decision process. Several other data collection instruments could be added by future researchers to strengthen "triangulation." For example, the use of the tape recorder, when permitted, would allow for better documentation and more accurate analysis of protocols and buyer–seller negotiations. Interviews with sales representatives and their managers should also be included to strengthen the development of the entire decision process. Interviews with supplier organizations will provide interesting information about their perceptions of the supplier choice process.

Understanding of buyflows will be increased from research on industrial organizations that use formal vendor rating systems to determine if supplier choice processes are different from those reported here.

The decision rules and evaluation criteria developed in this research can be viewed as hypotheses. Testing these hypotheses can be another area for further research.

An evaluation of the effect of change in the type of goods to be purchased upon the decision process is another area of possible research. For example, products involving MRO items or capital equipment could be studied.

Evidence in this study indicates that the management of the buying organization is willing to pay a premium price of approximately 4 to 6 percent to a supplier whose product and service performance is likely to be superior to other vendors'. The sample in this study was limited, and not specifically structured to answer this question. The question itself, because of its tremendous marketing implications, is another area in supplier choice process that warrants additional research.

This research should also be duplicated using a larger sample from other areas of the United States. Combining the research results of such future studies as these will contribute immensely toward the development of a theory of supplier choice.

Summary

An exploratory investigation has been reported that assessed the potential for using DSA in the evaluation of supplier choice decisions. The process by which choices are made has been examined, rather than the choices per se. In the simplest terms, this study was an attempt to probe deeply into what purchasing managers actually do, as opposed to what they say they do.

The results of this study indicate a clear distinction in choice criteria to qualify a supplier as an approved source, versus criteria applied to choosing suppliers for actually placing the order from those approved sources who submitted bids.

Purchasing agents, instead of using a single evaluation process model (for example, compensatory versus noncompensatory) use a combination of these evaluation models in their final choice of suppliers. Structural similarities were observed in all the choice processes investigated.

An interesting finding was that the choice criteria are of a dynamic nature. They are toughened or relaxed, depending upon the number of approved suppliers on the bid list, the number of suppliers submitting acceptable bids, and whether the situation warrants single or multiple sources. If the item to be purchased is new, and all of the potential vendors are new (not dealt with previously), the same criteria are applicable to all of them for qualifying as an approved source. If the potential vendors included some with whom the company has dealt previously, their past performance weighs heavily in both the qualifying and selecting process.

Once quotes are received, they are analyzed and made comparable. Those that meet product specifications and delivery remain for final evaluation. The price, thereafter, becomes a predominant factor in narrowing the choice. The supplier who provides the greatest value to the buyer receives the order.

The study demonstrated that it is possible to develop flow chart decision models for qualifying suppliers to receive RFQs, and for final vendor choice, using multiple methods of data collection. The buyers were observed to use specific choice heuristics during the entire decision process. These heuristics seemed to already exist in the purchasing agents' memories, but required further processing to apply, depending upon the situation. This observation supports the choice theory developed by Bettman and Zins (1977).

It seems appropriate at this time to quote Hamilton and Wilson (1972) again:

> Waste in marketing, were it only quantifiable, would, it is suspected, be of astronomic proportions. There are the problems of inadequate advertising, misdirected promotional efforts, expensive, over-elaborate and wasteful catalogues, abortive journeys and sales visits, junk direct mail; also the days and weeks of detailed planning, the operating and monitoring of complex marketing strategies, which are doomed from the outset to failure or at best to limited success because of the lack of understanding of buying.

Hopefully, this study has contributed to understanding industrial buying as it actually occurs.

Appendix:
Research Methodology

The need for research on supplier choices in long-term contract negotiations in naturalistic settings was shown in chapter 1. The supplier choice process occurs in five stages: (1) developing an RFQ; (2) searching for potential suppliers; (3) evaluating and selecting suppliers to bid on the required item; (4) analyzing the quotes; and (5) evaluating and selecting suppliers.

This research provides a detailed examination of the choice process during these five stages. In addition, the three objectives of this study are, as mentioned earlier:

Identifying persons (or departments) involved in the choice process, and learning how differences are resolved;

Determining if there is centralization in negotiating long-term contracts and if so, the reasons for this;

Determining what criteria are used in selecting suppliers for bidding, evaluating, and awarding contracts; this includes reasons for increasing or reducing a supplier's share of available business, dropping an existing supplier, or adding a new supplier for the contract period under consideration.

The research methodology used in accomplishing these objectives is explained in this appendix.

The most frequently used marketing research approach is to hypothesize a particular decision model, and then gather data in order to accept or reject this model. However, this method is not without pitfalls. First, this approach involves evaluating the data gathered against a hypothesized model, and more than one model may be consistent with the data. Even though the hypothesis may be accepted, there is no assurance that this is actually the decision process used. Thus, in most cases one tests only input–output relationships, and not the process used in decision making. On the other hand, if the hypothesis is rejected, one is no closer to learning the decision process than before formulating the hypothesis.

Second, and perhaps more critical in industrial purchasing, is the requirement that in hypothesizing a particular model for testing, the researcher should have some theoretical or empirical basis for choosing a particular model. The theoretical information currently available from which to develop a choice process model of the industrial buyer is limited in the literature.

The decision-making process in industrial buying is often complex, and the current state of knowledge about these processes is still in its infancy. There is a widespread recognition of the inadequacy of the industrial marketer's grasp of his customers' decision process (Robinson, Faris, and Wind 1967). Therefore, to gain a basic understanding of this process, a descriptive study was conducted, in which no attempt was made to manipulate specific predetermined independent variables.

The following basic characteristics of the research methodology should be noted:

1. The research emphasis is on collecting qualitative rather than quantitative data, in the natural day-to-day working environment of industrial organizations. The attempt is made to conduct "direct research," as described by Mintzberg (1979).
2. A combination of data collection methods, termed "triangulation," is used to investigate the decision process. The following methods of data collection were combined: protocol analysis; structured and unstructured interviews; experience survey; direct observations; and unobtrusive techniques.

The advantages and limitations of the above methods are discussed in the first section of this appendix. The second section describes in detail how each method is actually used in collecting the data required for the research.

Naturalistic Mode of Inquiry

The naturalistic method of inquiry results in a penetration of the everyday world of interaction in organizations. The fundamental goal of the naturalistic method is to develop theories that explain the attitudes, feelings, and actual behaviors of those observed. The language and commercial terms used by those studied must be understood. Their activities while at work, interactions within and outside of their departments, and the social relationships they form must all be described and analyzed to fit within the theoretical framework that reflects the everyday realities of participants. Central to such a method are research strategies such as participant observation, unobtrusive methods, historical–comparative techniques, interviews, grounded theory constructions, and triangulation (the combination of research methods). These strategies do not produce readily classifiable, quantitative data; rather, the data are qualitative in nature.

The quantitative method rests upon what may be termed the principle of objectivism. This principle holds that the closer one comes to the subject matter, the less objective the researcher can be in comprehending the behaviors studied. A distance must therefore be maintained between the investigator and the objects of investigation. Most typically, this is accomplished through the use of a structured interview format, or through the analysis of census data.

Neither the method of naturalistic inquiry nor its logic have been well understood through the years, though the method dates from Darwin in the nineteenth century. The naturalistic method has typically been designated as "soft science," as premature scientific inquiry (Lundberg 1929), and as non-scientific, nonproductive activity (Becker 1970; Blalock 1971).

Denzin (1978) attempts to explicate this method and the approach.

> Naturalists or symbolic interactionalists as they call them, consider this principle of "objectivism" to be a fallacy and base their philosophy of science upon the principle of subjectivism. Concurrent with the naturalistic method, this principle argues that one must become closely involved with those persons, situations and organizational groups for which one's theory is intended to account. Without such an involvement, a distorted account will invariably be presented.

The quantitative method assumes a world of causal analysis that rests upon clearly definable, independent, contingent, intervening, and dependent variables. Rather than asking how well its category system represents the empirical world, this methodology requires that the empirical world be fitted to the preconceived methods, techniques, and modes of inquiry. Rather than attempting to mirror empirical phenomena, this method accepts only those phenomena that are reflected through responses to attitude scales, social indicators, and census categories. The resulting picture of the world is a distorted image. The naturalistic mode of inquiry, on the other hand, reflects a respect for the everyday world of natural interaction. This method reflects the demands of that world, and attempts to reveal how the researcher's methods may be fitted to the study of ongoing patterns of organizational and social interaction.

Denzin (1978), working from this perspective, takes the position that the cardinal feature of any science must be its grounding in the empirical world. The ultimate test of the scientist's actions is an ability to reveal, describe, and explain the empirical world.

In addition to using the naturalistic method of data collection, Mintzberg's suggestions (1979) were constantly kept in mind while data was collected for the investigation. Mintzberg calls this approach "direct research," and describes seven basic themes of this activity:

1. Direct research is as purely descriptive as one is able to make it. Mintzberg believes that this pure form of research has illustrated that managerial work observed has more to do with interruption, action orientation, and verbal communication than coordination and controlling.

2. Direct research relies on simple, in a sense, inelegant methodologies. Mintzberg indicates that the field of organization theory has paid dearly for its obsession with rigor in the choice of methodology. Too often, results have been significant only in the statistical sense of the word. In his work, Mintzberg found that simpler, more direct methodologies yielded more useful results; for example, one direct methodology is sitting down in a manager's office and watching what he or she does. Given a hundred people, each prepared to do one year of research, is it better to have each person study a hundred organizations, resulting in superficial data on ten thousand organizations? Or, is it better to have each person study one company, providing in-depth data on one hundred companies? The choice is obviously dependent on what is being studied. However, the small sample must not be precluded, as it has often proven to be superior.

3. The direct research can be as purely inductive as possible. Deduction is certainly a part of science, but induction is just as much a part of scientific inquiry. Mintzberg thinks that induction is more interesting, challenging, and attractive because of its potential for discovering something new. The deductive approach often simply confirms or denies what is already thought to be known. The data do not generate the theory; only the researchers do. "Indeed it seems that the more deeply we probe into this field of organizations, the more complex we find it to be, and the more we need to fall back on so-called exploratory, as opposed to 'rigorous,' research methodologies."

4. Direct research is nonetheless systematic in nature. The direct research approach does not offer license to "fish at random." No matter how small the sample or what the interest is, the researcher always goes into organizations with a well-defined focus, to collect specific kinds of data systematically.

5. The research measures in real organizational terms. This involves, first of all, getting out into the field, into real organizations. Simply mailing questionnaires will not do; nor will conducting laboratory simulations, at least not in policy research. Mintzberg contends: "We do not yet understand enough about organizations to simulate their functioning in the laboratory. It is their inherent complexity and dynamic nature that characterize phenomena such as policy making. Simplification squeezes out the very thing on which the research should focus." Measuring in real organizational terms means measuring things that actually happen in organizations, as they are experienced.

6. Direct research, by its intensive nature, ensures that systematic data are

supported by anecdotal data. Theory building seems to require rich description, the richness that comes from anecdote. Mintzberg argues: "There is more and more need to be on site and to be there long enough to be able to understand what is going on. To miss this in research is to miss the very lifeblood of the organization."

7. Direct research seeks to synthesize, to integrate diverse elements into configurations of ideals or pure types. Pattern recognition is what the researcher is after. Mintzberg sums up his approach as follows: "Research based on description and induction instead of implicit or explicit prescription and deduction; reliance on simple, inelegant, as opposed to 'rigorous' methods of data collection, the measurement of many elements in real organization terms, supported by anecdote, instead of few variables in perceptual terms from a distance."

Triangulation

A researcher interested in studying the decision process of industrial buyers' supplier choices must consider a variety of approaches. Woodside and Sherrell (1980) advocate multiple methods of data collection for analyzing and describing purchase decision processes. Reaching valid conclusions on supplier choice processes that hold for more than one company requires cross-industry research, using more than one data collection method, and contacts with several persons in each firm.

Sociologists suggest that no single method of data collection is free of flaws; no single method adequately deals with all the problems of data analysis; and no single method yields all the data necessary for testing a theory. Consequently, the researcher must combine methods in a process termed "triangulation"; that is, empirical events must be examined from the vantage provided by utilizing as many methods as possible. Triangulation is broadly defined by Denzin (1978) as the combination of methodologies in the study of the same phenomena. The triangulation metaphor is from navigation and military strategy; this strategy uses multiple reference points to locate an object's exact position (Smith 1975). Given the basic principles of geometry, multiple viewpoints allow for greater accuracy. Similarly, organizational researchers can improve the accuracy of their judgments by collecting different kinds of data on the same phenomena.

In social science, the use of triangulation can be traced to Campbell and Fiske (1959), who developed the idea of "multiple operationism." They argued that more than one method should be used in the validation process to ensure that the variance reflected is that of the trait and not of the method. Thus, convergence or agreement between two methods enhances belief that the results are valid, and not a methodological artifact (Bouchard 1976).

This kind of triangulation is labeled by Denzin (1978) as the between (or cross) methods type, and represents the most popular use of triangulation. It is largely a vehicle for cross validation, when two or more distinct methods are found to be congruent, and yield comparable data. For organizational researchers, this involves the use of multiple methods to examine the same dimension of a research problem. For example, the reasons for switching suppliers of items purchased under long-term contracts can be studied by interviewing purchasing managers, surveying others in the purchasing departments, observing their behavior, and evaluating company records. The focus is always on the reason for the switch, but the mode of data collection varies. Multiple and independent measures, if they do reach the same conclusions, provide a more accurate and valid portrayal of the switching of suppliers.

Thus, no single research method is uniformly superior. Each has its strengths and weaknesses. Denzin (1978) suggests: "It is the time for organizational researchers to recognize this fact and move on to the position that permits them to approach their problems with all relevant and appropriate methods and to the strategy of methodological triangulation."

Companies

To meet the research objectives, research was conducted in six different industrial organizations in the southeastern United States. The purchasing managers of several organizations in this area were contacted, and asked to participate in the research. The contacts were achieved first by telephone and then in writing, followed by personal meetings in most cases. A 1978–79 roster published by the Purchasing Management Association of the Carolinas and Virginia, Inc., was used to obtain names, addresses, and telephone numbers of these organizations, including the names of purchasing managers. Formal permission was obtained from the Purchasing Management Association to contact members to request cooperation in research. The search was continued until permission was obtained from six organizations.

The organizations and individuals participating in this research prefer to remain anonymous. Therefore, the names of the companies and participants are disguised. The participating companies are described below:

1. A division of a large conglomerate referred to as Apex Products, manufacturing staple fiber and having its own purchasing department.
2. A division of a large international company called Chapman Machines, which builds heavy machinery, and has its own purchasing department that operates independently of purchasing departments of the company's other divisions.

3. A division of a large, high technology international manufacturer of sophisticated engineering products, referred to as Regal Technologies, this division has a local purchasing department.
4. A staple fiber plant operating under the chemical division of a very large international conglomerate, referred to as Evans Products, this plant has its own purchasing department.
5. One of the largest leading international chemical companies, called Diamond International, the company has centralized regional purchasing centers; each center is responsible for purchasing items required by eight to ten manufacturing plants located in a specific region. The southeast purchasing center cooperated in conducting this research.
6. A medium-sized electric utility company called Southeast Electric Company.

Detailed descriptions of each company are provided in chapters 4, 5, 6, 7, 8 and 9.

Although this is a convenience sample, it represents a broad cross section of industries manufacturing diverse products.

Long-term Contract Negotiations

Research efforts were focused on the decision process of choosing suppliers for items purchased under long-term contracts. In essence, these are open-ended, blanket-type purchase orders used by buyers to purchase a high volume of repetitive, sometimes off-the-shelf, standard products. Items purchased under long-term contracts are usually used in regular production to form part of the finished product, although some maintenance, repairs, and operations (MRO) items are also purchased under long term contracts. Items purchased on a one-time basis are excluded, such as capital equipment or items purchased in emergency situations, in which formal quotations may not be invited from other vendors. The contract period may vary from one year to an indefinite period. In the case of "evergreen" contracts, the contract is terminated only when the buyer or seller decides to terminate, and informs the other party of this decision in writing.

Selection of Items to Study the Decision Process

In order to collect the necessary data, the purchase decision process used in making supplier choices was studied in-depth for three items in each company. Thus, eighteen items were thoroughly investigated. As many different items as possible were selected for the study, meeting the following criteria: (1) the item is purchased on a long-term contract; (2) the dollar volume is high, preferably greater than $100,000 per year; and (3) there is input from at least two or three individuals from the company in the purchasing process.

A detailed description of each item regarding its use, quantity purchased, dollar volume, and specifications, is given in chapters 2 through 7.

Initial Interviews: Identifying the Buying Center

Several contacts were made by telephone and mail with the purchasing department heads of each division of the above companies, to gain their company's full approval for research. Prior to giving their approval, department heads were appraised of the objective of the research. Also, the need for their cooperation was stressed.

The initial face-to-face meeting was arranged with individuals in the purchasing departments. The purchasing manager introduced the researcher and explained the objective of the research to the employees. This provided an opportunity for the researcher to become acquainted with the company, and the individuals with whom he would be spending time conducting the actual research. This meeting was very helpful in attaining the necessary cooperation from persons involved in the purchasing process. Denzin (1978) points out:

> In a wide variety of instances, the research act comes alive during the interview, when the researcher is forced to confront the observational units on a direct, face-to-face basis. He or she must convince persons that they should be interviewed, get them to set aside time for the interview, and keep them conscious of what the interview is about. Silent, deviant, hostile, or overly verbal respondents represent problems which must be recognized.

These initial meetings were indeed useful in minimizing the above problems.

The second purpose of the meeting was to select three items per company to study, keeping in mind the criteria presented earlier. After the items were selected, each of them was discussed briefly with the purchasing agent responsible for the purchase of that item; the agent's manager was also included in this discussion.

One important question asked by the researcher during this meeting was: Who are the other individuals in the company contributing to the supplier choice decisions for the item under investigation? The names of these individuals were recorded, and a request was made to interview these people at their convenience. This was an attempt to identify the members of the "buying center." Moriarty and Baleson (1980) suggest: "If the conceptual problems in the study of organizational buying centers are to be resolved, then it is necessary to develop methodology capable of interviewing multiple members of the buying center. One approach to this methodological problem is the idea of snowballing."

The basic technique of snowballing is fairly straightforward. In a single-stage snowball, a known member of the buying center is asked to provide information on who else is involved in the decision-making process. These individuals are subsequently studied. Multiple-stage snowballing involves asking all of the respondents in the first stage who is involved in the buying center; this generates the second stage, and so on. In exhaustive snowballing, this process is continued until no new buying centers can be determined. The definition of involvement is highly complex, and depends upon (1) the category of the item purchased, that is, MRO, production, or capital equipment; (2) the cut-off selected to screen individuals according to their impact on the decision; and (3) the type of decision selected.

For example, in the case of a certain MRO item such as replacement parts for specific equipment, the maintenance supervisor may indicate that the part is made by a single manufacturer only, and may write "no substitutes" on the purchase requisition, because no other part will fit. The buying center for studying supplier choice in this case consists of two people; these are the maintenance supervisor and the purchasing agent. The purchasing agent makes the final decision on whether to buy the part from the manufacturer or a distributor, depending upon availability and price.

For the purpose of the present study, the second criterion (mentioned above) is crucial in screening individuals to consider including them as members of the buying center. During the initial interviews, it was found that for supplier choice decisions, individuals outside the purchasing department usually made only boundary decisions, such as accept/reject. In other words, only those individuals with the authority to tell the purchasing department if a certain supplier was to be accepted or rejected were included in the study. Using this criterion, exhaustive snowballing was used to select the respondents who were to be recognized as members of the buying center for supplier choice decisions.

Instruments of Data Collection

Questionnaires

To maintain the research focus, a fifteen-page detailed questionnaire was designed. The following data were collected for each item under investigation, with the help of the questionnaire:

Process of selecting suppliers to send RFQs:

number of suppliers sent RFQs

means of obtaining their names

type of information gathered about suppliers

criteria used in narrowing down the list of suppliers used for sending RFQs

if there is a maximum or minimum number of suppliers selected to be sent RFQs, and reasons for selecting that specific number of suppliers

Supplier selection for awarding contracts:

criteria used in comparing quotes

individuals involved in selecting suppliers

reasons for using a centralized or decentralized purchasing process

reasons for using single or multiple sources

criteria used in splitting the volume of available business in the case of multiple sources

influence of personal like/dislike toward sales representatives in supplier choice

influence of reciprocity

preference given to minority businesses

reasons for switching suppliers, and increasing/decreasing suppliers' share of available business.

In-depth Interviews

Using the above-mentioned questionnaire, an in-depth interview was conducted with members of the buying center for each item. This interview lasted from three to four hours per individual in the purchasing department. Next, the researcher requested an interview with persons outside the purchasing department who were involved in the decision process. In all cases, this request was granted. However, in some cases clearance from a department head was required.

During the interview, interruptions were minimal, with the exception of urgent phone calls, which were usually brief. Everyone interviewed had set time aside in daily work schedules for the interview.

Denzin (1978) draws some distinctions between the various types of interviewing techniques:

An interview is any face-to-face conversational exchange wherein one person elicits information from another, but a variety of types can be noted. There are those interviews that rest on a highly structured format. Here one set of questions, placed in the same order, is given to all respondents. This strategy, which has the potential of eliciting common information from all respondents, rests upon the assumption that questions can be worded and ordered in a way that will be understood by all respondents. However, this assumption may sometimes be unfounded. It can be argued that few respondents share the same perspective, and few words, terms, or concepts elicit the same response from different respondents.

A variation of the highly structured method is the focused interview or the nonscheduled standardized interview. Here, the interviewer works with a fixed list of questions or problems to be covered but alters that list and when required, rephrases questions to respondents. This is a strategy which has the benefits of eliciting common information grounded in the perspective of those observed.

For the purpose of this study, the focused interview technique, as suggested by Denzin (1978), was used, because the respondents interviewed came from different backgrounds such as engineering, purchasing, quality control, and production.

Most persons interviewed responded a good deal beyond the original questions. During the entire interview, the researcher kept a very low profile. The interview started with the researcher making the following statement: "Not much is known at the academic level as to how industry actually buys, especially the selection of suppliers for initial bids and the final supplier selection to award long-term contracts. This research is an attempt to learn and understand this important aspect of industrial buying."

This statement made the respondents feel important, and willing to give the researcher as much information as possible. They projected themselves to be experts, who gave vivid descriptions of interesting situations encountered during their purchasing careers with sales representatives, and other departments such as engineering, quality control, and production.

No attempts were made to interrupt the respondents, as it was clear that they found it a unique opportunity to talk to someone from the academic world about their experiences and activities. The researcher was initially apprehensive about whether the respondents would talk freely, or if they would devote the necessary time to the researcher from their busy schedules, or if they would express their feelings and ideas freely and openly. However, by the time the research was ended, these doubts were completely dispelled.

During the in-depth interviews, questions asked pertained to specific items under investigation. However, a majority of the respondents extended their answers to include other items, and gave examples of when the answer given was applicable, and when it was not. For example, this question was asked:

"Do you consolidate requirements from your other plants on long-term contracts for this item?" A typical answer:

> No, we don't for this item. The reason is that this item is special for this plant; no other plant uses it. However, we do have central purchasing at our corporate office. The corporate boys negotiate long-term contracts for other items such as computer cards or fluorescent lamps that all the plants use. But here again, if we can buy those same items locally for less money, we don't have to purchase through corporate contracts. You may like to note that in many instances we do get better prices locally. You know why? Because the corporate boys negotiate these contracts while wining and dining, and are taken for a ride by those big companies.

Thus, as the research progressed, the picture developed not only about the decision process for the specific items being investigated, but also about decisions applicable to long-term contract negotiations.

Interviews with members of the buying center were the basic source of data collection for this study in revealing the decision process of supplier selection. This was complemented by other research methods, as described below.

Protocol Analysis

In protocol analysis, the person being investigated talks aloud as he or she performs a specific cognitive task. The person's comments are recorded, and later analyzed. Inferences are made from the protocol data about the hidden mental processes used by the individual performing the cognitive task. Protocol analysis has been applied to marketing situations to reveal the brand choice and purchase decision processes of clothing, grocery, and beer consumers (Alexis, Haines, and Simon 1959; Bettman 1970; Woodside and Fleck 1979).

The length of time required for an industrial buying decision to be completed does create problems in using the protocol technique. One possible alternative to studying a "real-world" purchase decision would be to study a purchase decision in a hypothetical buying situation. Industrial buyers may be presented with information similar to that of a real-world situation. Upon receiving the information, the industrial buyer would proceed to make the purchase decision as a normal purchase decision. The use of hypothetical buying situations permits the researcher to control the variables of interest, and contract the time span to a length feasible for study. Normally the time span may be contracted to one or two hours. The buying game approach permits the use of protocol analysis in studying the industrial buying decision process. Cardozo and Cagley (1971) used this approach in studying a group of sixty-four industrial buyers.

Protocol analysis using hypothetical buying situations certainly solves the problem of length of time involved in the real-world buying situation, but it overly simplifies the entire purchase decision process. This simplification removes the very focus of the research; therefore, this method was not used in the present study.

Another approach that should be considered is a postpurchase protocol analysis. This approach has been used by Wind (1976) and Stiles (1973). Once the purchase decision has been completed, the researcher asks the industrial buyer to recall and record the thought processes he used in making the purchase decision. This method certainly provides more insight into the decision than hypothesizing a particular buying situation, but it also has limitations.

The use of postpurchase protocol analysis may permit the industrial buyer to introduce into the protocol some additional analyses and rationalizations that may not have actually been used at the time of the purchase decision. This is one shortcoming of the method. A second limitation is the amount of time involved in a purchase decision. Normally, an industrial purchase decision occurs over several days to several weeks. This may result in the industrial buyers' distorting or forgetting factors and rationales considered during the buying process. Further, because industrial buying is a joint decision-making process, a protocol taken from only one person may not accurately reflect the process being investigated.

An alternative to this approach is to use the protocol technique only for those stages in the decision process over which one person may have control. For lack of better terminology, this approach may be called the segmented protocol technique. This technique was used in this study during the in-depth interviews.

To further minimize the limitations of the postpurchase protocol described above, the items selected for study were those purchased as recently as possible. Most items investigated were for the contract period from January 1980, and the contracts were either negotiated just a few weeks prior to the interview, or were being negotiated at that time. Also, the postpurchase protocol was supplemented by document analysis to reduce the effect of possible distortion in the respondents' postpurchase protocol.

The respondents, when asked a question about making a choice crucial to the entire decision process, began to think aloud as if they were making that same choice again. At the same time, they suggested ways in which the choice might differ in other situations, and reasons for this. For example, the question was asked in the case of multiple sources: How do you split the volume between the two sources? A typical answer:

> Let's see. For this item the specifications are quite important. Suppliers X and Y both meet specifications and we have done business with both in the past.

However, if one of them was a new supplier, the choice will be to give the smaller volume of business, say 25 to 30 percent, to this new supplier and treat him as a secondary source. But in this case, it does not apply. On-time delivery record of both X and Y is pretty good, although X had some problems, but those are straightened out now. Both X and Y are known for their quality. Neither of these two have labor contract negotiations due in 1980. However, if any one of them had labor contracts expiring in 1980, I would be quite hesitant to give him a major share of the business. What's next? Yes, supplier X was our prime source in 1979. He is aware of our revised specifications. They worked closely last year with our industrial engineering and quality control people. Finally, it looks like they have understood our requirements and idiosyncracies. But look here—they are about 4.3 percent higher in price compared to Y. I would like to see supplier X as our prime source this year too, but not at this higher price. I will give them a chance and tell them their price is a little high and see if they can come down.

Will you reveal how much they are higher than Y?

Not really, not unless he asked. You know, you will be surprised to find the majority of salesmen don't ask for this type of information. Now, I don't usually give out this information to everyone, only when I am eager to do business with them. My usual response is "I can't tell you that." One thing for sure, I do not reveal the name of the competition. It's good to keep them guessing. A smart salesman really does not expect you to tell him exactly how much higher his bid is, but he normally starts probing. He is smart enough to know that if his price is higher than 10 percent as compared to competition, I would not have even called him. He knows that he should be around 5 to 7 percent higher. So he starts out, "Should we come down about 2 to 3 percent?" I may say, "No, that's not enough." He may say, "How about 4 percent?" I will then say, "Do the best you can and we'll see."

Now, if he comes down 4 percent, I will give him 60 to 70 percent of the business, and the remaining business to Y. But in this case, he did not reduce the price at all. Look—the salesman's hands are tied. He does not have the authority to reduce the price. He has to contact his plant personnel. They look at their cost, how much business they have on hand and so on. But again, because X did not reduce their price, I split the business 60–40 between Y and X, X getting 40 percent because his price is high.

As is evident from these comments, this is not strictly postpurchase protocol for the entire decision process of supplier choice, but only provides information on how the volume of business was split between sources. This is a protocol describing how the respondent would have generally made the choice, and how he actually made the choice of splitting the volume in a specific situation. This is a description of the process as it occurred, rather than a hypothetical situation with other things held constant.

Unstructured Interviews

Two respondents indicated that there were certain matters, such as the "role of personal friendship in supplier choices," that could not be discussed freely during office hours. Therefore, separate meetings were arranged after hours, ranging from three to four hours per respondent. During these meetings, respondents talked freely about the ethics of purchasing, how actual negotiations occurred, how the purchasing agent could help his favorite source if he wanted to, how top management might favor certain suppliers, and problems faced by his department.

Detailed notes were taken during each meeting. These interviews were extremely helpful in increasing understanding of the role of human elements in the decision-making process, and achieving a balance between the two extreme points of view. One extreme is the belief that industrial supplier choice decisions are rational, based solely on hard data; the other is that the decision process is idiosyncratic, irrational, and based primarily on likes and dislikes of those making the choices.

The Unobstrusive Method: Analysis of Purchase Documents

The unobtrusive method removes the investigator from direct participation in the events at hand. The logic underlying this approach is simple; because known observers create reactive effects, the researcher is removed from the situation. The investigator can undertake serious document analysis in an uncontaminated fashion, fitting findings into a naturalistic, interactionist perspective.

In addition, the unobtrusive approach offers a means of buttressing the findings from more traditional interview and survey methods. Findings from these reactive methods can be complemented and assessed by the nonreactive findings of the unobtrusive approach. Whereas the interview serves as a means to probe the subjective side of respondents' actions, the unobtrusive method basically probes the public side of their conduct.

After the formal in-depth interview, the researcher requested permission to study the file pertaining to the item under investigation. The researcher was able to obtain the files on every item studied. However, in one case he was instructed that no copies could be made of documents in the file, because of the confidential nature of the item studied. For the remaining items, permission to make copies of certain important documents was obtained, under the condition that they would be used only for analyzing the data, and not included as part of this book. The files contained valuable information and documents, concerning the entire decision process for that particular item, such as:

1. Specifications, including drawings for the item to be purchased;
2. Purchase requisition(s) from the user department, indicating quantity needed for the contract period, and the delivery schedule;
3. Interdepartmental memos concerning comments on vendor literature, minutes of meetings held with vendors, evaluation of sample performance, and test results;
4. Reports of vendor plant visits made by individuals from purchasing, engineering, and quality control departments;
5. List of names and locations of possible suppliers;
6. Copies of the RFQ sent to various suppliers;
7. Quotations submitted by various suppliers;
8. Written comments on vendor bids when requested by the purchasing department from other departments such as engineering, operations, and quality control;
9. Communications with vendors requesting clarifications on the bids when required, including the supplier's response;
10. Bid evaluation chart prepared by the purchasing department, including the final selection of vendors;
11. Copy of the formal purchase order sent to successful vendors;
12. If the order was not placed with the bidder with the lowest price, a written explanation by the purchasing agent for rejecting lower bids; this is a requirement of the company's auditors; and
13. Interdepartmental memos on vendor evaluation, long-range supply situation for the item under consideration, risk involved in single-source situations when applicable, means available for cost reduction, and reasons for reducing or increasing the quantity ordered, or for cancelling the order when situations dictate such actions.

The researcher spent two to four hours studying the documents on file for each item. If the file contained a name of or communications from someone within the company who influenced the supplier choice decision for that item, and if that name was not mentioned by those interviewed, it was added to the interview list.

If the researcher had questions pertaining to documents in the file, these were answered by the appropriate people. At least two persons were interviewed for each item investigated; at least one of these was from outside of the purchasing department. When the individual to be interviewed was outside the plant visited by the researcher, he or she was interviewed by telephone. Copies of important documents on file were made by the researcher when he had obtained permission to make such copies.

The documentation of purchasing is considered to be a very important aspect of record keeping by industrial organizations. Company auditors have access to these files, and purchasing records are subject to audit at any time. Thus, purchasing records were well kept in the company files, and were a very convenient data collection tool for the researcher.

Direct Observations in Natural Settings

Direct observation can be used as a tool of scientific inquiry. Such observations are scientifically planned and recorded to relate to the specific phenomenon of interest. This method represents commitment on the part of the investigator to study as intimately as possible the experiences of those being investigated. This requires that the investigator learn their language, and understand their actions. Denzin (1978) pointed out: "The observer must, as much as possible, learn to view the world of the subjects from their perspective. Preconceptions and stereotypes must be forsaken; a flexible and relativistic stance must be adopted."

The observer may subtly influence the subjects' actions when this method is used. This is because in direct observation, the observer makes his or her presence known, and attempts to become accepted within the group's activity structure. Denzin (1978) specifies the following criteria that the direct observation method of data collection should meet:

1. The observer must gain entry into the group to be studied, and this entry must permit repeated returns.
2. The observer must establish and maintain an identity that will permit ongoing social (organizational) relationships and continuing observations.
3. The observer must attempt not to alter the behavior of those observed, but must attempt to fit into the natural flow and rhythm of the social (organizational) structure.
4. The observer must remain objective in the face of new experiences, and must not be taken in by those being studied.
5. The observer must develop a reliable and dependable method for recording field notes.
6. The observer must be prepared to leave the field situation at the proper time, and must have a theoretical grasp of the data so that the exit time is easily discernable.

These suggestions were constantly kept in mind while data was collected during direct observations.

The researcher spent a week to ten days at each company location. During this time, many sales representatives from various organizations visited the purchasing department and other personnel at the companies visited. The researcher, with the permission of the purchasing department, sat in on at least one meeting with a sales representative of any supplier making a sales call related to an item under investigation. The researcher was introduced to the participants at the beginning of meetings, which lasted fifteen minutes to two hours.

These observations were useful in helping to understand how sales representatives try to establish a rapport with individuals in buying organizations, and how they act as sources of information to those in purchasing departments on price trends, raw material availability, management changes in their organizations as well as in competing organizations, and changes in manufacturing processes for items of interest to buying organizations.

Observing how sales representatives tried to establish trust and credibility was also valuable.

Experience Survey

The experience survey attempts to tap the reservoir of knowledge and expertise of those familiar with the general subject being investigated. Therefore, a probability sample is not used for an experience survey, as it would be a waste of time to interview those with little competence or relevant experience with the object of study. It is important that in such a survey, the purposeful selection of respondents should be of persons from a number of different groups.

In a structured questionnaire, questions are presented in exactly the same words and in exactly the same order to all respondents. The reason for this standardization is obviously to ensure that all respondents reply to the same question. In a typical structured, undisguished questionnaire, responses as well as questions are standardized. Fixed alternative questions are used, in which the subject's responses are limited to stated alternatives. The purpose of the question is clear and undisguised.

There are several advantages to the structured, undisguised questionnaire. Perhaps its greatest advantage is that it is simple to administer, and easy to tabulate and analyze. The respondent should experience little difficulty in answering questions. Thus, responses should be reliable; that is, if the respondent was asked the same question again, the response would be the same (assuming no change in attitude).

The fixed alternative questionnaire is reliable for several reasons. First, the frame of reference in which the respondent replies is often obvious from the alternatives. Second, the provision of alternative responses often helps to make the question clear. The provision of dimensions in which to frame the reply helps to assure the question's reliability.

The reliability of fixed, alternative questions sometimes has an associated cost of less validity, in that answers do not necessarily reflect the true state of affairs accurately. This loss of validity occurs for several reasons. First, the provision of fixed alternatives may force a response to a question on which the subject does not have an opinion. This is particularly true when "no opinion" or "not a reason" categories are not provided as alternatives. Another possible way the fixed alternative response may reduce validity is that the response categories themselves may introduce bias. This is particularly problematic when an appropriate response is omitted because of an oversight, or insufficient prior research into appropriate response categories. The provision of an "other" category may eliminate this bias. However, in using a fixed alternative question, one should be reasonably certain that the alternatives adequately cover the range of possible replies.

Keeping in mind the advantages and limitations of fixed alternative questions, a survey questionnaire of this type was developed. This was an attempt to focus on the question of what factors affect the increase or decrease in a supplier's share of available business, as well as the factors responsible for adding or dropping a supplier. The fixed alternatives were developed after in-depth interviews were conducted with purchasing agents, and an "other" category was included to improve the validity of the results.

The questionnaires were given to forty-three purchasing agents in the companies visited. They were asked to complete them at their convenience, and either mail them to the researcher, or hand them to him while he was still with the company conducting research. All of the questionnaires were returned, some by mail; the rest were picked up personally by the researcher after a couple of reminders to respondents.

The information received through the questionnaires supplemented that collected through other data collection methods. It also allowed statistical analysis and tests on data collected by this method to be performed.

Decision Process Flow Charts

Based on the data collected from structured and unstructured interviews, analysis of documents, and direct observations, flow charts were prepared for each item studied. These depict the decision process of selecting suppliers for initial bids, and then choosing suppliers with whom to place orders, among those who submitted bids. These flow charts were then shown to individuals involved in the decision process, who were to confirm whether the flow chart accurately depicted the process under investigation. With minor modifications, all respondents agreed that these flow charts were a good representation of what actually occurred.

These flow charts were extremely valuable in developing two models of supplier choice processes: one to select suppliers for inviting bids, and the other to select suppliers to award contracts after receiving bids.

Summary

Multiple methods of data collection were combined in this research study. Further, data collection was done in the naturalistic setting. Direct research methodology, as advocated by Mintzberg (1979), was used most advantageously in conducting this research. This approach is largely qualitative, but at the same time, scientific. Downey and Ireland (1979) concur:

> Both qualitative and quantitative data have their place in organizational research. The objectivity that is desired in scientific inquiry refers to objectivity on the part of the researcher. Subjective behavior on the part of those being studied, however, may well be a legitimate topic for scientific inquiry.

References

Abernathy, W.J., and J.A. Utterback. 1975. "Innovation and the Evolving Structure of the Firm." Unpublished paper, HBS 75–18. Harvard University.

Alexis, M., G. Haines, and L. Simon. 1959. "Consumer Information Processing." In *Marketing and New Science of Planning.* Edited by R. King. Chicago: American Marketing Association.

Berman, H.J. 1969. "Rating System Has Vendor's Number." *Journal of Purchasing* 7:71–74.

Brand, G. 1972. *The Industrial Buying Decision.* London: Cassell/Associated Business Programs.

Bubb, P.L., and D.J. Van Rest. 1973. "Loyalty as a Component of the Industrial Buying Decision." *Industrial Marketing Management* 3:145–153.

Buckner, H. 1967. *How British Industry Buys.* London: Hutchinson & Company.

Buzzell, R.D., B.T. Gale, and R.G.M. Sultan. 1975. "Market Share—A Key to Profitability." *Harvard Business Review* 75:97–106.

Cardozo, R.N., and J.W. Cagley. 1971. "Experimental Study of Industrial Buyer Behavior." *Journal of Marketing Research* 8:329–334.

Corey, E.R. 1978. *Procurement Management: Strategy, Organization and Decision Making.* Boston: CBI Publishing Company.

Crow, L.E. 1974. "An Information Processing Approach to Industrial Buying: The Search and Choice Process." Ph.D. dissertation, Indiana University.

Cunningham, M.T., and J.G. White. 1973. "The Determinants of Choice of Supplier." *European Journal of Marketing* 7:55–67.

Cyert, R.M., and J.G. March. 1963. *A Behavioral Theory of the Firm.* Englewood Cliffs, N.J.: Prentice-Hall.

Cyert, R.M., H.A. Simon, and D.B. Trow. 1956. "Observation of a Business Decision." *Journal of Business* 29:237–248.

Dauner, J.R. 1967. "The Attitude of the Purchasing Agent toward Reciprocity." *Journal of Purchasing* 3:5–15.

Dean, J.W. 1987. "Decision Processes in the Adoption of Advanced Technology." Unpublished paper. University Park: College of Business Administration, Pennsylvania State University.

Denzin, N.K. 1978. "The Logic of Naturalistic Inquiry." In *Sociological Methods: A Sourcebook.* Edited by N.K. Denzin. New York: McGraw Hill.

———. 1983. "Interpretive Interactionism." In *Beyond Method* pp. 129–146. Edited by G. Morgan. Beverly Hills: Sage Publications.

Deutcsch, C.H. 1973. "Reciprocal Trade: It's Still an Issue." *Journal of Purchasing* 11:37–41.

Downey, H.K., and R.D. Ireland. 1979. "Quantitative versus Qualitative: The Case of

Environment Assessment in Organizational Studies." *Administrative Science Quarterly* 24:630–637.
Dowst, S. 1967. "Purchasing and Vendor Evaluation." *Journal of Purchasing* 4:50–52.
Ellis, P.R. 1971. "Supplier Rating Sticks to Basics." *Journal of Purchasing* 9:35–36.
Hakansson, H. 1982. *International Marketing and Purchasing of Industrial Goods.* Chichester: Wiley.
Hill, R.W., and T.J. Hillier. 1977. *Organizational Buying Behavior.* London: Macmillan Press.
Hirschman, E.C. 1986. "Humanistic Inquiry in Marketing Research: Philosophy, Method, and Criteria." *Journal of Marketing Research* 23:237–249.
Hulbert, J.M. 1981. "Descriptive Models of Marketing Decisions." In *Marketing Decision Models*, pp. 19–53. Edited by R.L. Schultz and A.A. Zoltners. New York: North-Holland.
Johnston, W.J., and T.V. Bonoma. 1981. "The Buying Center: Structure and Interaction Patterns." *Journal of Marketing* 45: 143–156.
Luffman, G. 1974. "The Processing of Information by Industrial Buyers." *Industrial Marketing Management* 3:363–375.
March, J.G., and J.P. Olsen. 1986. "Garbage Can Models of Decision Making in Organizations." In *Ambiguity and Command*, pp. 11–35. Edited by J.G. March and R. Weissinger-Baylon. Marshfield, Mass.: Pitman.
Miller, D.W., and M.K. Starr. 1967. *The Structure of Human Decision.* Englewood Cliffs, N.J.: Prentice-Hall.
Mintzberg, H. 1979. "An Emerging Strategy of 'Direct' Research." *Administrative Science Quarterly* 24:582–589.
Mintzberg, H., D. Raisinghani, and A. Theoret. 1976. "The Structure of 'Unstructured' Decision Processes." *Administrative Science Quarterly* 21:246–275.
Mintzberg, H., and J.A. Waters. 1985. "Of Strategies, Deliberate and Emergent." *Strategic Management Journal* 6:257–272.
Moller, K.E.K. 1986. "Buying Behavior of Industrial Components: Inductive Approach for Descriptive Model Building." In *Research in International Marketing*. Edited by P.W. Turnbull and S.J. Paliwoda. Kent, U.K.: Croom Helm.
Monoky, J.F. 1973. "Preferences and Attitudes towards Sources of Information by Industrial Purchasing Agents as a Function of Buying Situations." Ph.D. dissertation, Pennsylvania State University.
Moriarty, R.T., and J.E.G. Baleson. 1980. "An Investigation of Alternative Research Strategies for the Study of Industrial Decision Making Units." In *Proceedings*. European Academy of Advanced Research in Marketing.
Nolan, D. 1970. "Supplier Rating Program Helps Buyers Too." *Journal of Purchasing* 8:40–41.
Parket, I.R. 1971. "The Industrial Buyer: Human But Rational." *Journal of Purchasing* 7:202–209.
Peter, J.P. 1981. "Construct Validity: A Review of Basic Issues and Marketing Practices." *Journal of Marketing Research* 18:133–145.
Pettigrew, A. 1975. "The Industrial Purchasing Decision as a Political Process." *European Journal of Marketing* 9:4–21.

Pfeffer, J. 1981. *Power in Organizations*. Boston: Pitman.
Pingry, J.R. 1972. "An Examination of the Purchasing Process of Technical Industrial Products." Ph.D. dissertation, Ohio State University.
Purchasing Survey. 1968. "Vendor Ratings: Everybody Wins." *Journal of Purchasing* 5:52–55.
Robinson, P.J., C.W. Faris, and Y. Wind. 1967. *Industrial Buying and Creative Marketing* Boston: Allyn & Bacon.
Spekman, R.E. and L.W. Stern. 1979. "Environmental Uncertainty and Buying Group Structure: An Empirical Investigation." *Journal of Marketing* 43:54–64.
Stiles, G.W. 1973. "An Information Processing Model of Industrial Buyer Behavior." *American Marketing Association Proceedings* 35:534–535.
Strauss, G. 1962. "Tactics of Lateral Relationships: The Purchasing Agent." *Administrative Science Quarterly* 4:154–171.
———. 1964. "Work-Flow Frictions, Interfunctional Rivalry and Professionalism: A Case Study of Purchasing Agents." *Human Organizations* 14:77–89.
Thain, D.H., C.B. Johnston, and D.S.R. Leighton. 1959. *How Industry Buys*. Toronto: Business Newspapers Association of Canada.
Turnbull, P.W., and S.J. Paliwoda, eds. 1986. *Research in International Marketing*. Kent, U.K.: Croom Helm.
Vyas, N.M., and A.G. Woodside 1986. "Micro Analysis of Supplier Choice Strategies: Industrial Packaging Materials." In *Industrial Marketing: A German-American Perspective*, pp. 41–68. Edited by K. Backhaus and D.T. Wilson. Berlin: Springer-Verlag.
Weigand, R.E. 1966. "Identifying Industrial Buying Responsibility." *Journal of Marketing* 30: 81–84.
Wilson, E.J. 1984. "A Case Study of Repeat Buying for a Commodity." *Industrial Marketing Management* 13 (August): 195–200.
Wind, Y. 1966. "Industrial Buying Behavior: Source Loyalty in the Purchase of Industrial Components." Ph.D. dissertation, Stanford University.
———. 1970. "Industrial Source Loyalty." *Journal of Marketing Research* 7:450–457.
Witte, E. 1972. "Field Research on Complex Decision Making Processes: The Phase Theorem." *International Studies of Management Organization* 2:156–182.
Woodside, A.G. ed. 1987. *Advances in Business Marketing*. Greenwich, Conn.: JAI Press.
Woodside, A.G., and R. Fleck. 1979. "Consumer Choice Processes: An Intensive Study of Two Cases." *Journal of Advertising Research* 19:23–32.
Woodside, A.G., and D.R. Lichtenstein. 1980. "Reasons Buyers Change a Supplier's Share." Unpublished paper. University of South Carolina.
Woodside, A.G., and D.M. Samuel. 1981. "Observation of Centralized Corporate Procurement." *Industrial Marketing Management* 10:191–205.
Woodside, A.G., and D.L. Sherrell. 1980. "New Replacement Part Buying." *Industrial Marketing Management* 9:123–132.
Zaltman, G., K. LeMasters, and M. Heffring. 1982. *Theory Construction in Marketing: Some Thoughts on Thinking*. New York: Wiley.

Index

Acetylene gas, 135
A.G. Whaley, 26, 27
Air Products, 136
Air tools, 57–64, 68
Alexis, M., 204
Amerada Hess, 92, 93, 94, 95
American Steel and Iron Institute specifications, 65, 67
Approved bidders list, 13
Arco Welders, 136
Argon, 135
Arizona Public Service Co., 187
Atlanta, Ga., 101
AT&T, xi
Automotive components manufacturing, 55

Bale caps, 79, 80–83, 158
Bale ties, 18–19, 22 27
Baleson, J.E.G., 200–201
Bar stock. *See* Steel rods
Batch mix tanks, 18, 19–22
Belton Bagging, 26
Bid submission, selection of vendors for, 23–26, 142–144, 152, 156–157; and bale caps, 81; and bale ties, 23–26; and batch mix tanks, 20–21; and cable, 142–144; and coal, 129–130; and cooling and purging gases, 136–137; and corrugated boxes, 31–32; criteria, 185; and directional valve castings, 49–50; dropping of, 60, 61; and fuel oil, 92–94; and hydraulic motors, 43–44; and investment castings, 59–60; maximum number of 50, 60, 152, 167; minimum number of, 21, 32, 50, 60, 152, 167, 169–170; no-bid response, 156–157, 174; and oleic acid, 105–106; and sealing gaskets, 117; and steel rods, 66–67; and wooden pallets, 112, and woodhog blades, 72
Boiler scaling, 93, 95
Bonoma, T.V., 8
Bounded rationality, decision theory of, 5, 182
Buzzell, R.D., xi
Buying centers: and bale caps, 80–81; and bale ties, 23; and batch mix tanks, 22; and cable, 139–142; and coal, 129; and cooling and purging gases, 136; and corrugated boxes, 30–31; and directional valve castings, 48–49; and front axles, 40–41; and fuel oil, 89–92; and hydraulic motors, 41–43; identifying, 7–8, 200–201; and investment castings, 59; and lift truck parts, 87–88; and oleic acids, 103–105; and sealing gaskets, 117; and steel rods, 66; theoretical concept, 182; and wooden pallets, 111–112; and woodhog blades, 69–72

Cable, 138–145, 155
Cagley, J.W., 186, 204
Caprolactum, 17
Carbon dioxide, 135
Cardoza, R.N., 186, 204
Carolina, Clinchfield, and Ohio Railroad, 127

Caterpillar Company, 83, 87, 88
Centralizing of purchasing. *See* Decentralization of purchasing
Charleston, S.C. 92, 93, 101, 102
Chemical production, 17, 77–78, 99–120
Chesapeake and Ohio Railway, Co., 127
Chevron, 93
Choice, economic theory of, 3–4
Choice rules. *See* Heuristic rules
Chrysler Corporation, 40
Coal, 124–135, 151; forecasting needs, 127–128; price negotiation, 181; specifications, 128–129; and transportation, 127, 130, 155
Colonial Oil Industries, Inc., 93, 94–95
Commodity prices, 59, 126, 128
Communications industry, xi
Conflict resolution, 184–185
Container Corporation, 33
Continuity of supply: and long-term contract, 72, 83–86, 104, 138, 149–151; and multiple sources, 92, 159; and price, 104–105, 159; and quantity buying, 150; and spliting order, 178; and tooling costs, 76
Contracts. *See* Long-term contracts
Contract coal, 126–127
Cooling and purging gases, 135–138, 181
Corey, E.R., 1
Corporate purchase agreement (CPA), 13, 165
Corrugated bale caps. *See* Bale caps
Corrugated boxes, 19, 27–33
Cost control, 31; and long-term contract, 65–72
Crown Zellerback, 33
Customers of vendors, contact with, 20
Cyert, R.M., 3, 5, 171, 175

Dacron, 100
Darwin, Charles, 195
Dean, J.W., 5
Decentralization of purchase, 18, 37–38, 104, 164–166, 187; and transportation costs, 105; *see also* Regional purchasing

Decision center, 4; *see also* Buying center
Decision system analysis (DSA), xiii, 6–8, 168, 185–186, 190
Delivery: late, penalty for, 181; and price, 14, 26, 32, 44, 67, 73, 82, 94–95, 106, 112, 158, 175; reliability and vendor selection, 67, 72, 137, 143, 153, 175, 177, 188; time, 144
Denzin, N.K., 6, 195, 197, 198, 200, 202–203, 209
Design engineer: and batch mix tanks, 20, 21, 22; and specifications, 20, 22, 69, 73; and woodhog blades, 69, 72, 73; and vendor evaluation and selection, 20, 21, 22, 43, 69, 72, 73
Differential choice process, 182–183
Direct observation research, 168, 169, 209–210
Direct research, 196–197
Directional valve castings, 38–39, 45–51
Distributors, buying from, 65, 116
Document analysis, 8; *see also* Records and research
Downey, H.K., 212
DSA. *See* Decision system analysis

Eastern Strapping, 26
Electric utilities, 121–147
Electrical equipment, 17
Electronics, 55
Energy departments, 100–102
Environmental concerns, 20, 89, 94, 122–123, 128
Environmental Protection Agency, 20, 128
Essex Group, Inc., 143–144, 145
Ethical issues, 69, 162, 207
Evaluation of alternatives and decision process, 4, 5
Evaluation of vendors. *See* Vendor evaluation and selection
Evergreen contracts, 39, 93, 150–151, 199
Expectancy-value model, 179
Experience survey, 168, 169, 210–211
Exxon, 92, 93, 94, 157

Faris, C.W., 185, 194
Federal Energy Regulatory Commission, 122
Feedback and decision making, 182
Fiber manufacturers, 17, 18, 78, 100, 103–110
Finishing ingredients, 102, 103–110
Fleck, R., 204
Flow diagrams, xiii, 6, 182, 211–212; development of, 8, 190–191; and management decision making, 186
FOB destination/job site prices, 14, 26, 32, 44, 67, 73, 82, 106, 112, 158, 175
FOB shipping point prices, 14, 44, 158
Foreign suppliers, 180
Formal vendor rating scale. See Vendor rating scale
Front axle assemblies, 38–41, 150, 171, 175
Fuel oil, 79, 88–97, 150, 171; and new suppliers, 179; purchase requisition, 151; and transportation, 155

Gale, B.T., xi
Gargill-Tennants, 26
Gas cylinders, 135, 136, 137, 138
General Dynamics, 40
General Motors, 40
Gifts, acceptance of, 162
Grounded theory construction, 195
GTE, xi

Haines, G., 204
Hakansson, H., xi, 1
Health care industry, xi
Heffring, M., 6
Heuristic rules, 4, 8–9, 169, 190–191
Hill, R.W., 184
Hirschman, E.C., 6
Hulbert, J.M., 6, 182
Humanistic inquiry, 6
Hydraulic motors, 38–39, 41–45, 174
Hydrogen gas, 135
Hyster Truck Co., 83, 87, 88

Inductive research, xii, 6
Industrial engineering: and corrugated box design, 30, 31, 32; and specifications, 59; and woodhog blades, 69

Industrial tools, 56–57
Information search, 4, 152, 167, 169–171; and new vendors, 154–155, 171–174; and sales representatives, 139, 152
Integrative choice process, 182–183
International industrial purchasing, 1, 6
Interviews, 168, 195, 202–204, 207
Inventory, 66
Investment castings, 57, 58–64, 154
Ireland, R.D., 212

Johnston, W.J., 8

Keystone Coal Industry Manual, 129–130

Labor relations and vendor selection, 82, 83, 106, 107, 144, 158, 178
LeMasters, K., 6
Lift truck parts, 79, 83–88
Lighting poles, 2
Linear attitude models, 182
Liquid Air, 136
Local purchasing, 18
Local rationality, 185
Location and vendor selection, 21, 67, 130, 136, 155, 171
Long-term contracts, 149–166; and bale caps, 80; and bale ties, 23; and batch mix tanks, 20; and coal, 130, 131, 135; and continuity of supply, 72, 83–86, 104, 138, 149–151; and cost savings, 65, 72, defined, 14, and design system analysis, 6; and electric utilities, 123; and fuel oil, 93–94; and lift truck parts, 83–86; and multiple sources, 92, 159; and oleic acid, 104–105; and price, 72, 104–105, 159; and research design, 199; and small industrial organization, 189; and steel bar, 68; and tooling costs, 76; and woodhog blades, 72, 76
Louisville and Nashville Railroad, 127
Lyere, 100

Maintenance department and vendor selection, 86, 87, 88, 95

Maintenance, repair and operations items, 14, 188, 189, 201
Management strategy theories, 2–6
March, J.G., 5, 171, 182
Market information, search for, 125
Marketing, 187–188, 190
Materials: alternative, 11; and chemical industry, 101; and price variability, 72, 106, 144, 150
Materials manager, 57, 69, 72
Minority suppliers, 112–113, 154, 167, 174, 178, 185
Mintzberg, H., xi, 6, 194, 195–196, 212
Moller, K.E.K., 6
Moriarty, R.J., 200–201
Multiple operationism, 197
Multiple sources, 44–45; and bid evaluation, 176; criteria for selection, 181; and long-term contract, 92, 159
Mylar sheets, 110

NAPA, 86
Napco Industries, 39, 40
National Welders, 136, 137
Naturalistic mode of inquiry, 194–197
Negotiation, 187, 188; lack of, 180–181; objections to by purchasing agents, 27, 45, 61, 110, 180–181; and price, 27, 33, 45, 61, 110, 112, 125–127, 137, 138, 145, 150, 163–164, 175–176, 179, 180–181; training program, 181
New items, 169–170, 190
New vendors, 79, 154; and bale ties, 26; and coal, 130; and engineering approval, 43; evaluation costs, 107–110, 152, 175; evaluation criteria, 171–174; financial check, 49; and fuel oil, 93; information search, 154–155, 171–174; and multiple source needs, 185; and payment terms, 113; and prices, 11, 26, 82, 83, 104, 113, 120, 158; and quantity of order, 155; and sales representative, 59–60, 86, 117, 152, 153, 155–156; search for, 40–41, 59–60, 88, 93, 112, 179; share of total order, 4, 11, 158
New York state, 89

Nitrogen, 135
Norfolk and Western Railway Co., 127
Normative model, 14
North Carolina Public Service Commission, 122
Nuclear Regulatory Commission, 122
Nylon, 17, 19, 22–23, 100

Oleic acid, 103–110, 155
Olsen, J.P., 5
Original equipment manufacturer (OEM), 55; price schedule, 41; and rubber gaskets, 116
Orlon, 100
Oxygen, 135

Packaging engineer, 80, 111–112
Paliwoda, S.J., xi, 1
Parket, I.R., 186
Participant observation, 195
Payment terms, 14, 26, 44, 50, 61, 67, 73, 82, 106, 112–113, 117; negotiation, 181; and new vendors, 113; and single source, 175; uniformity of in bids, 158
Performance and vendor selection, 67, 137, 158, 174, 178, 190; premium for, 177, 189–190
Performance reviews, 11
Personal factors and purchasing, 139, 162–163, 181, 207
Piedmont Welders, 136
Periodicals: and new vendor search, 60; and price information, 43, 59
Petroleum products, 17
Pettigrew, A., 5, 138
Pfeffer, J., 5
Phase theorem, 3–5
Phases of industrial purchasing, 8–9
Phenomenology, 6
Photographic products, 77
Pirns, 27, 30
Plant purchasing agreements (PPAs), 6–7; *see also* Long-term contracts
Plastics manufacture, 100
Political model of decisionmaking, 5
Postpurchase protocol analysis, 205–206
PPAs. *See* Plant purchasing agreements
Precedence and decisionmaking, 182

Predictive models, 14
Premium payment for good performance, 177, 189–190
Premium/penalty clauses, 126, 128–129, 131
Price: and collusion, 73, 76; competitive, checking for, 21; controlled, 150; conversion, 44, 94, 176; and delivery, 14, 26, 32, 44, 67, 73, 82, 94–95, 106, 112, 158, 175; differences allowable, percentage, 61, 177, 178, 179; firmness, 26, 33, 50, 67, 82, 106, 112, 117, 137, 144, 150, 158, 163–164; increases, prior notification, 61, 181; increases and selection of vendor, 26–27, 164, 174; information on, 42–43, 59; and inside information, 73; and long-term contracts, 72, 104–105, 159; and materials, 72, 106, 144, 150; negotiation of, 27, 33, 45, 61, 110, 112, 125–127, 137, 138, 145, 150, 163–164, 175–176, 179, 180–181; and new vendors, 11, 26, 82, 83, 104, 113, 120, 158; and original equipment manufacturer, 41; and single source, 175–176; and splitting order decision, 44, 113, 159, 178; and technical evaluation, deletion from, 157; and volume buying, 104–105, 150
Primary suppliers: displacing, difficulty of, 83, 104, 154; dropping of, 153, 154
Production control, 23, 30, 32
Production engineers: and batch mix tanks, 20, 22; and specifications, 20; and vendor evaluation, 21
Production items, purchasing, 18
Protocol analysis, 168, 169, 201–206
Purchase requisition, 151, 152
Purchasing audits. *See* Performance review
Purchasing Management Association of North Carolina and Virginia, Inc., 198
Purchasing World, 43

Qiana, 100

Quality control: and bale caps, 80–81; and coal, 128–129; and corrugatedboxes, 32; inspection, 30; and specifications, 49, 80–81, 105; and vendor evaluation, 26, 32, 130, 183
Questionnaire, 168, 169, 201–202, 210–211
Quotations. *See* Bid submission

Rail-laying machines, 41, 45
Railroad delivery, 94–95; and coal, 127, 130; tariffs, 127
Railroad equipment, 37, 41, 45
Realized industrial purchasing strategies, xii–xiii
Reciprocity, 184
Recommendations for purchasing managers, 9–11
Records and research, 168, 207–209
Regional purchasing, 101–102, 105–106, 187
Regulation, 20, 122–123
Repeat purchases, 169, 171
Request for quotation (RFQ), 7, 14, 152, 156
Research: company selection, 198–199; further needs, 189–190; limitations, 188–189; methodology, 168–169, 193–213; objectives, 167–168
Reward-balance model, 174
RFQ. *See* Request for quotation
Robinson, P.J., 185, 194
Rockwell Industries, 40

Sales representatives, 167, 187–188, 210; frequency of visits, 8, 163; friendship with, 139, 162–163, 207; as information source, 139, 152; and new vendors, 59–60, 86, 117, 152, 153, 155–156; and other departments, 155–156, 160–161; and technical personnel contact, 138; and vendor rejection, 153
Samples, 31–32, 171; testing, 88, 129, 155
Samuel, D.M., 6, 181
Savannah, Ga., 93
Sealing gaskets, 102, 113–130, 179

222 • Index

Search for vendors, 9, 152–155, 169–175, 178–179; see also Information search
Second bid opportunity, 11
Securities and Exchange Commission, 122
Selection of vendors. See Vendor evaluation and selection
Service charges, 181
Service quality and vendor selection, 67, 137
Sherrell, D.L., 197
Simon, H.A., 3, 175, 182
Simon, L., 204
Single-source buying, 27, 40, 45, 171; and bid evaluation, 175–176, 179; and coal, 131; criteria for selection, 181; and price, 175–176; and tooling costs, 60–61, 76
Snowball interviewing, 8, 201
South Carolina, 89
Southern Railway Co., 127
Special items, 72
Specifications, 151–152, 160, 188; and cable, 138–140; and coal, 128–129; and design engineer, 20, 22, 69, 73; deviations from and negotiation, 176; and oleic acid, 104; and production engineer, 20; and quality control, 49, 80–81, 105; revision, 111; and value engineer, 69
Spekman, R.E., 8
Spicer Industries, 39–41
Splitting orders, 44, 158, 159–160, 205–206; and bale caps, 82–83; and coal, 131; and costs, 113; criteria, 177–179, 181; and friendship with vendor, 162; and fuel oil, 94–95; and oleic acid, 107; and new vendors, 4, 11, 158; and price, 44, 113, 159, 178; and wooden pallets, 113
Spot market, 65, 125–126; and coal, 130, 131, 135, 151
Steel rods, 57, 65–68, 151
Stern, L.W., 8
Stiles, G.W., 205
Stochastic model, 15
Strategic market planning, xi
Sulphur content regulation: and coal, 128, 129, 157; and fuel oil, 89, 94

Sultan, R.G.M., xi
Suppliers. See Bid submission; New vendors; Vendor evaluation and selection

Technical evaluation. See Design engineer; Industrial engineer; Quality control; Value engineer
Thomas Register, 152
Tooling costs, 178; and long-term contract, 76; and single source, 60–61, 76; and woodhog blades, 73–76
Trade manager, 152, 171
Training programs, 179, 181, 187; and negotiations, 181
Transportation costs, 92, 94, 111; and coal, 127, 155; and decentralization of purchasing, 105; and fuel oil, 155; and proximity, 130, 136, 171; see also Delivery
Triangulation of evidence, xiii, 2–3, 168, 169, 189, 194, 197–198
Trow, D.B., 3, 175
Truck delivery, 94
Turnbull, P.W., xi, 1

U.S. Department of Health and Human Services, 122
U.S. Department of Labor, 122
University of Wisconsin, 48
Unobstrusive research method, 168, 169, 195, 207
Utility companies, 2, 121–145

Value analysis, 9–10, 179, 180
Value engineer, 57, 59, 72; and electric utilities, 123; and steel rods, 67, 68; and specifications, 69; and woodhog blades, 69, 72, 73, 76
Vanadium and fuel oil, 93, 94, 157
Vendor evaluation and selection, 15, 153–154; and bale caps, 82–83; and bale ties, 26–27; and batch mix tanks, 21; and cable, 144–145; and coal, 130–131; and commercial evaluation, 158; and cooling and purging gases, 137; and corrugated boxes, 32–33; criteria, 181, 185–186; and design engineer, 20, 21, 22, 43, 69, 72, 73; and

directional valve castings, 50–51; final stage, 158–159; and finishing goods, 106–107; and fuel oil, 94–95; and hydraulic motors, 44–45; and investment castings, 60–61; and labor relations, 82, 83, 106, 107, 144, 158, 178; and location, 21, 67, 130, 136, 155, 171; and maintenance department, 86, 87, 88, 95; model, 175–179; and oleic acid, 106–107; and past performance, 67, 137, 158, 174, 178, 190; and price increases, 26–27, 164, 174; and production engineer, 21, 22; and quality control, 26, 32, 82, 130, 183; and research, 167–169; and sealing gaskets, 117–120; service quality, 67, 137; and single source, 175–176, 179; and steel rods, 67–68; and technical evaluation, 157–158, 176; theoretical implications, 182–185; time period, 160; and wooden pallets, 112–113; and woodhog blades, 72–76

Vendor rating system, 27, 31, 33, 135, 137, 145, 167, 179, 181, 187; opposition to, 159; and research, 189; theoretical implications, 184
Volume buying, 18; and price, 104–105, 150
Vyas, N.M., 6

Wall Street Journal, 59
Warranty periods, 175, 181
Waters, J.A., xi
White Motors, 40
Wilson, E.J., 2
Wind, Y., 171, 174, 185, 194, 205
Witte, E., 4
Wood-boring drills, 68–69
Wooden pallets, 11, 102, 110–113, 155, 174
Woodhog blades, 57–58, 68–76
Woodside, A.G., 6, 181, 197, 204
Written communications by purchasing, 156

Zaltman, G., 5–6

About the Authors

Arch G. Woodside is president of ARC Consultants, Inc., a marketing consulting firm specializing in marketing and advertising strategy and research. He is the editor of *Successful Advertising Strategies*, a newsletter on using effective advertising to increase sales. He has worked on designing and testing the marketing strategies for several small and large retail, consumer, and industrial firms.

He is also the Malcolm S. Woldenberg Professor of Marketing at the Freeman School of Business, Tulane University. His studies on planning successful marketing strategies have appeared as articles in the *Journal of Marketing, Journal of Advertising Research, Industrial Marketing Management, Journal of Applied Psychology, Journal of Marketing Research, European Journal of Marketing*, and the *Journal of Retailing*. He is a past-president of Division 23, Consumer Psychology, American Psychological Association. He is the current editor-in-chief of the *Journal of Business Research*.

He has completed industrial and consumer research studies for GT&E, Ocean Spray Cranberry Company, Renault, South Carolina Peach Board, Park Seed Company, Shakespeare Fiberglass Division, tourism planning departments for several states and Canadian provinces, hospitals, banks, savings and loan associations, pizza restaurant chains, office furniture dealers, copier equipment dealers, campgrounds, and meat packing companies.

Niren Vyas is product planning manager for controller products at Square D Company in Columbia, South Carolina. He has participated in purchasing decisions for a number of large construction projects, including a major airport, a shopping center complex, cement and steel mills, petroleum and chemical plants, nuclear power plants, and paper and pulp mills. Before joining Square D Company in 1970, he worked with Larsen & Tenbo Ltd., Bombay, India, a large manufacturer of industrial equipment. He also served as a design engineer for Sargent & Lundy Consulting Engineers in Chicago.

He has published several papers in *Power Engineering Magazine, Journal of Marketing*, and *Journal of Purchasing*.